FIN DE SIÈCLE

Library of International Relations

Volume
1   The Business of Death: Britain's Arms Trade at Home and Abroad
Neil Cooper
2   The Age of Terrorism and the International Political System
Adrian Guelke
3   Fin de Siècle: The Meaning of the Twentieth Century
edited by *Alex Danchev*
4   On Liberal Peace: Democracy, War and the International Order
John MacMillan

FIN DE SIÈCLE

THE MEANING OF THE TWENTIETH CENTURY

edited by

ALEX DANCHEV

BLOOMSBURY ACADEMIC
LONDON • NEW YORK • OXFORD • NEW DELHI • SYDNEY

BLOOMSBURY ACADEMIC
Bloomsbury Publishing Plc
50 Bedford Square, London, WC1B 3DP, UK
1385 Broadway, New York, NY 10018, USA

BLOOMSBURY, BLOOMSBURY ACADEMIC and the Diana
logo are trademarks of Bloomsbury Publishing Plc

First published by I. B. Tauris in 1995
This paperback edition published by Bloomsbury Academic in 2021

Copyright © Alex Danchev 1995

Alex Danchev has asserted their right under the Copyright,
Designs and Patents Act, 1988, to be identified as Author of this work.

All rights reserved. No part of this publication may be reproduced or
transmitted in any form or by any means, electronic or mechanical,
including photocopying, recording, or any information storage or retrieval
system, without prior permission in writing from the publishers.

Bloomsbury Publishing Plc does not have any control over, or responsibility for,
any third-party websites referred to or in this book. All internet addresses given
in this book were correct at the time of going to press. The author and publisher
regret any inconvenience caused if addresses have changed or sites have
ceased to exist, but can accept no responsibility for any such changes.

A catalogue record for this book is available from the British Library.

Library of Congress catalog card number: 95-060220

ISBN: HB: 978-1-8504-3967-7
PB: 978-1-3501-8386-5

Typeset by The Harrington Consultancy

To find out more about our authors and books visit
www.bloomsbury.com and sign up for our newsletters.

What a disappointment the twentieth century has been
How terrible & how melancholy
  is [the] long series of disastrous events
  wh[ich] have darkened its first 20 years.
We have seen in ev[ery] country a dissolution,
  a weakening of those bonds,
    a challenge to those principles
      a decay of faith
        an abridgement of hope
          on wh[ich] structure & ultimate existence
            of civilized society ultimately depends.
We have seen in ev[ery] part of [the] globe
  one g[rea]t country after another
    wh[ich] had erected an orderly, a peaceful
    a prosperous structure of civilized society,
      relapsing in hideous succession
        into bankruptcy, barbarism or anarchy.

Winston Churchill, notes for election speech, 1922

The truth of our little age is this: nowadays no one gives a damn about what Henry James knew. I dare to say our 'little' age not to denigrate (or not only to denigrate), but because we squat over the remnant embers of the last diminishing decade of the dying twentieth century, possibly the rottenest of all centuries, and good riddance to it (despite modernism at the start and moonwalking near the middle). The victories over mass murder and mass delusion, West and East, are hardly permanent. 'Never again' is a pointless slogan: old atrocities are models (they give permission) for new ones. The worst reproduces itself; the best is singular. Tyrants, it seems, can be spewed out by the dozens, and their atrocities by the thousands, as by a copy machine; but Kafka, tyranny's symbolist, is like a finger print, or like handwriting, not duplicatable. This is what Henry James knew: that civilization is not bred out of machines, whether the machines are tanks or missiles, or whether they are laser copiers. Civilization, like art its handmaid (read: handmade), is custom-built.

Cynthia Ozick, *What Henry James Knew* (London, 1993)

CONTENTS

NOTES ON THE CONTRIBUTORS — vii

INTRODUCTION:
THE SARAJEVO CENTURY — Alex Danchev — ix

1. THE END OF HISTORY? — Chris Brown — 1
2. AMERICA — John A. Thompson — 20
3. RUSSIA — Edward Acton — 43
4. JAPAN — Ian Nish — 58
5. EUROPE — William Wallace and Piers Ludlow — 71
6. THE NUCLEAR REVOLUTION — Richard Wyn Jones — 90
7. ECONOMISM — Patricia Clavin — 110
8. NATIONALISM — James Mayall — 137
9. ISLAMISM — Maha Azzam — 158
10. COMMUNITY — Andrew Linklater — 177
11. THE FIN DE SIÈCLE — Charles Townshend — 198

INDEX — 217

NOTES ON THE CONTRIBUTORS

Edward Acton is Professor of Modern European History at the University of East Anglia. He is the author of *Rethinking the Russian Revolution* (1990) and *Russia: The Tsarist and Soviet Legacy* (1995).

Maha Azzam is Associate Fellow of the Royal United Services Institute for Defence Studies in London. She is the author of *Islamic Radicalism in Egypt* (1993) and is working on a book on ideology and development in Muslim states.

Chris Brown is Professor of Politics at the University of Southampton. He is the author of *International Relations Theory: New Normative Approaches* (1992) and editor of *Political Restructuring in Europe: Ethical Perspectives* (1994).

Patricia Clavin is Lecturer in Modern History at Keele University. She is the author of *The Failure of Economic Diplomacy: Britain, Germany, France and the United States, 1931–1936* and, with Asa Briggs, *Modern Europe: 1789 to the Present* (both forthcoming).

Richard Wyn Jones is Lecturer in International Politics at the University College of Wales, Aberystwyth, where he has special responsibility for teaching through the medium of the Welsh language. He is completing his doctorate on strategy, security and Critical Theory. **Andrew Linklater** is Professor of International Relations at Keele University. He is the author of *Men and Citizens in the Theory of International Relations* and *Beyond Realism and Marxism* (1990). He is working on a book on political community and global order.

Piers Ludlow is a research student at St Antony's College, Oxford. He is completing his doctorate on the reaction of the six original members of the European Community to the first British application to join.

James Mayall is Professor of International Relations and Chairman of the Steering Committee for International Studies at the London School of Economics. He is the author of the prize-winning *Nationalism and International Society* (1991).

Ian Nish is Emeritus Professor of International History at the London School of Economics. He is the author of *Japanese Foreign Policy 1869–1942* (1977) and *Japan's Struggle with Internationalism 1931–33* (1993).

John A. Thompson is University Lecturer in History and Fellow of St Catharine's College, Cambridge. He is the author of *Reformers and War: American Progressive Publicists and the First World War* (1987). His forthcoming book on US foreign policy develops the themes outlined in his essay in this volume.

Charles Townshend is Professor of Modern History at Keele University. He is the author of *Political Violence in Ireland* (1983) and *Making the Peace: Public Order and Public Security in Modern Britain* (1993).

William Wallace is Walter F. Hallstein Senior Research Fellow of St Antony's College, Oxford and Visiting Professor of European and International Studies at the Central European University in Prague. He is the author of a number of works on foreign policy and national identity.

INTRODUCTION:
THE SARAJEVO CENTURY

Alex Danchev

This book is the product of an entry in the Economic and Social Research Council (ESCR) Research Seminar competition of 1992. Its structure and focus (originally developed in discussion with Hidemi Suganami and Charles Townshend) sprang from a desire to liberate a number of our colleagues from the daily round and give them the opportunity to survey the whole of their domain, whatever it be, in long perspective and short compass. We wanted to attract top-class scholars and happily succeeded in so doing. We were not unduly concerned about disciplinary background but sought fruitfully to intermingle the cognate fields of History, Politics and International Relations. At Keele, in particular, we hoped to strengthen the intellectual and institutional links between International History and International Relations. Within certain well-understood constraints (chiefly space and accessibility), contributors would be free to roam, governed loosely by three overarching questions put to each of them:

(1) What are the salient characteristics of the twentieth century?
(2) What, if anything, is ending as the century ends?
(3) Was Winston Churchill right to call it a disappointing century?[1]

The seminars were designed to run over a two-year period 1992–4. It seemed inevitable that the opening session (now chapter 1) should confront the End of History.[2] Thereafter, the first year's seminars (chapters 2–5) would be organized geographically, or to be more exact, geopolitically; they would raise a familiar but unresolved question – whose century? Was it, for example, the American century after all? The second year's seminars (chapters 6–10) would be organized thematically; they would raise a less neat but perhaps more troubling question – what kind of century? A nuclear one, uniquely, but what other kind? It remained only to situate or eviscerate the very idea of the *fin de siècle* (chapter 11) and we could bid each other farewell, and pass the time – or let the time pass – in the manner of that quintessential twentieth-century documentarist, Samuel Beckett.

ESTRAGON: I can't go on like this.
VLADIMIR: That's what you think.
ESTRAGON: If we parted? That might be better for us.
VLADIMIR: We'll hang ourselves tomorrow. (*Pause.*) Unless Godot comes.
ESTRAGON: And if he comes?
VLADIMIR: We'll be saved.[3]

In this instance, strange to relate, a saviour did come, though not in the expected form – a contingency of which Beckett would surely have approved. Our scheme failed to move the ESRC, but it did excite the interest of the Nuffield Foundation. Funding from that enlightened quarter unlocked further contributions from a number of sources at Keele: the Departments of History and International Relations, Research Development and Business Affairs, and, last but not least, a doughty Vice-Chancellor. We were launched. The freshly minted Keele International Seminar convened for the first time in October 1992, in pitch dark, to the hypnotic strains of The Doors, Jim Morrison intoning apocalyptically – what else? – 'The End'.

It may be objected that the *fin* has come a little early this *siècle*. To that objection a number of responses can be made. In the first place, as many have observed, the end is always being declared. Hegel, so it is said, glimpsed the end of History when the French Revolution (in the person of Napoleon) defeated Prussia at the Battle of Jena in 1806.[4] Keynes identified 'the final destruction of the optimistic liberalism which Locke inaugurated' in 1940.[5] Karl Polanyi announced the end of Civilization in 1944, Daniel Bell the end of Ideology in 1960.[6] Bell recognized well enough that, 'while the old nineteenth-century ideologies and intellectual debates have become exhausted, the rising states of Asia and Africa are fashioning new ideologies with a different appeal for their own people. These are the ideologies of industrialization, modernization, Pan-Arabism, color, and nationalism' – many of which are examined in the pages below – but his gaze was fixed on his own society: on the West (above all the USA), and on the intellectual, especially that unhappy breed, the young intellectual.

> The young intellectual is unhappy because the 'middle way' is for the middle-aged, not for him [nor, presumably, for her]; it is without passion and is deadening. Ideology, which by its nature is an all-or-none affair, and temperamentally the thing he wants, is intellectually devitalized, and few issues can be formulated any more, intellectually, in ideological terms. The emotional energies – and needs – exist, and the question of how one mobilizes these energies is a difficult one. Politics offers little excitement. Some of the younger intellectuals have found an outlet in science or university pursuits, but often at the expense of narrowing their talent into mere technique; others have sought self-expression in the arts, but in the wasteland the lack of content has meant, too, the lack of the necessary tension that creates new forms and styles.

To which a young intellectual at Keele has felt moved to append the edifying marginal comment BOLLOCKS.[7] This is nothing if not a sceptical century.

More recently Francis Fukuyama declared the end of History, thunderously, in 1989 – early 1989, be it noted, while the Berlin Wall still held. 'In watching the flow of events over the past decade or so', he began, 'it is hard to avoid the feeling that something very fundamental has happened in world history.'

> The twentieth century saw the developed world descend into a paroxysm of ideological violence, as liberalism contended first with the remnants of absolutism, then bolshevism and fascism, and finally an updated marxism that threatened to lead to the ultimate apocalypse of nuclear war. But the century that began full of self-confidence in the ultimate triumph of Western liberal democracy seems at its close to be returning full circle to where it started: not to an 'end of ideology' or a convergence between capitalism and socialism, as earlier predicted, but to an unabashed victory of economic and political liberalism.

'The triumph of the West, of the Western *idea*', Fukuyama concluded, 'is evident first of all in the total exhaustion of viable systematic alternatives to Western liberalism.'[8] In short, as Chris Brown puts it in this book, 'Something Big has happened, and happened for reasons that are equally Big.'

Après Fukuyama, le déluge. Since 1989 Something Big *has* happened: of that we can be very sure. As like as not we watched it on television. For countless numbers of people, in Africa, in Asia, in Europe, in the Middle East, the world has been turned upside down. Walls have tumbled, empires have sundered, wars have been waged, people have been shot, starved, disappeared and ethnically cleansed. But what does it all mean? Is this the end of History or merely the end of the Cold War? Are they synonymous or causally related? Is it – whatever it is – a happy end, or a final one? Francis Fukuyama himself waxed elegiac:

> The end of history will be a very sad time. The struggle for recognition, the willingness to risk one's life for a purely abstract goal, the worldwide ideological struggle that called forth daring, courage, imagination and idealism, will be replaced by economic calculation, the endless solving of technical problems, environmental concerns, and the satisfaction of sophisticated consumer demands. In the post-historical period there will be neither art nor philosophy, just the perpetual caretaking of the museum of human history.[9]

Fatefully, Fukuyama's declaration, like so many others, was premature. The enervating state of affairs he describes may correspond to reality in the intellectual fug of the State Department or the cloudless cocoon of the RAND Corporation, but nowhere else. It is not only what we used to call the Third World that remains 'mired in history': it is the heart of Europe too. The only caretaking being done in *fin-de-siècle* Sarajevo is the caretaking of the graves – some, to our shame, mass graves – what Michael Ignatieff has called the wastelands of the new world order.[10] The condition of the former Yugoslavia, like many other former places, is more pre- than post-historical. Time has run out for these places, but not History. The twentieth century, Susan Sontag has suggested, began and ended in Sarajevo.[11] Centuries are more malleable than one might suppose. They can skid, as Charles Townshend says, and they can be lengthened or shortened according to taste – hence the long sixteenth, 1450–1640, or the displaced nineteenth, 1815–1914. After that, our little age may be seen as a Hobbesian one, nasty, brutish and above all short.[12]

Here Lies the Twentieth Century
1914–1991
RIP

INTRODUCTION: THE SARAJEVO CENTURY   xiii

This, then, is the Sarajevo Century. For most of us, of course, it is a Sarajevo of the mind.[13] But not for Susan Sontag. In 1993, in a brave and quixotic gesture, she staged 'Waiting for Godot' in Sarajevo. A half-starved cast performed miracles in a ruined theatre.[14] Godot, however, failed to materialize. Outside the theatre – all over the world – we are waiting still, and keeping hope, as we must, unquenchable.

Notes
1 See epigraph above. Printed in Martin Gilbert, *Winston S. Churchill*, (London, 1975), p.915. Later it was simply a 'terrible' century: Winston S. Churchill, *Lord Randolph Churchill* (London, 1950), p.12.
2 An issue rekindled by Francis Fukuyama, 'The end of history?', *The National Interest*, 16 (1989), pp.3–18, and *The End of History and the Last Man* (London, 1992). To sample the response see, variously, M. F. Burnyeat, 'Happily ever after', *London Review of Books*, 23 July 1992; Alan Ryan, 'Professor Hegel goes to Washington', *New York Review of Books*, 26 March 1992; E. P. Thompson, 'Ends and histories', in Mary Kaldor (ed.), *Europe from Below* (London, 1991), pp.7–25.
3 Samuel Beckett, *Waiting for Godot* (London 1965), p.94.
4 This is Alexandre Kojève's interpretation, or over-interpretation. On that mysterious figure see Tom Darby, *The Feast* (Toronto, 1990), and the discussion in chap. 1 below.
5 Quoted in Robert Skidelsky, *John Maynard Keynes*, ii (London, 1992) p.xv.
6 Karl Polanyi, *The Great Transformation* (Boston, 1944); Daniel Bell, *The End of Ideology* (Glencoe, IL, 1960).
7 Bell, *End of Ideology*, pp.373–5, copy in Keele University Library.
8 Fukuyama, 'The end of history?', p.3.
9 Ibid. p.18.
10 Michael Ignatieff, *Blood & Belonging* (London, 1993), p.186.
11 Susan Sontag interviewed by Alfonso Armada of *El País*, reprinted in *The Guardian*, 29 July 1993.
12 'For the first time in more than two centuries Hobbes has more message for us than Locke.' Keynes quoted in Skidelsky, *Keynes*, ii, p.xv. Susan Sontag is by no means the only one to shorten the century. Some prefer 1989; Eric Hobsbawm, for one, 1992. See his *Age of Extremes: The Short Twentieth Century* (London, 1994). See also chaps 1 and 12 below.
13 Salman Rushdie's phrase. 'Bosnia on my mind', *Index on Censorship*, 1/2 (1994), pp.16–20. It was not always so. Not only did the century begin and end in Sarajevo, but there was a forgotten middle passage. In 1947 an international contingent of 200,000 people including some 450 British – among them the young historians Edward and Dorothy Thompson – spent a satisfying socialist summer building the *omladinska pruga*, 'the youth railway', from Sarajevo to Samac (on the Bosnian–Croatian border). See E. P. Thompson (ed.), *The Railway: An Adventure in Construction* (London, 1948); Mark Thompson, *A Paper House* (London, 1992), pp.118–20.
14 Susan Sontag, 'Godot comes to Sarajevo', *New York Review of Books*, 21 October 1993.

1. THE END OF HISTORY?

Chris Brown

Can a century have a meaning? Hardly. The twentieth century is an arbitrary stretch of time, defined by the supposed year of birth of a religious figure important in European culture, and by the habit of counting in tens, and thus hundreds (and thousands). It would be strange if such an arbitrary system of reckoning were to create periods of any social significance, unless, of course, human beings adjusted their behaviour in accordance with expectations that a particular date *would* have such significance – as happened to some extent at the end of the first millennium, and may, indeed, happen again as 2001 approaches. For the most part, when we think of particular centuries having a particular character we rarely have in mind a neat hundred-year span beginning with the year 01. The study of nineteenth-century international relations usually refers to the years 1815–1914, or perhaps 1848–90, but never 1801–1900, while Wallerstein's notion of the 'long' sixteenth century stretches from 1450 to 1640.[1]

This much is obvious – pedantic even – but what is less obvious is whether even loose periodization of this sort conveys anything of real significance about the world. Unless, rather implausibly, we see the world as completely devoid of any kind of change, we cannot avoid producing some sort of temporally based characterizations, but it is by no means clear that these particular periods or 'ages' need be anything more than labels of convenience. As conservative historians, and some radical postmodernists, are given to asserting, it may be that there is no deep meaning to history, no metanarrative,[2] and thus a term such as 'the twentieth century' can be little more than a pointer to one or two sequences of events that happen to have coincided for no particular reason during an arbitrarily chosen stretch of time. From this viewpoint it would be unwise to expect that even a temporally adjusted twentieth century – from 1919 to 1989, say – would actually provide a useful frame of reference for analysis, or a valuable stimulus to reflection.

Such scepticism may be justified, but in the recent past, this position has not had as much resonance as the alternative, developmental, approach to periodization: the view that there are historical 'stages', and that these stages succeed one another in ways that are not random, that, on the contrary, they convey a story, a metanarrative even, about human development. This point of view seems to have its origins in the late eighteenth and early nineteenth centuries. It can be found in a nascent form in Kant and earlier writers but it is first elaborated at great length by Hegel. In the nineteenth century it became an article of faith for liberals everywhere, but also, obviously in a rather different form, the centrepiece of Marx's 'materialist conception of history' and a major weapon in the armoury with which Marxism conquered much of the world in the first half of the twentieth century. And it is, of course, from this developmentalist, progressivist viewpoint that it may be possible to assign a meaning to the 'end of the twentieth century'.

Plausibly, part of this potential meaning is to be found in the end of the Cold War, the accompanying dramatic developments in Eastern Europe since 1989, and the even more dramatic developments in the former Soviet Union since 1991. On the face of it, these developments seem to constitute a sequence of changes which herald something more than simply an extreme version of the usual shifting patterns of world power. Apparently, something rather basic and genuinely meaningful is going on here – but what exactly? One of the most ambitious attempts to answer the question in this form has been that of Francis Fukuyama in his article – and subsequent book – on the 'End of History'.[3] Although, in the last resort, the answer Fukuyama gives is not defensible, he deserves a great deal of credit, much more than he has received, for asking the right sort of question. As a kind of tribute, in the first part of what follows, his way of setting up the issues will be used in order to present a marginally different view of the nature of the changes in the world revealed by the events of the last few years. The following section will, tentatively, suggest what mutations to the nature of international order might be expected in the light of these other changes. Finally, and perhaps even more tentatively, the possibility that, especially from a non-European viewpoint, postmodernist scepticism about history arranging itself in stages makes more sense than attempts to characterize the current stage will be examined.

Fin de socialisme?

Fukuyama can be taken to be presenting a multilayered thesis, composed of a number of different positions of varying degrees of generality: first, that Something Big has happened, and happened for reasons that are equally Big; second, that this Something Big is the victory of 'Western Liberalism' over its last remaining systematically constituted Alternative; third, that this victory can be characterized in the light of Kojève's reading of Hegel's phenomenology as bringing about the 'end of History';[4] and, finally (a point elaborated in Fukuyama's book in particular), that this in turn is leading to a crisis which threatens humanity, as the 'Last Men' described by Nietzsche in the Prologue to *Thus Spake Zarathustra* come to inherit the earth.[5] To summarize the response to these positions adopted in what follows, the first is met with total agreement, the second is accepted with important qualifications, the third is rejected – at least in the form presented by Fukuyama/Kojève – while the fourth is not addressed at any length.

It seems difficult to deny that something momentous has indeed happened over the last few years, namely the fall of communism, the end of the Soviet empire, and, ultimately, of the Soviet Union itself. Clearly whether these events took place as a result of deep underlying causes is a matter of possible controversy. It may be that the system collapsed for contingent reasons. Some of the defeated leaders of the East European satellites seem to hold Gorbachev responsible for their fate, as though had he found the right move at the right time all would have been different and the system might have survived.[6] For all we know, Gorbachev may hold the same view – some of his former colleagues certainly hold him responsible for the downfall of the system. From another angle, some US commentators on the right of the political spectrum believe that their policies brought about the downfall of communism – high defence budgets, symbolic aid to dissidents in Eastern Europe, material aid to Afghan rebels having put the system under intolerable strain.[7] Bad luck – in the shape of poor harvests, earthquakes and (more dubiously attributable to luck) the Chernobyl disaster – also can be seen as having played its part.

Some combination of these factors clearly has been important in shaping the day-to-day course of events over the last few years, and there are all sorts of reasons why, most of the time, it makes sense to assume that accidents and contingencies determine world history. It certainly would not be difficult to construct a counter-factual history of the 1980s in which the Soviet system at least survived the decade. However, this should not preclude us from recognizing large-scale, irresistible forces in action when they are staring us in the face, and they have been doing just that for the last decade. Regimes can survive weak leadership, poor economic performance and a whole range of natural disasters, always supposing they are granted a basic minimum of legitimacy by their peoples. The USSR was not granted this basic minimum – or, rather, it possessed just about enough legitimacy to allow it to stagnate but not enough to allow its leaders to try to deal with this stagnation. In the 1980s it suffered a Habermasian 'Legitimation Crisis'.[8] There is a genuine irony here; writing in the 1970s, Habermas posited that Western societies were increasingly dependent for their legitimacy on an ability to deliver the economic goods and that failure to do so would lead to crisis and a new politics. In the 1980s many Western countries *did* experience acute economic differences and this *did* lead to a new politics. But it did *not* lead to the delegitimation of Western regimes, which clearly had non-economic sources of legitimacy upon which to draw. Not so the Soviet system: it seems that this regime drew its legitimacy solely from the basic economic security it provided to its peoples. When this very security became perceived as an obstruction to economic reform the Soviet leadership attempted to undermine it, with the result that legitimacy was withdrawn. Real change could take place only under a new, differently constituted system.[9]

It is here that we can see something of fundamental importance happening before our eyes; the different constitutions that most of the successor states of 'really existing socialism' have constructed, are based on positions which have been realized, albeit imperfectly, in the twentieth-century politics of the Western liberal democracies. Put differently, a consensus about politics in advanced industrial societies is emerging, not on the basis of some kind of 'convergence' between the two systems, but on Western terms. Two such terms are crucial.

The first has been given characteristic expression by Václav Havel, then Czechoslovakian President, in his 1991 essay 'What I Believe':

> Though my heart may be left of centre, I have always known that the only economic system that works is a market economy, in which everything belongs to somebody – which means that somebody is responsible for everything. ...This is the only natural economy, the only kind that makes sense, the only one that can lead to prosperity because it is the only one that reflects the nature of life itself. The essence of life is infinitely and mysteriously multiform, and therefore it cannot be contained or planned for, in its fullness and variability, by any central intelligence.[10]

Westerners tend to take the essential features of a market economy for granted and are obviously rather less conscious of its metaphysical significance and more conscious of its practical drawbacks than Havel, but there seems no reason to doubt that he has identified a key factor which shapes politics in advanced industrial societies. The failures of central planning affect the legitimacy of regimes in a way that market failures do not. Even in its own terms, central planning is self-avowedly 'unnatural'; its only justification is success. Markets, on the other hand, are seen to be 'natural' and can cope with failure without arousing the wrath of the people. It may be that this is a case of 'false consciousness'; it is certainly not the case that the market is some kind of ahistorical institution, universal to all societies. Perhaps the political success of markets is an instance of the rule of unreflective 'common sense', the nature of which is captured by Gramscian ideas about Hegemony in bourgeois society.[11] But be this as it may, the basic generalization holds: market-based regimes can cope with failure in ways that planned systems cannot.

The second sense in which the East has adopted the West's political agenda is captured by the political theorist Brian Barry in his paper 'Is Democracy Special?' (1979). Barry first examines the view that there is something special about majority decisions *qua* decisions, and comes to the conclusion that there is not: there is no reason to think that decisions will be 'better' in accordance with some kind of objective criteria simply because they are made by majority vote. However, he goes on to argue that there is one respect in which democracy is special, namely that it is the only claim to rule that is compatible with ideas of natural equality.

> Once a society reaches a level of development in which there is widespread education and where the bulk of the population enjoys independence from grinding poverty and continuous toil, the choice can *only* be between repression ... and a system of representative government. This may appear to be a quite banal generalization and yet if it is true (and it seems to stand up well empirically) it is surely a remarkable fact.[12]

This *is* a remarkable fact, and the power of the generalization is attested to by the number of times in recent years that old-style communist leaders have been forced to deal with the fatal question 'Who *elected* you?' The Chinese leadership answered this question with bursts of machine-gunfire and, clearly, some Eastern European leaders at different times toyed with the idea of a similar response; however, in the Soviet Union, at the heart of the old regime, once Gorbachev had set his society on the road to 'reconstruction' and 'openness' he obviously felt unwilling to take the path of repression. Instead he tried to falsify Barry's generalization, ruling without repression, but also without attempting to gain democratic legitimacy. All he succeeded in doing was to prove Barry's point, finding himself caught between the genuine forces of repression – the plotters of 20 August 1991 – and those who *had* taken the electoral route – in particular, of course, Yeltsin and the Russian Parliamentarians. The victory of the latter demonstrated the weakness of both the old guard *and* of Gorbachev.

Fukuyama's summary of the emerging consensus around these two positions speaks of a 'triumph of the West' and the 'total exhaustion of viable systemic alternatives to Western liberalism'.[13] Is this a reasonable précis of events? Since one description of Western liberalism might well be a market economy plus representative government, Fukuyama's point cannot be taken to be positively wrong; it does seem plausible that there are no *systemic* alternatives to markets and free elections, though central planning does survive in some areas and *ad hoc* authoritarianism may even be on the increase. However, Western liberalism is a term that can have – and certainly ought to have – a rather less mechanistic meaning than the open-market/free-elections formula would suggest. A particular kind of political culture evolved in the liberal democracies which is not captured in this way. In philosophical terms, this involves individualism; constitutionally, the rule of law; normatively, the promotion of tolerance; in practice, a contest between the power of the vote and the power of money – all these are features of liberal democracies that are not simply captured by the markets/elections formula. Moreover, and this is of crucial importance, it seems they do not need to be present for a society to be economically successful and politically legitimate; Japan is a case in point, with at least the first and third of these characteristics hardly being present at all. The East Asian newly industrializing countries, the 'baby tigers', seem to be moving in much the same direction.

Thus, when Fukuyama says that Western liberalism has triumphed, he is taking too limited a view of the nature of this social form. His account of the triumph of consumerism is also slightly off the mark. The apparent desire of their peoples for Western consumer culture may have been one of the reasons why the communist regimes felt they had to launch themselves into the processes of reconstruction that led to their demise, but it was only one such reason – potential second-class status in the military sphere was most likely more important – and in any event, a legitimate political system would have been able to cope with this pressure. Nonetheless, for all his tendency to overgeneralize, Fukuyama is, surely, closer to the truth than a great many of his critics who are unwilling to acknowledge that the Cold War has ended with a victory for one side and a loss for the other. As Fred Halliday has remarked, the Cold War *was* a genuine ideological, inter-systemic conflict which the advanced capitalist West really *did* win, albeit at some cost.[14]

End of history?

But is this the 'End of History'? Fukuyama's aim in using this formula is to take on Marx on his own ground. For the last hundred years, the Marxist claim to be able to discern the pattern of world history has rested on Marx's supposed achievement in taking the idealist categories of Hegelian thought and standing the dialectic 'on its feet' – as he put it in the Postface to the first volume of *Capital*.[15] Fukuyama gives the dialectic another turn, suggesting that the triumph of Western liberalism constitutes a vindication of Hegel's original notion that the sequence of societies that can be traced in the movement of Spirit in history culminates in the rational, ethical, constitutional state described in the *Philosophy of Right*.[16] Marxists see this state as bourgeois and subject to internal contradictions; they envisage its eventual 'withering away' under communism.[17] Fukuyama reads recent events as putting an end to this vision of a more perfect society; there is no superior state to that described by Hegel.

However, and perhaps unfortunately, Fukuyama wants to take the point further, drawing as noted above on Alexandre Kojève's interpretation of Hegel's *Phenomenology of Spirit*. Part of this interpretation consists of a spectacularly obscure and complicated account of Hegel's view of the role of Time in constituting Man as distinct from Nature, but in the middle of the fog there is a moment of clarity to be found in a footnote to the second edition of Kojève's work, which is in turn layered by comments added in 1946, 1948 and 1959. In this note, Kojève addresses the idea that Man might disappear at the end of History, reverting to animality once the working through of Spirit has taken place, Action has Negated the Given, the Subject–Object distinction has disappeared, and so, somewhat obscurely, on. Will the end of Man mean the end of art, play and love? So it would seem, thinks Kojève, but then he announces that, between editions of his lectures, and rather to his surprise, he has come to realize that all this was not to come in the future, but had already taken place. He had come to see that Hegel had been right to see the Battle of Jena in 1806 as the end of History properly so called, because:

> In and by this battle the vanguard of humanity virtually attained the limit and the aim, that is, the *end* of Man's historical evolution. What has happened since then was but an extension in space of the universal revolutionary force actualised in France by Robespierre–Napoleon.[18]

Kojève goes on to describe the 'American Way of Life' as the type of life specific to the post-historical period, prefiguring the 'eternal present' future of all humanity.[19]

This strange position has been set out at some, though doubtless inadequate, length, in order to draw a contrast between Fukuyama and Kojève. It seems that Kojève really does mean by the 'End of History' a state in which Man reverts to animality, happy perhaps (who could tell?), but no longer happy through the arts, love and play, but happy in an unreflective animal-like way. To him, the end of History means the end of *events* – an end to wars and bloody revolutions is specifically mentioned[20] – and of philosophy. Now, although his discussion of the (not wholly dissimilar) *Nietzschean* idea of the Last Man suggests that Fukuyama is sensitive to the argument here, his use of the 'End of History' formula does not seem to involve such connotations. What he seems to mean is something more like this: that whereas previous societies have produced either unreflective freedom only, or reflective freedom for the few, the modern constitutional state, first described in detail by Hegel, provides freedom for everyone; and since the provision of freedom is the purpose of History (Spirit's self-realization), there is nowhere else for History to go, no-one else to be liberated. Hence History with a capital 'H' comes to an end – but there is no implication that history in the more usual sense of the term will come to a full stop.

Given this contrast, it is interesting to ask why Fukuyama feels the need to use Kojève in what is, in fact, a rather unKojèvian argument. Possibly the influence of Allan Bloom, an interpreter of Kojève and, apparently, Fukuyama's mentor, can be traced here. But, for whatever reason, Fukuyama ends up using a very complicated and metaphysical notion of the meaning of Time, Man and Nature instead of a somewhat clearer point about the relationship between freedom and particular political institutions. Moreover, the effect of this substitution is to help him to get away with a much more important – and contestable – substitution of meanings. In his account the constitutional, ethical state described by Hegel as the embodiment of rational freedom is described simply as 'liberal' and equated to the market-economy/free-elections-based states which are coming to dominate in the modern world. Clearly this is not a substitution that Hegel would have accepted, and its plausibility in Fukuyama's argument depends on the confusion spread by Kojève's ruminations.

To summarize a long, too long, diversion, something important has happened in recent years and this 'something' *does* seem to involve an emerging consensus about the most basic elements of a successful political formula for advanced industrial societies. However, it does not clarify matters to describe this formula as 'Western liberalism'; talk of the end of History confuses and obscures more than it illuminates. But, finally, is it helpful to talk of the end of *Socialism*? In certain respects, perhaps. The collapse of the Soviet planning system does have implications which go beyond the traditions out of which that state emerged. It may well be the case that some of the most disastrous features of the Soviet system were specific to *Russian* circumstances – although Marx's contempt for so-called bourgeois constitutionalism should not be discounted as one important source of Stalinism[21] – but the idea of planning is not one of these culture-specific factors. For most of its history, socialism has involved claims about the proper way to run society, and most of the time these claims have involved the employment of human agency to manage and regulate economic and social life – albeit sometimes through bureaucracies, sometimes, more optimistically, through democratic procedures. In this sense at least the failure of communist planning is a failure of socialism in general, unless someone can provide good reasons to believe that a planning system could be set up that would avoid the failures of the Soviet model.[22]

However, this certainly does *not* mean that social democratic ways of managing states which are essentially liberal cannot work; on the contrary there is every reason to think that the most successful capitalist societies in Europe at least have been those which are based on a strong social democratic tradition – Federal Germany in particular. Nor does it mean that the basic ethical impulse of socialism, the drive for equality, the reaction against poverty and against unearned privilege is in any way outmoded or passé. What it does mean is that, at least for the time being, if this impulse is to be realized and social democratic polities are to function, it can only be within the sort of economic framework outlined by Havel.[23] There seems no reason to think of this as too strict a limiting condition – Texas and North-Rhine Westphalia both have liberal–capitalist politics, but they most definitely do not have the same way of life. The triumph of the open-market/free-elections formula does not involve the irrelevance of socialist *values*, much less an end to pluralism or the imposition of a stifling uniformity.

Post-historical international society

A consensus may have emerged as to the basis of politics in advanced industrial societies. A good question would be whether this consensus will extend also to non-industrial societies – the non-Western 'third world' (a suspect term now that the 'second world' has disappeared).[24] This issue will be examined below, but first it may be helpful to look at the sort of international society that could be expected to emerge if all the major power centres *do* conform to the emerging consensus.

Here talk of the end of History is singularly unhelpful. As outlined above, Kojève evidently thinks that there will be no more *events* in the future, no more wars, no more revolutions, because there will be no more human beings; without history Man will revert to animality and thus 'men' will be no more capable of having international relations or an international society than any other group of primates. Fukuyama clearly does not take this seriously – although he ought to if he is going to use Kojève – and instead seems to think international relations in the future will be like international relations in the past, but without the ideology. If this is what post-historical international relations means, the key question becomes, what would international society look like without ideological contestation?

One way of turning round this question is to ask what international relations would be like in a world composed only of 'liberal' states.[25] The answer, simply put, is that we do not know. There is no reliable empirical evidence on the matter. There have been a number of studies which suggest that liberal states are more peaceful in their relations with each other than non-liberal states, but all of these studies are based on empirical circumstances in which the liberal states that do exist are either in a minority in a largely non-liberal world, or are faced with powerful anti-liberal opponents.[26] Such circumstances make intra-liberal peace quite easy to explain, but they tell us little about the conditions that would apply were liberal states to be the only effective participants in world politics. Peace within capitalist–liberal clubs such as the Organization for Economic Co-operation and Development (OECD) or the European Union (EU) since the Second World War may be a function of the presence of an external, anti-capitalist enemy – or it may not, there is no way to tell.

There *are* conceptual arguments to the effect that the constitutional arrangements of liberal states are such as to promote generally peaceful behaviour. Most of these arguments stem from the first true classic of international relations theory, Kant's *Perpetual Peace: A Philosophical Sketch*.[27] Kant believed that a 'republican civic constitution' would be inherently peaceful and that a Federation of Free States – actually, more like a treaty between such states than a federation as such – would form the basis for a pacific union which would gradually become larger as the attractions of republican forms become more apparent. One of these attractions would be the fact – as he saw it – that republican institutions would not treat war as a sport, in the frivolous manner of kings.

However, the problem with this – and cognate positions such as those of the nineteenth-century Manchester liberals – is that it is based on a highly stylized and implausible characterization of the nature of liberal states. Kant's republican constitution has the rule of law and the separation of powers but no provision for a large-scale bureaucracy; it is premised on the assumption that the only role of the state is to provide law and order, internally and externally. Liberal states have no interests, and therefore there can be no clash of interests between liberal states, and hence no grounds for conflict. The sort of liberal states that actually exist now, and will exist in the future, are obviously *not* like this at all. 'Really existing liberalism' is a far messier business, with large-scale bureaucracies competing for power with elected representatives: the representatives themselves are elected on the basis of their supposed ability to promote the welfare of the people, and there is the clear possibility that this process of welfare promotion could lead to conflict between different countries whether similarly constituted or not.

Really existing liberalism is what the open-markets/free-elections formula provides, and there are no clear-cut conceptual reasons to think that it leads to a peaceful international order. Conversely, and contrary to the arguments of Marxist theorists of imperialism, there is no reason to think that really existing liberalism is necessarily unpeaceful and expansionary. Just as the messiness of actual liberal states undermines the Kantian position, so it also undermines the alternative Leninist view that the capitalist state has been captured by Finance Capital which, unlike the competitive capitalism of the previous era, does have its own foreign policy of imperialism.[28] There is no clear formula that can be used to describe these states, and, therefore, there is no set of generalizations that can be made about their foreign policy behaviour, at least not on the basis of their internal characteristics.

This might seem to suggest a move in the direction of structure. Perhaps talk of the international relations of liberalism is simply one more illustration of the 'reductionist' fallacy of which virtually everyone is accused in Kenneth Waltz's neo-realist tract *Theory of International Politics*.[29] Perhaps so; and yet there is, intuitively, something very seductive about the idea that liberal states do not go to war with each other, and although intuition is not a reliable guide, neither is it to be dismissed out of hand. Perhaps the peacefulness of liberal states is a side-effect, a function of some other feature of liberal states apart from their liberalism?

It would take too long to vindicate this position, but it seems plausible that rather than looking to Kant, we should look to Norman Angell's *Great Illusion*, or perhaps Karl Kautsky's notion of 'ultra-imperialism'.[30] Both of these writers stress the irrelevance and stupidity of war between advanced industrial states, not because these states are liberal, but because it is inconceivable that advanced industrial states could actually gain from war with each other more than they would lose. Of course, Kautsky puts the argument differently from Angell; he sees the real contradiction in world politics as being between classes and regards an inter-imperialist war as contrary to the interests of any of the bourgeoisies involved. But the argument is, in essence, the same – a reliance on the capacity of elites to make at least the most basic calculations about their own self-interests.

The advantage of seeing things in these terms is that it does not imply peacefulness as such, only a tendency towards a calculated pacifism. As an argument it is perfectly compatible with a decision on the part of the advanced industrial countries to go to war with, for example, an Iraq-like state which is disturbing the peace yet can be dealt with at relatively little cost – in military terms at least – by the marshalling of overwhelming force. Of course, such a war may not actually solve any problems – the point is that it is not self-evidently counterproductive in the way that, for example, an attempt to settle US–Japanese trade relations by war would be.

But if this way of putting things be accepted, why did war break out in 1914 – or, for that matter, in 1939 and 1941? And why are some of the post-communist regimes in Eastern Europe and the former territory of the Soviet Union engaging in war at this very moment? There are, I think, two sorts of answer to be given here, neither of which is wholly satisfactory. In the first place, if peace depends on calculation, it is more or less certain that sometimes war will break out, because the idea of calculation always implies the possibility of *mis*calculation. It is always possible that leaders will get things wrong – there are complicated ways of putting this point, perception and misperception, victims of groupthink and so on, but the reality is that people make mistakes, sometimes on big issues.

But, equally to the point is the fact that although rational calculation may lead to peace there are always other things involved in international politics – such as, most typically at the moment and in 1914, the emotions generated by nationalism. A contest between an emotional response and a rational response is not always going to be decided in favour of the latter; even if Hume overstated the case in making reason *always* the slave of the passions, there is no guarantee that rational self-interest will always win through.[31] At the moment in many of the post-communist regimes nationalism is a very strong force, partly because communism suppressed national conflicts which are now breaking through, but also because communism actually promoted nationalism, albeit usually unintentionally. In a system of rule in which political action outside the control of the state is banned, political identity will be formed around those factors that the state cannot control – such as ethnic identity, language differences, religion, race – and this is a source of many of the current ills of the post-communist world.[32]

The basic point here is that whatever *tendency* there may be towards peace between industrial societies in the new international system, there is absolutely no guarantee that war will always be avoided. Nor should we expect to be able to produce social theories that would provide accounts of international relations that eliminate contingencies. When asking ourselves what kind of international society will emerge on the ruins of the post-1945 international order, the best we can do is produce very tentative generalizations. Since at least some reasons for conflict have disappeared with the ending of ideological contestation, and although some new bases for conflict may emerge in their place – or old bases become revitalized – still, on the whole, the best forecast would be for a more peaceful, less fraught, *global* international order at the end of this century and the beginning of the next. Global needs to be stressed here, because such a forecast is quite compatible with increased insecurity in some *regions* – perhaps the idea of 'zones of peace' and 'zones of turmoil' is a depressingly possible scenario.[33] This opens up questions addressed in the final section of this chapter.

Beyond the pacific union?

If there is reason to believe that a consensus on domestic politics is emerging in the industrialized world, and that this is likely to have some consequences for the better in terms of the international relations of these countries, is it possible to generalize about the extent to which these trends will be found operative outside the industrialized world, outside this nascent 'pacific union'?

The evidence available so far points in contradictory directions. On the one hand, a number of non-Western countries are experiencing the same sorts of pressure towards open markets and free elections manifested in the former socialist countries. The undermining of one-party states in Africa – Zambia, Kenya and, perhaps temporarily, South Africa – points in this direction, as does the replacement of military rule by elected governments in most Latin American countries. India has transformed its long-standing planning system, making a bid for free-market investment from multinationals after two generations of *dirigisme*. Much of this change has taken place as a result of pressure from the outside – from Western aid donors and the International Monetary Fund (IMF) – but it clearly has also chimed with a growing internal acceptance of a new economic 'realism', and awareness of the long-term fragility of corrupt, authoritarian, governments.

On the other hand, there are clear pressures pushing some states away from convergence with the industrial world. In India, moves towards economic liberalization have been accompanied by secessionist ethnic struggles, and the increasing significance of communal Hindu–Muslim tensions. Democracy in Africa may yet be undermined by 'tribalism' – as the defenders of the one-party states always claimed it would be. Democratic politics in the Arab/Muslim world, where it exists, seems more likely to place in power radical Islam rather than liberal democracy. Most interestingly, in the Muslim areas of the former Soviet Union there is a fascinating struggle under way between secular authoritarianism sponsored by Turkey and Islamic so-called 'fundamentalism' sponsored largely by Iran.

This was one part of the world where the former communist regime could genuinely be said to have represented the 'West', and its fall here may have very different consequences from those to be seen in areas where communism clearly was in opposition to Enlightenment values.

What these different trajectories put into question is an issue raised in the opening paragraphs of this chapter but then set aside – namely whether there is actually a single path for the development of human societies in the way that both the classical liberal and Marxist traditions believed. For Hegel, the realization of freedom takes place via a unique historical sequence that culminates in the modern, rational State – which latter is an achievement available to all cultures, but produced by one in particular, that of modern Europe.[34] Marx's 'modes of production' are similarly shaped by European history, with the Asiatic mode sitting uneasily outside the sequence.[35] These two grand narratives both claim to be universal, but both, in effect, privilege European history.

In this, at least, they do no more than historicize the universalism of the eighteenth-century European Enlightenment. Figures such as Hume and Voltaire, Rousseau and Kant differed on much else but agreed that they were producing accounts of the world and of knowledge that were for all time and all places. The most ambitious attempt to 'transcend' – to produce universal and necessary knowledge – was the Critical Theory of Kant, but his universal categories are simply the most elaborate exemplars of the belief of the Enlightened that their self-emancipation was of world-historical significance. The achievement of Hegel – upon which Marx built, or, perhaps, which Marx trivialized – was to see that 'rationality' does not have a fixed meaning, that different kinds of societies think about the world in different ways, but even he in no respect challenged the superiority of the modern European world-view over its contemporary rivals.[36] About the only thinker of the period who was prepared to be genuinely pluralist and to respect all cultures was Herder, but, unfortunately, this aspect of his thought was not influential.[37] Later on, Marx himself can stand as the exemplar of a complacent, Victorian, progressivist Eurocentrism, his writings on India, for example, positively dripping with contempt for the local culture and religion.[38]

Today's heirs of Kant, Hegel and Marx are generally politer about these matters, but they remain convinced of the uniqueness of the West. This takes us full circle, to the comments with which this chapter began. Discourse on the 'meaning' of an era – a literal or metaphoric 'century' – can take place only in the context of some notion of stages, of a historical sequence that is not random. Since there are a great many different histories available – associated with different peoples, cultures and societies – to employ any one history in this way is necessarily to make a claim about its priority over the others, to privilege its account of temporality. But one of the features that, perhaps paradoxically, gives meaning to the end of the twentieth century, is an increasing awareness that this sort of privileging must be put in question. The cultural critic Paul Ricoeur has best captured this feeling and its potential consequences:

> When we discover that there are several cultures instead of just one and consequently at the time when we acknowledge the end of a sort of cultural monopoly, be it illusory or real, we are threatened with destruction by our own discovery. Suddenly it becomes possible that there are just *others*, that we ourselves are an 'other' among others.[39]

From this viewpoint, instead of the 'end of History' with a capital 'H', all that the events of the last few years add up to is the end of one particular history, with a small 'h'. It does now seem clear that the contest over how to run advanced industrial societies is coming to an end with the victory of a liberal–capitalist conception of society, but what is by no means clear is what status this particular contest had in the wider scheme of things. The developmentalist models of history generated by the post-Enlightenment West made this contest central to human existence, but it clearly did not play this role in the Islamic world – nor, for that matter, is it clear that Japanese culture puts the sort of emphasis on wealth-creation that one might expect from a people so good at it. From the point of view of Teheran or Tokyo, the fact that one variety of Western thought has triumphed over another, in a decade which has a certain amount of resonance in the context of European methods of timekeeping, is not necessarily of great significance.

And yet, before endorsing a postmodern eclecticism, it is worth remembering that postmodern thought is post*modern*, and not the same as *pre*modern thought, or post-something-else thought. The claim of Enlightenment thinkers was that they could understand themselves *and* everyone else. The claim of postmodern thinkers is that such an understanding is not available *to anyone*, themselves or everyone else. When postmoderns challenge Western conceptions of history, they do so from the viewpoint of a Nietzschean perspectivism which is subversive of *all* claims to privilege, not simply those of the West. In a strange way, the refusal to privilege becomes a kind of privileging, in the sense that 'we' can still understand 'them' while they still cannot understand us – even though what understanding might mean has been radically problematized to the point that it now almost amounts to a confession of ignorance. If this last point holds, it seems to suggest that it is impossible to avoid attributing universal significance to the various shifts in consciousness felt within Western and Western-affiliated societies in recent years. We are doomed to find, or at least seek, a meaning to the end of the century whether we want to or not – the Western world-view within which such a meaning could only emerge has become unavoidable; all we can do is choose which Western narrative we wish to espouse. Perhaps this sense of closure, this ending of the possibility of difference, is the final and conclusive disappointment of our century?

Notes

1. Immanuel Wallerstein, *The Modern World-System: Capitalist Agriculture and the Origins of the European World Economy in the Sixteenth Century* (New York, 1974), pp.67 ff.
2. Jean-François Lyotard defines postmodern as 'incredulity toward metanarratives'; see *The Postmodern Condition: A Report on Knowledge* (1979), trans. G. Bennington and B. Massumi (Manchester, 1984), p.xxiv.
3. Francis Fukuyama, 'The end of history?', *The National Interest*, 16 (1989), pp.3–18, and *The End of History and the Last Man* (London, 1992).
4. See Alexandre Kojève, *Introduction to the Reading of Hegel* (1947), trans. J. H. Nichols, ed. A. Bloom (New York, 1969).
5. *The Portable Nietzsche*, ed. and trans. Walter Kaufmann (New York, 1959), p.129. Whereas the original article was largely Hegelian in tone, the spirit of Fukuyama's book is decidedly Nietzschean – and not simply

Part V which explicitly addresses 'The Last Man'.
6 See, for example, the interview with Bulgaria's Todor Zhivkov on Channel 4's 'The World this Weekend', 29 September 1992. George Schöpflin in *Politics in Eastern Europe* (Oxford, 1993) suggests that a number of East Europe's dismissed leaders had good personal reason to take this view – see chapter 9, 'The end of communism in Central and Eastern Europe' – but he also stresses the more general point that there were deep-seated causes of these events in addition to the particular decisions of the individuals concerned.
7 This was a major theme of the Republican Party's Nominating Convention in Houston, August 1992, and was nicely satirized in Gary Trudeau's 'Doonesbury' cartoon strip in 1989, with ticker-tape victory parades down Wall Street in New York, and an amnesty for imprisoned insider-traders.
8 Jürgen Habermas, *Legitimation Crisis* (1973), trans. Thomas McCarthy (London, 1976).
9 A new regime was a necessary not a sufficient condition for successful change; as events since 1989–91 have shown, simply changing the regime did not, of itself, guarantee successful reform.
10 Václav Havel, 'What I believe', in *Summer Meditations on Politics, Morality and Civility in a Time of Transition*, trans. Paul Wilson (London, 1992), p.62.
11 See Antonio Gramsci, *Selections from the Prison Notebooks*, ed. and trans. Q. Hoare and G. Nowell Smith (London, 1971), esp. Part II, 2.
12 Brian Barry, 'Is democracy special?', cited from *Democracy, Power and Justice: Essays in Political Theory* (Oxford, 1989), p. 56.
13 Fukuyama, 'The End of History?', p.3.
14 Fred Halliday, 'An encounter with Fukuyama', *New Left Review*, 193 (1992), p.91.
15 Karl Marx, *Das Kapital*, i (Hamburg, 1867); trans. B. Fowkes as *Capital* (Harmondsworth, 1976), p.103.
16 Georg W. F. Hegel, *Philosophie des Rechts* (1821); ed. A. Wood, trans. H. B. Nisbet as *Elements of the Philosophy of Right* (Cambridge, 1991).
17 The *Ur*-text for this position is Marx's early 'Towards a critique of Hegel's Philosophy of Right: Introduction' (unpublished in his lifetime); see *Karl Marx: Early Texts*, ed. and trans. D. McLellan (Oxford, 1971), pp.115–30.
18 Kojève, 'Introduction', p.160. Kojève might have been better off adopting the (perhaps apocryphal) approach to the French Revolution of Chou En Lai; when asked once to comment on its significance he is alleged to have replied that it was 'too soon to tell'.
19 Ibid., p.161.
20 Ibid., p.159.
21 Marx's defence of the Paris Commune in 'The Civil War in France' makes plain his contempt for the view that the powers of the leaders of the revolution should be shackled by constitutional restraints, an attitude that was used by the Bolshevik leaders in defence of the dictatorship they established. See 'The Civil War in France', *Marx and Engels: Selected*

Works (London, 1968), pp.248–309.
22 The best such attempt is Alec Nove, *The Economics of Feasible Socialism* (London, 1983) and *The Economics of Feasible Socialism Revisited* (London, 1991).
23 Recent interest in the notion of 'market socialism' reflects this point; see, for example, Ian Forbes (ed.), *Market Socialism* (London, 1986), Julian Le Grand and Saul Estrin (eds), *Market Socialism* (Oxford, 1989) and David Miller, *Market, State and Community* (Oxford, 1989).
24 If, in fact, the countries of really existing socialism were the 'second world', which was never clear. The original term 'Third, World' was used by analogy with the French Revolutionary Third Estate (i.e. the People); clearly, on the same lines, the advanced West was cast as the Second Estate, the Nobility – although often, incorrectly, termed the First World – but who were the equivalents of the real First Estate, the Clergy? Obviously there are sound reasons for abandoning this terminology!
25 What follows draws on Chris Brown, '"Really existing liberalism" and international order', *Millennium: Journal of International Studies*, xxi/3 (1992), pp.313–28.
26 The most famous, and best, because simplest, of these empirical studies is Michael Doyle, 'Kant, liberal legacies and foreign affairs' (Parts 1–2), *Philosophy and Public Affairs*, xxi/3–4 (1983), pp.205–35, 323–53.
27 Most conveniently to be found in *Kant's Political Writings*, trans. H. B. Nesbit (Cambridge, 1977).
28 This view is best set out in Rudolf Hilferding, *Finance Capital*, ed. Tom Bottomore (London, 1981).
29 (Reading, MA, 1979), chap. 4, 'Reductionist and systemic theories'.
30 (London, 1911) and, for Kautsky, 'Ultra-Imperialism' [1914], trans. in *New Left Review*, 59 (1970), pp.41–6.
31 David Hume, *A Treatise on Human Nature* (Harmondsworth, 1969), p.662.
32 This point is made by Zarko Puhovsky in 'The moral basis of political restructuring', in Chris Brown (ed.), *Political Restructuring in Europe, East and West* (London, 1994), pp.201–20.
33 Max Singer and Aaron Wildavsky, *The Real World Order: Zones of Peace/Zones of Turmoil* (Chatham, NJ, 1993).
34 See Georg W. F. Hegel, *Philosophy of History* (1821), trans. J. Sibree (New York, 1956).
35 This sequence is outlined briefly in the Preface to the *Critique of Political Economy*; see David McLellan (ed.), *Karl Marx: Selected Writings* (Oxford, 1977), p.388.
36 Although he *does* avoid the bigotry and anti-Semitism characteristic of so many of the thinkers of the age, including Kant: see *Philosophy of Right*, Section 209.
37 See F. M. Barnard, *Herder's Social and Political Thought: From Enlightenment to Nationalism* (Oxford, 1965).
38 See Shlomo Avineri (ed.), *Karl Marx on Modernisation and Colonialism* (New York, 1969).
39 *History and Truth* (Chicago, 1965), p.278.

2. AMERICA

John A. Thompson

'Consider the twentieth century', wrote Henry R. Luce in 1941. 'It is ours not only in the sense that we happen to live in it but ours also because it is America's first century as a dominant power in the world.'[1] Usually considered bombastic, Luce's claim might well be judged too modest. Few now would question that the USA has been *the* dominant power in the world since 1945. Its relationship with the rest of the non-communist world has been variously described as one of 'leadership', 'hegemony' and 'empire', and the non-communist world was always larger as well as much stronger economically than that over which the Soviet Union held sway. Earlier in the century, too, the course of world politics was greatly affected by the actions (and non-actions) of the USA.

The nature of international affairs is such that the influence of one state can rarely be assessed precisely, but it is nevertheless clear that the United States has not only been on the winning side in the three major geopolitical conflicts of the twentieth century but has also been decisive in their outcome. In the First World War the allies had become dependent on American supplies and finance even before the USA entered the war but in the end the American military contribution also became vital. When, following the collapse of Russia, the Germans made their final thrust on the western front in 1918, it must be doubtful whether Foch would have been able to turn the tide without the rapidly increasing flow of fresh troops from across the Atlantic. In the Second World War the brunt of the land fighting against Germany was borne, of course, by the Russians, but it was the more than eightfold increase in American armaments production between 1941 and 1943 that gave the allies the tremendous superiority in *matériel* that carried them to victory on all fronts. By 1943, about 60 per cent of all the combat munitions of the allies was being produced in the USA.[2] In the Cold War the United States not only largely organized the effort to contain Soviet and communist power but also provided the major part of the resources. In more peaceful enterprises, too, the United States has played a leading role. No doubt, broader forces lay behind the development of the international organizations that have become such a prominent feature in world affairs but as a matter of historical fact the League of Nations and the United Nations (and their associated agencies), the IMF, the World Bank and the General Agreement on Tariffs and Trade (GATT), have all been the products of American initiative and leadership. Whatever the economic importance of Marshall aid *per se*, it is hard to imagine the postwar recovery and integration of Western Europe without American assistance and encouragement, to say nothing of the confidence generated by the security guarantee institutionalized in NATO. The development of modern Japan, likewise, has been much affected by US policy, during the occupation and since. The American role has been crucial in the creation and survival of the state of Israel. And in many less dramatic and precise ways, the activities of the US Government and its agents, and signals and rumours of what 'Washington' wants, have had a significant influence on the course of events in Latin America and other parts of the Third World as well as in those countries formally allied to the United States.

While the important consequences of America's exercise of power in world politics are fairly clear to see, its causes are less transparent. Most of the broader explanations that have been offered have been linked to general theories of one kind or another. Thus writers in the 'realist' tradition emphasize the need of states to protect their own security in the anarchic environment of world politics and the effects on the behaviour of individual states of the distribution of power in the international system. Another tradition (which includes the heirs of Charles Beard as well as some of those of Karl Marx) stresses the pervasive influence of economic interest. Although, as we shall see, the course of American policy in the twentieth century fits none of these theories very well, examining it in terms of such universally applicable concepts as 'power', 'security' and 'economic interest' does help to illuminate its dynamics and provides the basis for some speculations about its future course.

Power-based theories

There would be little dispute that the impact of the United States on world affairs has resulted principally from the nation's pre-eminent command of the resources necessary for the exercise of power in international politics. It was in the 1880s that America overtook Britain as the world's leading producer of manufactured goods and it has retained this position ever since. Indeed, for most of the twentieth century, its output of such goods has been more than twice as great as that of any other country; for some years after the Second World War it was almost equal to that of the rest of the world combined.³ This productive capacity, in combination with advanced technology and a large and comparatively well-educated population, has provided the basis not only for formidable military strength but also for the provision of economic aid and the development of a large and sophisticated apparatus for the conduct of foreign policy, including the gathering of intelligence.

For some analysts, the extent of America's power provides not only a necessary but also a sufficient explanation for the nation's extensive role in world politics. To Michael Mandelbaum, for example, the course of US foreign policy since 1945 represents 'the Natural History of a Great Power':

> American expansion followed a pattern common to other countries similarly situated in the international system. ...There is a family resemblance between the United States, the Soviet Union, and Great Britain, on the one hand, and ancient Rome, on the other. The Romans in their day were also stronger than others. They too dispatched soldiers and governors far from the imperial city.⁴

'As the power of a state increases, it seeks to extend its territorial control, its political influence, and/or its domination of the international economy', Robert Gilpin has written. 'The phenomenon ... is universal.'⁵

If one asks why great powers are bound to expand, various answers are given. To some, it is simply a consequence of human nature. 'Of the gods we believe and of men we know that it is a necessary law of their nature that they rule wherever they can', Thucydides has the Athenians telling the Melians. This aphorism is cited by Hans J. Morgenthau in support of his assertion that the drive to dominate is one of 'those elemental biopsychological drives by which in turn society is created'.[6] Such an assumption apparently underlies the common image of power as a sort of liquid substance, flowing automatically into hollows and 'vacuums'. Thus Martin Wight approvingly quoted Lord Acton's dictum that 'power tends to expand indefinitely, and will transcend all barriers, abroad and at home, until met by superior forces'.[7]

To other 'realist' writers, however, the imperatives of power derive less from some internally generated drive to dominate than from the demands of the international system. Kenneth Waltz, for example, has observed that 'in a world of nation-states, some regulation of military, political, and economic affairs is at times badly needed'. In Waltz's view, such regulation and the provision of other 'collective goods' inevitably falls upon the shoulders of the larger states since 'great power gives its possessors a big stake in the system and the ability to act for its sake'.[8] The idea that the international system imposes special tasks on its most powerful members has been most developed in the version known as 'the theory of hegemonic stability'. According to this theory, a multilateral trading system can function successfully only when there is a 'hegemon' to manage it, to ensure an acceptable distribution of benefits, and when necessary to enforce adherence to the rules. In the nineteenth century and until 1914, it is said, this role was played by Britain; since the Second World War it has been assumed by the USA. 'A liberal economic system is not self-sustaining', Robert Gilpin has insisted, 'but is maintained only through the actions – initiatives, bargaining, and sanctions – of the dominant power'.[9]

Whether they focus on internal or external dynamics, theories that assume that the possession of power will automatically lead to its exercise are open to the objection that they neglect the costs of wielding power. For, of course, every means by which a state can exert leverage in international affairs involves some sacrifice on its part. This is obvious in the case of wars, where the price is bound to be paid in the form of casualties as well as money. But it also applies to the deployment (or even maintenance in being) of armed forces, military or other foreign aid, economic sanctions or preferential terms for trade or investment. These last, as Klaus Knorr has pointed out, always involve some sort of opportunity cost through 'diverting trade or capital investments from the channels indicated by purely economic criteria'.[10]

Recognizing that the exercise of power requires effortful activity involving the sacrifice of other desirable goods makes it much less plausible to see it simply as a universal human instinct. The psychological restraints on the drive to domination do not consist only of altruistic feelings and ethical considerations; they may also include the desire for an easy and comfortable life. These restraints are likely to be overcome only if the benefits to be gained appear to outweigh the costs. In this calculation both elements are variables. In other words, whether a state acts will depend upon the value it attaches to the objects at stake as well as its assessment of its capacity to achieve them at an acceptable cost. For the same reason, the mere fact that a state possesses the capability to provide 'collective goods' for the international system will not necessarily provide it with the motivation to do so; it must also perceive sufficient benefit to itself to justify the costs involved.

That these are not merely theoretical objections is well illustrated by the behaviour of the USA itself. As we have seen, its latent power has been greater than that of any other state throughout the century. In terms of steel-making capacity, for example – described by Churchill as 'a rather decisive index of conventional military power' – the United States in 1913 possessed about twice that of Germany, which in turn produced more steel than Britain, France and Russia combined.[11] In 1920, after the European powers had suffered the devastating effects of the First World War, the United States produced 59 per cent of the world's steel – a proportion even higher than in the years following the Second World War.[12] Yet after the failure of the Senate to approve American membership of the League of Nations, the United States did not deploy any significant portion of the country's ample resources in efforts to affect the course of events in the outside world. Its definition of its security interests did not expand beyond the Western hemisphere and it did not assume any responsibility for managing either the international economic system or the world balance of power. Nor can it well be argued that this was because the 'collective goods' were being adequately provided by others. On the contrary, the credibility of the League of Nations was greatly reduced by the non-participation of the United States. When the Axis powers challenged the international order in the 1930s, the resistance of Britain and France was much weakened by the unlikelihood of American support in any war. As for the international economic system, Charles P. Kindleberger's conclusion that it was 'British inability and US unwillingness to assume responsibility for stabilizing it' that caused the 1930s depression to be so severe and prolonged was the origin of 'hegemonic' theory.[13]

Interest-based interpretations
Power alone, then, provides neither a theoretically adequate nor a historically persuasive explanation for the extensive role in world affairs that the United States has played in the twentieth century. To understand why the nation came to devote a significant proportion of its resources to efforts to affect developments beyond its borders we need to know what interests led it to do so. For most states, the most important national interests are military security and economic prosperity. Each of these goals has been seen by an influential school of historians as providing the basic motivation for the expansion of American foreign policy.

The most developed economic interpretation of America's world role has been the 'Open Door empire' thesis of William Appleman Williams.[14] The premise of this is that the continued prosperity and thus the internal political stability of the United States as a capitalist economy has depended upon (or been believed to have depended upon – there is some ambiguity here) a continued expansion of overseas markets and investment opportunities. The pursuit of an 'Open Door world' in which goods and capital could move freely has been the overriding goal of US foreign policy. Among the obstacles and threats to this objective have been traditional European imperialism, Nazi Germany with its autarkic ideals and state trading practices, communism, and revolutionary Third World nationalism. Consequently the USA has been committed to eliminating, or at least containing, all these forces.

Although this interpretation has had persistent appeal to those ideologically disposed to see American foreign policy as a manifestation of capitalist imperialism, it is open to powerful objections. The most basic of these is that foreign trade has been of much less relative importance to the United States than to most other industrial countries. Indeed, the American economy has been rather more self-sufficient in the twentieth century than it was earlier. Whereas in the second half of the nineteenth century exports constituted 6–8 per cent of GNP, in the period 1920–70 the figure was no more than 3–5 per cent. (These percentages, low as they are in comparative terms, would be reduced even further if the North American economy were considered as a unit, since between a fifth and a quarter of US exports have been to Canada and Mexico.)[15] As far as overseas investment is concerned, there *has* been an increase in the postwar period – but it followed rather than preceded the assumption of a world role politically and militarily. Moreover, the scale of US investment abroad – for all the impression it has made on people in the countries concerned – has remained small in proportion to the enormous American economy. Even in 1968, following two decades in which more capital flowed out of the United States than at any time before or since, direct investment abroad represented only about 6 per cent of total American investment, and the return on foreign investment amounted to only 9.3 per cent of domestic corporate profits. (Again, the proportion invested in Canada was approximately equal to that invested in the whole of Europe.)[16]

Nor is it at all obvious that America's overseas economic interests have either depended upon or shaped its foreign policy. The logic of such a connection seems clearest in the case of countries in the Third World where the rights of property and the sanctity of contractual obligations might have needed to be enforced by outside intervention. But such places have never absorbed more than a small proportion of US exports, the great bulk of which have always gone to other industrial countries.[17] In preventing discrimination against US exports in the developed world, the greatest leverage has been provided by the size of the American market, which has meant that the trade in question has always been proportionally more important to the other countries involved than to the United States.[18] By contrast, America's security commitments have yielded little economic benefit even when such a linkage has been sought, as in the recent relationship with Japan; in the early postwar years, national economic interests were subordinated to geopolitical ones to the extent that the US government actually promoted a scheme that discriminated against American exports.[19] Moreover, there has been no reason to assume that other nations' interest in trade relations with the United States would cease if ideologically hostile regimes came to power; that was certainly not the case with the Communist governments in Russia and Eastern Europe. Nor would the balance of economic power have been altered by such political developments.

American investment has been much more sensitive than trade to the political conditions obtaining in foreign countries. Nevertheless, American business interests have rarely needed diplomatic support in this respect either; the desire of other countries to attract capital investment has generally given corporations a strong enough bargaining position to protect their interests. When American-owned assets have been expropriated, the response of the US government has hardly suggested that opening the world to American capital was its highest priority. Heavy losses were incurred by American investors during the Mexican Revolution of 1911–20 but, despite much agitation by these investors and their political supporters, the Wilson administration did little on their behalf.[20] The legal right of other governments to nationalize foreign property has never been denied by the United States although it has stood by the principles of no discrimination and of prompt and adequate compensation. Yet, as Stephen D. Krasner has pointed out, neither overt nor covert force has ever been employed solely for the purpose of upholding these principles.[21] By contrast, of the 40 examples of British armed intervention in Latin America between 1820 and 1914, at least 21 were to protect property.[22] Again, one reason for this difference might be the scale of the interests involved; whereas overseas investments had provided as much as 8 per cent of Britain's national income in 1910, the comparable figure for the United States in 1973 was 1.6 per cent.[23]

A further problem for the 'Open Door' interpretation is that a drive generated by the very structure of the American economy might be expected to produce a much steadier form of expansionism than is apparent in the history of US foreign policy in this century. The response given by Williams and his followers to this objection is that the retreat from formal imperialism after 1900 or the return to 'isolationism' following the First World War represented changes of 'tactics'; the strategy of seeking an 'Open Door world' remained the same.[24] But this means that for those interested in understanding the reasons why the United States came to play a more strenuous role in international affairs, the important question becomes why the 'tactics' changed.

The timing of America's entry on to the world stage seems to be much better explained by those who attribute it to the requirements of national security. The thesis here is that the nation's traditional policy of non-involvement had to be abandoned because the conditions that made it possible ceased to exist. During the nineteenth century, it is argued, the USA had been protected by its isolated position, British command of the seas, and the balance of power that prevailed in Europe between 1815 and 1914. However, in the twentieth century, the barrier constituted by the oceans was first reduced, and then virtually eliminated, by advancing technology in the form of steamships, aircraft and intercontinental missiles. British control of the Atlantic became dependent upon American assistance, as was shown in 1917, more dramatically in 1940–41, and unmistakably with the sharp decline in British capabilities in the period following the Second World War. The maintenance of a balance of power in Europe (or Eurasia) similarly came to require the throwing of America's weight into the scales.

The weakness of this explanation for America's adoption of a world role is that it ignores the effects of the great growth of the nation's power upon its security position. It is easy to see that, in the changing conditions of the twentieth century, the United States could not prudently have continued to spend less than 1 per cent of its GNP on defence, as it had through most of the nineteenth century; the days of 'free security' were over.[25] It is much less clear, however, that the nation could no longer rely solely on its own efforts to deter or defeat any assault upon it. Not only did it become the most formidable military power in the world but its ability to defend itself was also enhanced rather than diminished by most of the technological advances in warfare. The transition from sail to steam, for example, reduced the range of battleships and thus made the oceans more, not less, of a barrier to hostile navies. As John Keegan has delighted in pointing out, the 'wooden walls' of Nelson's day had a range far greater than that of later 'fossil-fuel fleets' constrained 'by the capacity of their coal bunkers or oil tankers'.[26] Likewise, the dependence of modern armies on sophisticated and customized munitions meant that a trans-oceanic invasion would face much greater logistical problems than had been the case during the war of 1812. The development of aviation also aided the defence more than the offence, despite frequent claims to the contrary.

With the development of intercontinental bombers and missiles, together with nuclear weapons, a devastating attack upon the American homeland did become technically feasible in a way that it had never been before. However, this did nothing to increase the extent to which the defence of the United States depended upon the assistance of other countries. The threat was countered by the deterrent effect of the nation's retaliatory (second-strike) capability, which has been entirely self-generated. Indeed, a good case can be made that the physical security of the United States in the nuclear age has been reduced rather than increased by its involvement in world politics, and especially by its commitment to 'extended deterrence'. As that tough-minded analyst Robert W. Tucker has repeatedly observed, 'the loss of allies, even the most important allies, would not significantly alter the prospects of an adversary surviving an attack upon the United States' but 'the risks that might have to be run on behalf of allies could lead to a nuclear confrontation that would escape the control of the great protagonists.'[27]

A historical approach

The question of why America came to play such an extensive role in world politics is not, then, convincingly answered by any of the general theories that attribute a determining influence to a single factor, be it 'power', 'economics' or 'security'. If we seek a more particular and historical explanation, we are led to focus on the decade of the 1940s. For what has been called 'the revolution in American foreign policy' occurred in the ten years that separated the fall of France from the outbreak of the Korean War.[28] At the beginning of 1940, the United States was still following a policy of unilateral non-involvement; by the end of 1950, it had not only assumed the leadership of such international organizations as the UN, the IMF, the World Bank, and GATT, but also committed substantial resources to efforts to affect the course of political developments across the globe.

In probing the reasons for this dramatic change, we need to concern ourselves with more than the minds of a small number of officials. The nature of the foreign-policy-making process in the United States is a controversial as well as complex subject. However, few would dispute that any policy which makes a significant demand upon resources needs a broad and deep basis of political support if it is to be sustained. Although policy makers, and particularly the president, have several important assets in developing such public support, they cannot, in an open and competitive political system, take it for granted.

An implication of these aspects of the way American foreign policy is made is that it is even more difficult than in the case of most countries to assimilate it to the model of a single, rational actor. Developing the necessary consensus behind a foreign policy of any significant degree of strenuousness is a process very similar to that required to put into effect a domestic policy. Indeed, in many cases it, too, involves mustering a congressional majority – whether for a declaration of war or a treaty or, more commonly, for the appropriation of the necessary funds. Such a process requires an aggregation of support, which is almost always the product of a coming together of people and groups with various interests and priorities, and also of individuals who are themselves responsive to more than one type of appeal.

This being so, the search for a single dynamic for US foreign policy seems fundamentally misconceived. On the other hand, the nature of the process does open the possibility that concern with economic interests or national security may have played a greater part in shaping American actions than would be deduced from a detached analysis of the nation's relationship to the rest of the world. In the first place, a disproportionate influence on policy may have been exercised by elements in society that were particularly involved in overseas economic activities or which had a vested interest in exaggerating the nation's vulnerability to attack. Furthermore, even those without any special reason for doing so may have misperceived the real situation.

The role of interest

Whether concern with the nation's economic or security interests played a decisive role in generating the necessary political support for US actions abroad is not a question that can be conclusively answered. Despite the vast body of material recording the opinions expressed by American policy makers, politicians, commentators, lobbyists and ordinary citizens about foreign-policy issues, weighing the considerations which were most important to people (and which may not have been articulated) must always be a matter of judgment. Moreover, for the majority of Americans, the only evidence of their views is that provided by poll data, which tells us much more about the level of support for particular policies than about the reasons for it. Nevertheless, one can make some inferences by looking at the record of American actions as well that of the almost continuous debate from which those actions emerged.

The influence of economic interests seems most significant in the case of the 'eastern establishment'. The heart of this lay in New York City, the home of banks and corporations that acquired substantial overseas assets during the First World War and the 1920s.[29] Since the great majority of these were in Europe, it hardly seems surprising that prominent New York bankers and lawyers associated with them wanted the United States to assist in the economic and political stabilization of that continent. They were among the keenest supporters of Wilson's attempt to lead the United States into the League of Nations and, after this had been defeated, took the initiative in organizing the Dawes and Young Plan loans in an attempt to resolve the war debts/reparations tangle. Throughout the interwar period, some of the firmest opponents of 'isolationism' such as Henry Stimson and the members of the Council on Foreign Relations were associated with New York banks and law firms.[30] Augmented by other capital-intensive and internationally competitive businesses from the late 1930s, this financial and corporate elite has been seen as the driving force behind the Marshall Plan.[31]

Although this is the most persuasive version of an economic interpretation of American foreign policy, some caveats need to be entered. The first is that the sense of involvement with Europe felt by most upper-class Americans in the first half of the twentieth century was based on much more than an economic relationship. Indeed, the financial links can be seen as reflecting these other ties. Most of the American capital that went to Europe before the Second World War took the form of the purchase of some form of government bonds rather than of direct investment or portfolio investment in business enterprises.[32] This process began on a large scale with the loans to the Allies during the First World War before the USA itself became belligerent. They were handled by J. P. Morgan & Co., whose actions seem to have been inspired much less by financial motives than by the partners' passionate sense of commitment to the Allied cause.[33] European reconstruction in the 1920s was a cause with wider appeal on Wall Street because firms with German–American directors could enter into it more wholeheartedly. But the support for such reconstruction both then and after the Second World War cannot really be understood unless the cultural milieu of the 'eastern establishment' is taken into account. As Walter Isaacson and Evan Thomas have written of the 'small, tightly knit group of men' who conceived and carried through the Marshall Plan:

> it was not just the United States they sought to serve but, in a broader sense, the culture and civilization of the West. ... As children, they had strolled with their parents through Europe's Edwardian autumn; as young men they had immersed themselves in the tangled economies and politics of the Continent on the eve of its Nazi ordeal.[34]

The second caveat is that this elite did not have the political leverage to shape American policy; the interwar period demonstrated that. In building the broader consensus necessary to sustain an active and strenuous 'internationalism', invocation of the nation's economic interests played at best a minor role. It is true that in the battle against isolationism in 1940–41, Franklin D. Roosevelt and others painted a dire picture of the consequences for American living standards of a Hitler-dominated world. But their arguments were vigorously contested and there is little reason to believe that this was a major factor in developing public support for Lend-Lease and other 'short-of-war' measures.[35] More often, it has been opponents of intervention who have attributed it to economic motives, notably in the cases of the First World War and Vietnam. This has reflected a common assumption that overseas economic interests have been essentially sectional rather than national in character as well as the related belief that they were not worth the lives of American boys.

Security from attack, by contrast, has been generally agreed to be a national interest of supreme importance and the best (for some, the only acceptable) justification for military force. In a message to Hitler and Mussolini in April 1939, Roosevelt declared that 'nothing can persuade the peoples of the earth that any governing power has any right or need to inflict the consequences of war on its own or any other people save in the cause of self-evident home defense'.[36] It is not therefore surprising that 'national security' has been a principal justification for America's adoption of a world role. It first achieved this prominence in the period before the USA entered the Second World War when the case for abandoning neutrality was made by Roosevelt and others largely in terms of the threat that victory for Hitler would present to America itself; Lend-Lease, for example, was formally entitled 'an Act to Promote the Defense of the United States'. It was argued that the defeat of Britain would remove the shield of the Royal Navy and that, if the Axis powers controlled the resources of the entire Old World, the Western hemisphere would be out-matched. This last point was elaborated by writers such as N. J. Spykman and Walter Lippmann into the proposition that America's security depended upon preventing any single power achieving dominance of the Eurasian continent.[37] During the 1940s this became established as a premise of strategic thinking and it has remained a basic rationale of the nation's world role to the present day.[38] In one of its more widely cited versions, George F. Kennan often insisted on the importance of preventing the Soviet Union from acquiring control of any of the other 'five centers of industrial and military power ... which would enable people there to develop and launch the type of amphibious power which would have to be launched if our national security were to be seriously affected'.[39]

That such arguments have been advanced and reiterated does not, however, prove that they have been of decisive importance in building support for America's involvement in world politics. It is open to question how real a sense of danger was felt by Americans in the 1940s, before the development of intercontinental bombers and missiles. In a 'fireside chat' in September 1941, Roosevelt warned that if the Axis powers gained control of 'the world outside the Americas', they 'would have the manpower and the physical resources' to defeat the United

States.⁴⁰ In light of the military situation at the time, such a diagnosis would seem to have called for a stronger remedy than aid to the beleaguered Britain and Russia. The fact that the president did not call for war, and that the public showed little readiness to support such a move, suggests that neither really believed in this scenario. It is true that polls taken in the summer of 1940 found a majority of Americans expecting an attack on the Western hemisphere quickly to follow a conclusive German victory in Europe, but this apprehension seems to have declined over the next year as Britain's survival was taken to show that the sea, even when it was as narrow as the English Channel, remained a formidable military barrier. Whereas Selective Service had been adopted in September 1940 with large majorities in both houses of Congress, its extension was passed in August 1941 by a margin of only one vote in the House of Representatives. 'Fundamentally', Robert Divine has observed, 'the close ballot indicated that the American people were not convinced that Germany and Japan truly endangered the security of the United States. The near-panic which followed the fall of France had subsided.'⁴¹

It is nonetheless clear that 1940–41 saw a decisive change in public sentiment that made it possible for the United States to embark on a course of action carrying a real risk of war and that laid the basis for the post-Pearl Harbor 'internationalist' consensus. The very real prospect of a German victory led most Americans to approve such departures from a policy of strict neutrality and non-involvement as Lend-Lease and the destroyers-for-bases deal. Others wanted the United States to go further and enter the war as a full-scale belligerent. These attitudes reflected several concerns, of which fear for America's own safety was only one. Britain's fight for survival, so vividly and sympathetically reported across the Atlantic, pulled many emotional strings. Moreover, after the elimination of France it seemed clear that the Axis could not be defeated unless the United States threw at least some of its weight into the struggle. And in the fight against Hitler, few would deny that a moral and ideological issue was involved. 'You cannot say that you believe in freedom and democracy and then help to destroy it somewhere else', the columnist Dorothy Thompson observed in her testimony on behalf of the Lend-Lease Act.⁴²

Yet, whatever the impulse by which they themselves were moved, those who wanted America to do more had a strong incentive to emphasize – and exaggerate – the military threat that a victorious Germany would pose to the United States. Not only did this put the case against 'isolationism' firmly on the grounds of national interest but, since self-defence was by far the most widely accepted justification for the use of force, it also laid a basis for American entry into the war.[43] We should not, therefore, assume that security concerns were in reality the primary motive, as Henry Luce pointed out in his 'American Century' essay (itself a contribution to the Lend-Lease debate):

> We are *in* the war. ... How did we get in? We got in on the basis of defense. Even that very word, defense, has been full of deceit and self-deceit. To the average American the plain meaning of the word defense is defense of American territory. Is our national policy today limited to the defense of the American homeland by whatever means may seem wise? It is not. We are *not* in a war to defend American territory. ... If the entire rest of the world came under the organized domination of evil tyrants, it is quite possible to imagine that this country could make itself such a tough nut to crack that not all the tyrants in the world would care to come against us. ... No man can honestly say that as a pure matter of defense – defense of our homeland – it is necessary to get into or be in this war.

In truth, Luce maintained, 'we are in a war to defend and even to promote, encourage and incite so-called democratic principles throughout the world.'[44] The echoes here of the traditional idea that the United States has a special mission to uphold the cause of liberty and self-government reminds us that support for America's active role in world politics derived strength from the ideological and evangelical character of American nationalism. So it did, particularly in the crucial decade of the 1940s, from the strong ties between the preponderant part of the American population and Europe, which were, in the last analysis, a consequence of the fact that it was from that continent that they, or their forebears, had come. In assessing the importance of this last factor, it may be helpful to engage in a thought-experiment. Suppose that the economic and strategic relationship between the United States and Europe had been exactly as it was but that the countries there had been inhabited by peoples with whom Americans had little cultural connection, such as Hindus or Muslims. Would the 'objective' imperatives of national interest have still led to the same degree of political involvement and military commitment?

AMERICA

The role of power
Whether viewed 'objectively' or in terms of Americans' subjective perceptions of them, the nation's economic and security interests, then, do comparatively little to explain why the USA has played such a major role in world politics. On the other hand, the sheer extent of the nation's power has not only objectively facilitated the exercise of influence but also greatly strengthened the subjective inclination to become involved.

Objectively, the scale of American power has enabled the nation to achieve a large effect in the world at a relatively small cost. Victory in the Second World War established the USA and the USSR as the dominant powers in the world: it cost the latter at least 26 million dead, the former 323,000.[45] Of course, democracies tend to be particularly sensitive about this kind of cost, and American leaders have consistently sought to minimize casualties by using air and naval rather than land power wherever possible and by being prepared to spend money on extensive rescue and medical facilities as well as sophisticated weaponry. However, the sacrifices demanded by the deployment of American power have been moderate in other respects also. Even during the nation's greatest military effort in this century, the domestic standard of living (i.e. the total of goods and services available to the civilian population) continued to rise between 1940 and 1944.[46] Whereas in Britain total personal consumption had fallen by 1943 to only 70 per cent that of 1938–9, in the United States the wartime nadir (in 1942) was about 5 per cent *higher* than it had been in 1940.[47] The burden of the substantial overseas expenditures on economic aid, security assistance and the maintenance of US forces abroad during the 1940s and 1950s was greatly eased by America's accumulated gold reserves and chronic balance of payments surplus on private account. With the disappearance of these assets, foreign aid of all kinds fell from 2.4 per cent of GNP in 1949–52 to 0.5 per cent in the early 1980s.[48] However, because of the size of its economy, the United States in 1983 provided twice as much development assistance as any other country even though the proportion of its GNP devoted to such expenditure was the lowest of any industrial nation except Austria.[49]

Power on this scale obviously affects the cost/benefit calculation for foreign-policy enterprises; objectives that might have been judged not worth the price of the effort to achieve them can come to seem affordable. As the record of the United States in the interwar period shows, this does not mean that a state's foreign-policy goals will inevitably increase commensurately with its power. There are, after all, always domestic needs competing for the resources that a strenuous foreign policy requires. But the incentive effect of the relatively low costs of affecting the course of events beyond one's borders is strengthened by other, more psychological, concomitants of the possession of great power.

One such concomitant tends to be an enhanced sense of national pride and honour. These emotions are not, of course, felt only by the citizens of great powers, but the latter are able to derive a higher level of psychic gratification from their country's position in the world, and many Americans seem to have done so. Only a few, like George Liska, have been inspired by the glory of past empires to hope that America's achievements would in their turn become 'a feat to be remembered, and a model to be imitated, after the imperial creator has left the world of action for the realm of history'.[50] But the majority have shown themselves concerned that the USA should maintain its standing as the world's leading power, and have been ready to support vigorous action to uphold its prestige and the rights of its citizens.

Such nationalistic emotions have perhaps been more characteristic of 'mass' than of 'elite' opinion, and more strongly held by conservatives than by liberals.[51] The reverse has probably been the case with another concomitant of the possession of great power – a sense of responsibility for the course of events in other parts of the world. As a country gains in the capacity to influence such events, the consequences of inaction on its part come to seem more significant. This was the meaning of Theodore Roosevelt's declaration that 'we have no choice as to whether or not we shall play a great part in the world. All that we can decide is whether we shall play it well or ill.'[52] The idea that power brings with it responsibilities has been a recurring theme in the debates over US foreign policy throughout the twentieth century, and a leitmotif in the speeches of American leaders since the Second World War.

It is, as usual, difficult to assess exactly how influential such rhetoric has been in developing support for American foreign policy. Yet, there is little doubt that the knowledge that only the United States possessed the capacity to do what seemed to need doing weighed heavily with well-informed Americans in the 1940s. As we have seen, there were good grounds for questioning whether Hitler's victories in 1940 really posed a danger to the safety of North America. There was much less rational basis for doubting that they had produced a situation in which the outcome of the war would depend upon the actions of the

United States. If the nation continued to adhere to strict neutrality, within the terms even of the revised act of 1939, it was hard to see how Britain could hope to win the war against Hitler. (At this time, the Nazi–Soviet pact was still in being.) Nor was there any other power that had the means to contain further Japanese expansion in South-east Asia. In planning and establishing mechanisms to govern the postwar international economic and security order, policy makers in Washington operated on the assumption that America's strength brought with it a responsibility to act on behalf of the general welfare rather than its own narrow interests. So, many believed, had Britain done in the days of her pre-eminence; when Britain's capacities declined further in the postwar period, a similar motivation inspired the taking over of her geopolitical role in the Near and Middle East.[53]

Such behaviour tends to corroborate those 'structural' versions of realist theory that see great powers as compelled to shoulder the tasks of providing 'collective goods' for the international system. But before assuming this to be a universal tendency, we need to note that this motive would not have been sufficient in itself to develop the political support such commitments required. Notoriously, the Truman Doctrine and the Marshall Plan needed to be 'sold' on the basis of an ideological crusade against communism (a doctrine that had long been anathema to most Americans) and the threat of limitless Soviet expansionism.[54] One might wonder also whether the idea that power carries with it responsibilities would resonate as strongly in all capitals as it did in a Washington where the direction of policy was largely in the hands of Anglo-Saxon Protestants.[55] Finally, it might be observed that it took an extraordinary crisis in international affairs to precipitate the United States into action. The possibility that the whole world might be dominated by a sinister dictatorship has rarely seemed as real as it did in 1940–41 or, with that period in vivid memory, in 1948–51. It would be a pessimistic theory indeed that postulated an endless succession of Hitlers and Stalins.

Retrospect and prospect

This analysis suggests that the major role that the USA has played in world politics in the twentieth century has owed more to the scale of its power than to the requirements of its military security or economic prosperity. Yet although America's pre-eminent economic (and potential military) strength provided it with the wherewithal to exert great influence, it might well not have been prepared to meet the costs involved in the role it has assumed over the past half-century had it not been for such 'contingent' factors as the remarkable military successes of the Axis powers in 1940–41, the non-material ties with the European home of 'Western civilization' and the missionary character of American nationalism. If, throughout the century, America's capacity to influence events abroad has greatly exceeded that necessary to protect clear and important national interests, this may help to explain such frequently noted characteristics of its foreign policy as the amount of internal controversy it has generated, its tendency to oscillate, and the relative ease with which failure to achieve proclaimed objectives has been absorbed.

This analysis also implies that in the twenty-first century America's role in international affairs will be both smaller in extent and rather different in nature. Insofar as US foreign policy has had something of the quality of a 'luxury good', it is unlikely to find favour in a polity burdened by deficits and most reluctant to impose taxes. On the other hand, as the means available to policy makers decline, the demands of the nation's core interests may well increase. In security terms, it is true, it is hard to envisage any threat to the nation's self-sufficiency in the foreseeable future, but in the economic sphere the combination of increased interdependence and decreased competitiveness would seem to presage a greater concern with the political and diplomatic protection of narrow national interests.

Notes

1 'The American century', *Life*, 17 February 1941, pp.61–5 (64).
2 Paul Kennedy, *The Rise and Fall of the Great Powers: Economic Change and Military Conflict from 1500 to 2000* (London, 1988), pp.353–6.
3 Paul Bairoch, 'International industrialization levels from 1750 to 1980', *Journal of European Economic History*, 11 (1982), pp.296, 304.
4 Michael Mandelbaum, *The Fate of Nations: The Search for National Security in the Nineteenth and Twentieth Centuries* (Cambridge, 1988), pp.129, 133.
5 Robert Gilpin, *War and Change in World Politics* (Cambridge, 1981), pp.106–7.
6 Morgenthau seems to have seen this as one of the 'objective laws that have their roots in human nature' upon which he sought to erect his 'theory of international politics'. Hans J. Morgenthau, *Politics among Nations* (New York, 3/1965), pp.3–4, 33–5. Thucydides' sentence has been frequently quoted. Colin S. Gray is a recent writer for whom it captures 'the permanent realities of international politics'; see *The Geopolitics of Super Power* (Lexington, KY, 1988), p.33.
7 Martin Wight, *Power Politics*, ed. Hedley Bull and Carsten Holbraad

(Harmondsworth, 1979), p.144.
8 Kenneth N. Waltz, *Theory of International Politics* (Reading, MA, 1979), pp.195–209 (quotations on pp. 207, 195).
9 Robert Gilpin, *U.S. Power and the Multinational Corporation: The Political Economy of Foreign Direct Investment* (London, 1976), p.85.
10 Klaus Knorr, *The Power of Nations: The Political Economy of International Relations* (New York, 1975), p.94.
11 Kennedy, *The Rise and Fall of the Great Powers*, p.200. For the Churchill quotation, see Peter G. Boyle (ed.), *The Churchill–Eisenhower Correspondence. 1953–1955* (Chapel Hill and London, 1990), p.179.
12 Duncan Burn, *The Steel Industry 1939–1959: A Study in Competition and Planning* (Cambridge, 1961), table 105.
13 Charles P. Kindleberger, *The World in Depression 1929–1939* (Berkeley and Los Angeles, rev., enlarged 1986), chap. 14 (quotation on p.289).
14 The original, seminal statement of this thesis was William Appleman Williams, *The Tragedy of American Diplomacy* (Cleveland, 1959; New York, 1962, 1972). For a fuller critique of it, see J. A. Thompson, 'William Appleman Williams and the American "Empire"', *Journal of American Studies*, vii (1973), pp.191–104; and for a balanced assessment of its place in the historiography of US foreign policy, see Bradford Perkins, '"The tragedy of American diplomacy": twenty-five years after', *Reviews in American History*, xii (1984), pp.1–18.
15 US Bureau of the Census, *Historical Statistics of the United States: Colonial Times to 1970* (Washington, DC, 1975), pp.887, 903.
16 Robert W. Tucker, *The Radical Left and American Foreign Policy* (Baltimore and London, 1971), pp.128–9.
17 *Historical Statistics*, p.903.
18 For some examples of the assymetries involved, see Kenneth N. Waltz, 'The myth of national interdependence' in Charles P. Kindleberger (ed.), *The International Corporation* (Cambridge, MA, 1970), p.213. Robert O. Keohane points out that, strictly speaking, the relative strengths of bargaining positions depends on the opportunity costs involved, which will not necessarily be a function simply of the statistical value of the trade. He nevertheless accepts that other things being equal, one might expect that the country with the larger market would have more leverage. *After Hegemony: Cooperation and Discord in the World Political Economy* (Princeton, NJ, 1984), p.198.
19 The scheme was the European Payments Union; see Keohane, *After Hegemony*, pp.144–6.
20 Stephen D. Krasner, *Defending the National Interest: Raw Materials Investments and U.S. Foreign Policy* (Princeton, NJ, 1978), pp.156–78.
21 Ibid., *passim*, esp. pp.217–25, 274–7.
22 Charles Lipson, *Standing Guard: Protecting Foreign Capital in the Nineteenth and Twentieth Centuries* (Berkeley, Los Angeles and London, 1985), p.54.
23 Waltz, *Theory of International Politics*, p.158.
24 See, for example, *Tragedy of American Diplomacy*, pp.37–42, 106–8, 123; Walter LaFeber, *The New Empire: An Interpretation of American*

Expansion 1860–1898 (Ithaca, NY, 1963), p.416.
25 This phrase was coined by C. Vann Woodward in 'The age of reinterpretation', *American Historical Review*, lxvi (1960), pp.1–9.
26 John Keegan, *The Price of Admiralty: The Evolution of Naval Warfare* (Harmondsworth, 1988), pp.41–2.
27 Robert W. Tucker, *A New Isolationism: Threat or Promise?* (New York, 1972), p.46–7; *The Purposes of American Power: An Essay on National Security* (New York, 1981), p.121; 'Containment and the search for alternatives: a critique', in Aaron Wildavsky (ed.), *Beyond Containment: Alternative American Policies toward the Soviet Union* (San Francisco, 1983), pp.81–2.
28 William G. Carleton, *The Revolution in American Foreign Policy: Its Global Range* (New York, 1963).
29 See the figures in Jeff Frieden, 'Sectoral conflict and foreign economic policy. 1914–1940', *International Organization*, xlii (1988), pp.60–90.
30 On this tradition, see Robert D. Schulzinger, *The Wise Men of Foreign Affairs: The History of the Council on Foreign Relations* (New York, 1984) and Priscilla Roberts, '"All the right people": The historiography of the American foreign policy establishment', *Journal of American Studies*, xxvi (1992), pp.409–34.
31 Michael J. Hogan, *The Marshall Plan: America, Britain, and the Reconstruction of Western Europe, 1947–1952* (Cambridge, 1987), pp.10–18. Hogan here draws upon the analysis of Thomas Ferguson, 'From Normalcy to the New Deal: industrial structure, party competition, and American public policy in the Great Depression', *International Organization*, xxxviii (1984), pp.41–94.
32 John Braeman, 'The New Left and American foreign policy during the age of normalcy: a re-examination', *Business History Review*, lvii (1983), pp.85, 88. The total of overseas portfolio investment (very largely in government securities) was only slightly larger than that of direct investment, but it was much more heavily concentrated in Europe.
33 Priscilla Roberts, *The American "Eastern Establishment" and World War I: The Emergence of a Foreign Policy Tradition* (PhD diss., Cambridge University, 1981).
34 Walter Isaacson and Evan Thomas, *The Wise Men: Six Friends and the World they Made* (New York, 1986), pp.406–7
35 Justus D. Doenecke, 'Power, markets, and ideology: the isolationist response to Roosevelt policy, 1940–1941', in Leonard P. Liggio and James J. Martin (eds), *Watershed of Empire: Essays on New Deal Foreign Policy* (Colorado Springs, 1976).
36 Samuel I. Rosenman (ed.), Public *Papers and Addresses of Franklin D. Roosevelt 1939* [hereafter *PPA*] (New York, 1941), pp.202–3. In the UN Charter, 'the inherent right of individual or collective self-defense if an armed attack occurs' (Article 51) is the only qualification on the commitment by member states to 'settle their international disputes by peaceful means' (Article 2(3)).
37 Nicholas John Spykman, *America's Strategy in World Politics: The United States and the Balance of Power* (New York, 1942); Walter

Lippmann, *US Foreign Policy: Shield of the Republic* (Boston, 1943).
38   Thus Henry Kissinger recently defined America's 'vital interest' in world politics as preventing 'the domination by a single power of either of Eurasia's two principal spheres – Europe or Asia'; see *Diplomacy* (New York, 1994), pp.812–13.
39   John Lewis Gaddis, *Strategies of Containment: A Critical Appraisal of Postwar American National Security Policy* (New York, 1982), p.30; George F. Kennan, *Realities of American Foreign Policy* (Princeton, NJ, 1954), pp.63–4; idem, *Memoirs 1925–1950* (Boston, 1967), p.359.
40   *PPA: 1941* (New York, 1950) p.388.
41   Robert A. Divine, *The Reluctant Belligerent: American Entry into World War II* (New York, 1965), p.131.
42   For a fuller statement of the argument in this and the preceding paragraph, see John A. Thompson, 'Another look at the downfall of "Fortress America"', *Journal of American Studies*, xxvi (1992), pp.393–408.
43   The tendency to exaggerate American vulnerability has been a recurrent one throughout the twentieth century, and has usually been associated with the desire to exercise American power abroad. See John A. Thompson, 'The exaggeration of American vulnerability: the anatomy of a tradition', *Diplomatic History*, xvi (1992), pp.23–43.
44   'The American century', pp.61–2.
45   This point is made in David Reynolds, 'Power and superpower: the Impact of two world wars on America's international role', in Warren F. Kimball (ed.), *America Unbound: World War II and the Making of a Superpower* (New York, 1992), p.22.
46   John Morton Blum, *V was for Victory: Politics and American Culture during the Second World War* (New York, 1976), p.91.
47   Harold G. Vatter, *The U.S. Economy in World War II* (New York, 1985), p.20.
48   David A. Baldwin, *Economic Statecraft* (Princeton, NJ, 1985), p.296.
49   Susan Strange, *States and Markets* (London, 1988), p.220.
50   George Liska, *Imperial America: The International Politics of Primacy* (Baltimore, 1967), p.113.
51   See generally, Michael Mandelbaum and William Schneider, 'The new internationalisms: public opinion and American foreign policy', in Kenneth A. Oye, Donald Rothchild and Robert J. Lieber (eds), *Eagle Entangled: U.S. Foreign Policy in a Complex World* (New York, 1979), pp.34–88; William Schneider, 'Conservatism, not interventionism: trends in foreign policy opinion, 1974–1982', in *Eagle Entangled*, pp.33–64.
52   Quoted in Howard K. Beale, *Theodore Roosevelt and the Rise of America to World Power* (Baltimore, 1959), p.173.
53   For Washington officials' perceptions of Britain's traditional role and the responsibility of the USA to take it over, see Joseph M. Jones, *The Fifteen Weeks* (February 21–June 5, 1947) (New York, 1955), esp. pp.40–4, 130–1.
54   On this see, for example, Robert A. Pollard, *Economic Security and the Origins of the Cold War, 1945–1950* (New York, 1985), pp.19–25. In January 1939, in answer to the question, 'If you had to choose, which kind

of government would you prefer to live under – the kind in Germany or the kind in Russia?', 26 per cent opted for the first, 24 per cent for the second, and 52 per cent refused to choose; see Jerome S. Bruner, *Mandate from the People* (New York, 1944), p.108. In 1937 Gallup found 59 per cent of the public saying that, if forced to choose, it would rather live under the kind of government in Nazi Germany than under the kind in Russia; see Ralph B. Levering, *American Opinion and the Russian Alliance. 1939–1945* (Chapel Hill, 1976), p.17. This reflected a depth of antagonism fostered by countless denunciations of communism as the enemy of all that most Americans believed in – not only the free enterprise system but also religion. Such denunciations, particularly by Catholic spokesmen, were not stemmed by the Second World War and in 1941 Roosevelt had made a point of emphasizing that 'the Nazis are as ruthless as the Communists in the denial of God' (radio address, 27 May 1941); see *PPA: 1941*, p.184.

55   It is sometimes argued that the largest state in the system has so much the greatest interest in it that its share of the benefits from 'collective goods' will outweigh the total cost of producing them. But this argument subsumes in the concept of size the two variables of capability and interests, which need not be equivalent. As we have seen, in the American case the former has been much larger than the latter in both economic and security terms. In such cases, the impetus to provide collective goods has to come from a sense of 'responsibility' which, in international affairs as in other realms of life, will not necessarily accord with a narrowly defined self-interest.

3. RUSSIA

Edward Acton

Whereas the twentieth-century history of some societies may be written as drama, and perhaps a very few as comedy, that of Russia and the Soviet Union is unmistakably tragedy. The opening Act (1900–28) saw the overthrow of autocracy, the failure of liberal and moderate socialist efforts to restrain popular determination to smash the social legacy of Tsarism, and the emergence from within a popular revolution and civil war of a highly autonomous and centralized Communist government. In Act II (1928–41) this government launched a momentous industrialization drive accompanied by forcible collectivization of agriculture, political terror and mass repression. Act III (1941–53) saw the Soviet Union in turn devastated and triumphant in the Great Patriotic War, and then in the Cold War elevated to superpower status while enduring acute deprivation and vicious repression. In the fourth Act (1953–75), the system enjoyed a period of stability based upon the party's jealously guarded political monopoly, sustained economic growth and upward social mobility, and alternating doses of international pride and paranoia. The denouement (1975–91) was brought on by the economy's failure to maintain the growth necessary to sustain superpower status and meet the demands of an increasingly sophisticated population. Gorbachev's reforms unleashed forces he could not control and a somewhat aged and tainted Fortinbras, in the person of Yeltsin, emerged to preside over the banning of the Communist Party and the final lowering of the Red Flag.

The moral of the tale

Given the spurious claims made on behalf of the Soviet system at the height of its power, it is scarcely surprising that few tears were shed over its collapse or that the negative verdict passed upon it should be almost unanimous. The regime based its claim to legitimacy on the assertion that it was the product of a law-governed historical process which foreshadowed the destiny of all societies. Lenin, Stalin, Khrushchev and Brezhnev in turn insisted that the Soviet system was the most progressive in the world, the harbinger of humanity's future, and would in the long run prevail over its doomed capitalist rival. They proclaimed the system the fulfilment of history and asked that it be judged in those terms. History has spoken. The story of the Soviet Union is the most blood-curdling lesson in what not to do, the supreme cautionary tale of the twentieth century.

The question is: what is the moral of the tale? Naturally enough those who had most loudly and consistently denounced the USSR during its heyday saw no difficulty in explaining it. The champions of the free market, having enjoyed an ideological resurgence during the 1970s and 1980s, hailed the collapse of communism as the final proof of their case. With delight they watched as Gorbachev's efforts to reform and revitalize the Soviet system foundered and as voices rose across Eastern Europe for a drastic shift towards a market economy. The favourable impact which the Soviet model had once had on the prestige of economic planning was thrown into reverse. Whereas in the 1930s the dynamic image projected by the USSR provided ammunition for those in the West who sought to promote planning and state intervention, in the 1990s it has been the turn of free marketeers to point to the Soviet model – and its abject failure. Like latter-day mirror-images of the Webbs, they seem quite happy to explain away a temporary dose of economic and social desolation en route to the market working its magic.[1] The debate over which the nineteenth century expended so much intellectual energy and the twentieth century so much blood, they have pronounced, has come an end. Planning has been tested and found wanting. The shades of Saint-Simon, Marx and the Fabians must concede victory to the spiritual descendants of Adam Smith.

This verdict quickly gained the status of conventional wisdom, endorsed by newspaper columnists, heavyweight weeklies and countless radio and television commentaries. It was one of the central themes of Fukuyama's thesis in *The End of History*. With the collapse of the Soviet experiment, left-wing challenges to capitalism have reached the end of the line. Capitalism alone can accommodate technologically driven economic modernization; no other economic system is compatible with constant innovation and the ever more complex division of labour involved. The centrally planned economy and the totalitarian oppression implicit in it have also come up against the universal human drive in the direction of liberal democracy.² The Soviet débâcle, we are urged, has rendered three truths self-evident. First, a planned economy is a denial of the 'natural order' and, in terms of wealth-creation, a disaster. Second, a planned economy is inherently incompatible with democracy. Third, as a logical consequence of the obstacle it presents to economic growth and political democracy alike, planning is in long-term retreat.

Putting planning to the test

Before assessing this reading of the Soviet experience and the twentieth century, it is worth pausing momentarily to consider how we would explain the matter to a Victorian advocate of planning. Take, for example, Alfred Wallace, Darwin's sometime collaborator, a mild and hopeful socialist. In his declining years, reflecting on the meaning of his own century and drawing up a balance sheet of its successes and failures, he urged 'all earnest and thinking men and women' to look beyond the existing system of 'capitalistic production and distribution' towards a form of planning to cure 'those ulcers [that] are the necessary product of competitive individualism'.³ How would he have reacted had he learned that in its wisdom humanity had chosen the Russian Empire as the location for a conclusive test of planning? Whereas a tearaway young Fabian might well have eagerly endorsed the experiment without a second thought, one can imagine at least a shadow of doubt crossing the mind of an elderly gentleman like Wallace. Had not Russia at the beginning of the twentieth century only just emerged from serfdom? Of all the major powers, was she not the one with the lowest level of literacy and the most explosive population growth? Did she not suffer from the shortest growing season, the least predictable climatic conditions, and the highest incidence of harvest failure? Did she not have the lowest GNP per head, the most backward and uneven economy, parts of which were barely integrated into the national market and much of which was served by the worst communications network in Europe? Was she not the country furthest from a law-governed state, administered by a bureaucracy which was a byword for corruption, incompetence, abysmally unreliable statistics and an almost paranoid concern for secrecy? He might also have regretted the choice of a society made up of over a hundred different nationalities and one in which the single most powerful cultural influence had for centuries been exerted by, of all the world's great religions, Russian Orthodoxy.

All this would have been enough to give our Victorian shade pause. But he would have begun to have real reservations had we also told him that the experiment was to be launched in the aftermath of a double dose of military defeat and revolution, first in 1905 and then repeated in spades in 1917, and to be inaugurated amidst the most savage and destructive civil war Europe had ever seen, bringing the industrial economy to a virtual halt, driving much of the educated population into exile, and contributing to deaths through violence, disease and famine totalling some 9 million.[4] Indeed, this was enough to make H. G. Wells and, for a time, even the Webbs take a very gloomy view of the whole Bolshevik enterprise.[5] Wallace would have become distinctly restless had we gone on to tell him that in the course of the first three Five-Year Plans the combination of political repression, forced collectivization and famine would cost another 10 million lives, and that the immediate sequel to the first phase of Soviet-style 'planning' would be invasion by the most powerful army the world had ever seen; indescribably brutal occupation; the destruction of much of the country's economic capacity; four years of total war; and the death of at least 26 million and, by some estimates, anything up to one-fifth of the pre-1939 population.[6] Had we then warned him that the experiment was to be concluded in an atmosphere of grave international tension and be dominated by an open-ended arms race against an alliance of the wealthiest and most powerful nations of the world that for years on end would consume up to 20 per cent of GNP, he would have begun to object that perhaps the dice were being somewhat loaded.

But when all is said and done, these surely are matters of detail. They ignore the country's vast, unrivalled natural resources and they do nothing to alter the plain fact before all our eyes that the Soviet experiment in central planning ended in fiasco.

Planning Soviet-style

So let us turn to the lessons to be drawn about the nature and fate of planning. There is no consensus on the precise meaning of the term but for a working definition we could do worse than consult that great anti-planning Cassandra, Friedrich Hayek. 'An economic plan, to deserve the name, must have a unitary conception', he wrote; it is 'a complex whole in which all the parts must be carefully adjusted to each other'.⁷ The cap seems, at first glance, to fit perfectly. Successive Soviet Five-Year Plans, and the shorter-term interim plans, took a comprehensive view of the economy – investment, labour, output, foreign trade, balance of payments, wages, consumption, productivity, heavy and light industry, grain and dairy produce, education and training, housing and welfare. On this basis they drew up targets for every sector, every region, every enterprise. The Communist Party leadership then implemented the plan through the vast administrative apparatus at its disposal. This great Leviathan, rigidly hierarchical and centralized, looks on the face of it the ideal instrument for planning. State officials and economic managers were supervised and monitored by a party apparatus, itself subject to the disciplines of democratic centralism and shadowed in turn by a vast secret police force armed with sweeping powers and supported by a seemingly ubiquitous information network. The lines of command for the implementation of the plan could hardly look firmer. Officials in every arm of the state – industry, agriculture, soviets, education, the military – would defy orders at peril not only of their jobs but of their liberty and, at times, their lives. Through this army of officials, the leadership proceeded to instruct, urge and if necessary force peasants and workers to carry out the plan to the letter. With the state in effect the sole employer, the masses were dependent on it for survival; not only did it provide their living wage but it was through employment that they secured housing and welfare; and all this was backed up by the unlimited legal and coercive sanctions the state could impose upon them. In short, the 'totalitarian' state looks ideally equipped to put the centrally planned economy to the test.

The problem is that the more closely we examine the command economy created by Stalin, the less it looks like an economy where all parts are 'carefully adjusted to each other'. In the formative years, it lurched from crisis to crisis, time and again fell hopelessly short of its production targets, wildly overshot the planned level of wages and labour, began massive programmes only to halt them half-finished, entailed waste on a colossal scale, and virtually abandoned vast and vital areas of the economy as residues left to fend for themselves. Every archive excavated bears witness to the cavalier treatment of variables as critical as foreign trade and health provision, the 'bacchanalian' assumptions, the minimal allowance made for unforeseen contingencies.⁸

In part this arose from political interference and the imposition of unrealistic targets upon Gosplan. In part, too, it arose from the deeply flawed information on which the centre relied. The problem was not only that the statistics were so poor, the bureaucracy so overburdened with paper work, the educational level of officials so low, and communications across the vast country so difficult. The misinformation was more deeply rooted in the efforts of industrial, agricultural and party officials to exaggerate output, underestimate potential, and evade the supervision of Moscow. But information was not the only casualty of this tension between the centre and its servants. In seeking to achieve their targets and ensure that their commissariat, region, city or enterprise secured scarce labour and raw materials, officials bucked the will of their masters and were drawn into semi-officials and often corrupt networks lubricated by patronage and bribery.

Moreover, the methods used by the regime to overcome the real and perceived resistance from within its own apparatus could hardly have been more disruptive. It empowered plenipotentiaries to override the regular administration and cut through normal regulations. During the First Five-Year Plan it orchestrated a campaign against 'bourgeois' specialists and replaced them with 'red' specialists and managers, tens of thousands of workers given crash courses in higher education and promoted off the factory floor. Part of the purpose in 1930 of despatching the famous 25000ers, handpicked workers chosen to help enforce collectivization, was to enable Moscow to reassert control over local officials deemed to be showing either excessive or inadequate zeal in handling recalcitrant peasants.[9] Another strategy was to invite pressure from below, to encourage workers to denounce instances of inefficiency, corruption and 'wrecking' on the part of state officials and economic managers. An important motive behind the official support for the Stakhanovite movement in the mid-1930s was to compel management to adopt new production methods by combining pressure from above with demands by model workers from below.[10]

Most drastically, under Stalin, the centre resorted to the arrest and in many cases the execution of suspect officials. The precedent was set in the notorious Shakhty trial of 1928 when 55 specialists in the coal industry in the Donbass were found guilty of using their position deliberately to sabotage economic planning. In 1930 and 1931 fabricated cases against the 'Toiling Peasant Party', the 'Industrial Party' and the 'Menshevik Union Bureau' took a heavy toll of economists, agrarian and industrial specialists and other officials involved in the state planning agencies. In the course of the First Five-Year Plan period there was a massive purge of rural state and party officials and of trade union officials. An even more extensive and far bloodier attack on officialdom formed an integral part of the Great Terror of 1936–8. Although this was not all that there was to the Terror, a powerful case is being assembled by several recent pieces of work on the 1930s that it does explain the main thrust of the horrors of 1936–8.[11] Unable to admit or possibly even to understand that abuse and rule-breaking was endemic and not the product of ill-will, Stalin's group sought to stamp them out in the most drastic fashion possible. To his surprise, the decimation of the country's skilled and experienced specialists and administrators proved a poor remedy for inefficiency, corruption and tension between centre and periphery rooted in the very nature of the Soviet economic system. It made a nonsense of planning.

In the decades after Stalin's death, the centre retreated from terror, but resignation in the face of defiance by officialdom was scarcely more conducive to planning. Indeed, the more closely 'planning' became based on past performance or attained levels of output, the less leverage the centre had to alter the behaviour of enterprises. Reviewing the Khrushchev and Brezhnev years, senior figures like Nazarbaev, subsequently President of Kazakhstan, confessed that 'I don't believe that in the past three decades we have really had a planned economy.'[12]

With the state's own servants failing to implement orders and deliberately misleading the centre, rational planning and coordination of different branches of the economy was quite simply impossible. But even if the state machinery had been the streamlined mechanism of myth, its ability to direct and control the mass of the population beneath it was severely limited. Two aspects of this limitation deserve emphasis. The first concerns the collectivization of peasant agriculture.[13] The state was confronted by the bitter hostility of the vast majority of peasants and found there was a point beyond which it could not bend them to its will. Symbolic of this were the household plots it was forced to concede to the peasantry. Each household was permitted to retain a plot of land of somewhat less than an acre for its own use, together with a small amount of livestock, and to market its surplus produce. And, contrary to the whole ethos of collectivization, the peasantry devoted an entirely disproportionate amount of their time and effort to these small plots. Soviet agriculture was bedevilled from the start. Every device used to motivate and discipline peasant labour on collective farms proved dismally unsuccessful. Monetary incentives were minimal, limited as they were to the meagre surplus left after both the state's insatiable appetite and the farm's running costs were met. In this situation even the most diligent farm managers found the problems intractable. Intervention by local party and state authorities into the detailed running of the farms did little to improve matters. Based as it often was on minimal knowledge of agriculture in general and local conditions in particular, it served only to alienate the peasantry further. Nor did Khrushchev's massive organizational reforms tackle the underlying problem.[14] The apathy, neglect and petty insubordination of the peasantry amounted to a form of passive resistance which the seemingly unlimited power of the state could not overcome and which ensured that agricultural shortfalls constantly unbalanced the 'plan'.

An analogous situation limited the state's control over industrial workers. True, collective protest was kept to a minimum. But the state proved unable to approximate the degree of control over the individual worker to which it aspired. What prevented it from doing so was that, despite their lack of independent collective organizations, workers retained a rudimentary amount of autonomy and bargaining power. This was guaranteed by the chronic labour shortage created by overtaut targets. The effect was to compel managers to compete with each other in order to secure and retain labour, thereby limiting their ability to discipline workers. No matter how furiously the state hurled down decrees against high labour turnover, absenteeism, slipshod work, alcoholism, defiance of foremen and damage to machinery, managers were severely inhibited about implementing them. What happened on the factory floor was in large measure beyond the control of the planning authorities.[15]

Before permitting the Soviet experience to cast a pall over planning as such, therefore, we need to be clear about what it is that is being written off. If the definition of a centrally planned economy is one in which all parts are 'carefully adjusted to each other', there are grounds for questioning whether the label is appropriate for the Soviet economy.[16] There is no denying, of course, the lengths to which the regime went to portray itself thus or the political advantage it derived from the pretence that every facet of the economy was integrated into an overall plan: the mobilizing role of each successive Five-Year Plan and the mythical status they acquired have rightly been stressed.[17] But the reality was very different. The regime was quite incapable of implementing a plan embracing the whole economy. What it was able to do was to identify a strictly limited number of priority objectives and to wrench the economy out of its groove to achieve them, effecting fundamental shifts in the pattern of investment and labour by deliberate acts of government policy in defiance of the market. If this is the sense in which we use the term 'planning', there is no doubt towards which end of the spectrum the Soviet economy belongs. But of course once a balance sheet is attempted in these more narrow terms, rather more attention has to be paid to the extent to which such priority goals were achieved. First and foremost among the objectives it set itself was to develop heavy industry and the defence sector, to defeat Hitler, and to match the nuclear capability developed by its much wealthier rival superpower after the Great Patriotic War. The twenty-first century may be more inclined to dwell on why 'success' here came at such an awesome price and why it could not be generalized rather than to consign the whole ordeal to the rubbish-heap of history.

In a sense, then, the Soviet economy masqueraded as a planned economy. The regime took infinite pains to uphold the myth that it operated upon rational lines to achieve coherent goals embracing every facet of social life. In time, now that that vast propaganda machine is no more, the myth can be expected to fade. It should be no surprise if it does not do so immediately. For champions of the free market there is every incentive to seek to perpetuate the identification of planning with the record – and fate – of the USSR. But as that record recedes into the past and archival work advances, it may become increasingly difficult to do so.

Planning and democracy
This raises the second proposition urged by warriors enjoying the afterglow of their triumph in the Cold War, namely that there is now conclusive evidence about the relationship between planning and democracy. The lesson of this supremely oppressive regime, we are told, is that planning and democracy stand virtually in inverse proportion, that planning is incompatible with democracy. To turn to Hayek again, this of course was one of his basic theses. Central planning requires consent on a phenomenal range of issues. Since in terms of judgment, interests and morality the common ground between individuals is distinctly limited, it is impossible to obtain such consent by democratic means. The road to the centrally planned economy is therefore the road to serfdom.[18]

But the point that emerges from a study of Soviet so-called planning is that democracy was never even tried. The relationship between the state and the peasantry established under Stalin was based in its very essence upon coercion. The entire industrialization drive denied the democratic voice and civil rights not only of peasants but of workers, the intelligentsia, and indeed the rank and file of the party itself. This 'planning' process did not destroy democracy. It arose from and was launched upon a fundamentally undemocratic order.

It might be objected that the limitations on the power of the centre – the notion that there was bargaining between officials, peasants and workers on the one hand, and the government on the other; that the government was frustrated by its own officials; that the state could not impose its will on workers; that it failed to make peasants do its bidding; and that it enjoyed a measure of support from below – that all this amounts to a form of consultation, of interest-group politics, even of informal democracy. That this is what is being implied by much recent Western work on the 1930s is the prime charge made against so-called 'revisionists'.[19] It is claimed that by studying what they call the social dynamics of the period, by noting the minority who materially benefited from upward mobility, the residual autonomy retained by workers, the extent to which official policy was affected by pressure from below, these 'revisionists' are attributing to Stalin's regime a form of pluralism, of give-and-take between state and society, of political manoeuvre and popular pressure which sounds all too much like any other government, whether democratic or not, operating in difficult conditions. It is not clear, in fact, that a single 'revisionist' would accept this implication of his work. To do so would be profoundly misguided. The overweening coercive power of the state and the unprecedented extent of its autonomy were defining characteristics of the early Soviet period. This was the very antithesis of a democratic state. The deliberate and unwitting frustration of the government's will, both by its own servants and by peasants and workers, bears no relation to democratic control and participation.

This is not to deny that there were elements of positive support for the regime, and that they form a vital part in the drama. Support came from those grateful that unemployment had ended, resentful of the seemingly privileged position of so-called kulaks and intelligentsia in the 1920s, convinced by the class-war rhetoric in terms of which Stalin's industrialization drive was launched, alarmed by the apparent threat from abroad, enthused by the vision of a socialist future for their children, motivated by opportunities for upward social mobility.[20] But the idea that this renders Soviet-style 'planning' in some sense democratic is a non-starter. For one thing the support was that of a small minority. For another, even that minority was not engaged in detailed consultation and collective decision-making. Indeed, it is a misnomer even to speak of this amounting to a 'social base' for the state. The point that needs to be made is that those elements to benefit from being promoted off the shop floor into managerial and official positions were in effect absorbed into the state. Workers involved in collectivization who remained in the countryside took up positions in the local party and state hierarchies; enthusiasts for cultural revolution were set to work to enforce increasingly centralized political control over scholarship, art and education; shock workers and the upwardly mobile generally were appointed to positions in which they wielded a modicum of state power. They blazed a trail followed by millions who, over ensuing decades, came to occupy posts in the vastly expanded administrative, economic and coercive apparatus. In so doing they crossed the notional line between state and society without forming a social base outside the state itself.

This points to a conception of the relationship between planning and democracy rather different from that posited by Hayek. The Soviet experience suggests that far from being a necessary condition for planning, the absence of democracy was a severe constraint upon it. Much of what bedevilled Soviet-style 'planning' arose precisely from the lack of consultation over, support for, and consensus behind its proclaimed goals.[21] In this respect, perhaps the most indicative phase of Soviet history was that of the Great Patriotic War. It was then that the regime enjoyed the greatest support and it is arguable that it was then that the greatest economic feats were achieved. As the pre-war years had shown, force and a battery of draconian decrees could not ensure that orders from above were obeyed. Moreover, amidst the chaos of invasion, with key economic sectors thrown into confusion, communications disrupted, most of the central party and state apparatus evacuated from Moscow and relocated in the east, and the administrative system drained of hundreds of thousands of key personnel called to the front, the centre was fully stretched in trying to mobilize resources for the military. Yet what was most striking, in many ways, was the resilience of the civilian economy. And this is largely explicable in terms of the fact that the 'command economy' enjoyed the popular support whose absence had so profoundly handicapped it in peacetime. It was this which explains why millions gave far more to the war effort than coercion could ever have extracted, poured into the voluntary militia, engaged spontaneously in 'socialist competition' and worked to breaking point in industry and agriculture. It explains why industrial productivity held up as well as it did despite wartime disruption, mass malnutrition, barely human living and working conditions, and an industrial workforce drastically recast, as skilled and experienced men were called to arms and replaced by untrained ex-peasants, youths and women (almost 60 per cent by 1943). It explains how the country was fed at all, despite the German occupation of the best land, the loss to the army and industry of three-quarters of the able-bodied menfolk working on the collective farms, the requisitioning of most of the horses, and the virtual collapse of mechanization.[22]

The conviction that the command economy could take on new life only by winning popular endorsement was, of course, central to Gorbachev's ideological odyssey. And here, surely, was what our Victorian shade would have objected to most strongly about humanity's proposed experiment in the lands of the Russian Empire: the absence of democracy. If we had admitted that the whole thing was to be run by a vicious sectarian dictatorship sworn to an ageing ideology and possessed of unassailable intellectual arrogance, prepared to kill and imprison millions for years on end, and headed for three formative decades by a virtual psychopath, he would have ceased to take the matter seriously. The absence of democracy was the very root of the disease from which the Soviet economy suffered. Peasants did not seek collectivization or identify with collective farms; workers did not feel themselves masters of their own destiny; managers and officials scarcely more so. What this supreme cautionary tale demonstrated was that without democracy planning becomes a nightmare. How far it may be taken *with* democracy remains to be seen.

Planning in retreat?

This raises the third proposition made popular by the collapse of the USSR: the notion that, unable to harness either the ever-accelerating pace of technological innovation or democracy, planning is everywhere doomed and the future lies with the market. Given the investment made by the Soviet Union in projecting itself as the supreme model of economic planning, it is not difficult to see why this conclusion should so readily be drawn. Suddenly the number of countries ostensibly committed to a planned economy has fallen away to a handful and everywhere the advocates of planning appear on the defensive. What fed this conviction – a key thread running through Fukuyama's thesis – was the simultaneous popular repudiation across Eastern Europe and the Soviet Union of both Communist rule and the command economy. The apparent symmetry was irresistible. Given the chance, free peoples endorse economic individualism and the free market.

Yet here, too, there are grounds for scepticism. Reviewing the broader pattern of the twentieth century, Alfred Wallace would be bound to conclude that on balance history has been moving his way. Across the world, collective action to manage the 'natural economy' has made vast strides since Queen Victoria's death. For all the historic significance of the Soviet collapse, it should not obscure this wider trend – any more than should the frenzied Anglo-Saxon efforts of the 1980s to reverse the tide. An overview of Europe as a whole since the French Revolution, and especially in the twentieth century, would surely point to the pronounced growth in deliberate collective and state intervention in economic and social development. The proportion of national income passing through state hands has catapulted. The state's role in developing the infrastructure, sponsoring services, and guaranteeing welfare, from birth through education and training to old age and infirmity, has expanded out of all recognition. For all the current disillusionment with Keynsian demand management, the century has witnessed an enormous increase in active use of subsidies as well as monetary and fiscal measures to alter the pattern of economic activity. The array of regulations governing employment – from health and safety to conditions of employment and equality of opportunity – has multiplied a hundredfold. The state has intervened in a thousand and one ways to guide the market, protect the environment, inform the consumer.

Moreover, for all the inspiration champions of planning drew from the USSR in the 1930s, it is hardly plausible to see the Soviet débâcle as itself removing the major impulse behind this extension of state intervention. It began before the USSR came into existence and accelerated in the postwar period at the very time the once glittering image of the 'New Soviet Society' was becoming progressively more tarnished. More important has been the effect of the role played by the state in mobilizing resources during two world wars. But the critical factor, as champions of the free market have been close to acknowledging when looking West rather than East, has been the impact of democratization. The most striking correlation, in Northern, Southern, Central and Western Europe at least, has been between the establishment of democracy and the expanding role of the state. It is precisely as a result of swelling demands from an enfranchised population that state intervention – at local, national and international level has grown so vastly. Nor, given the range of moral, social and ecological problems and economic, scientific and cultural opportunities that lie before us, are those demands likely to tail away. In short, as the century comes to an end it is more tenable to locate the source of pressure for state intervention in sustained democratic pressure than in burned-out Jacobin adventure.

Conclusion

If this scepticism is justified, if what the Soviet attempt at planning proves is that its supreme, insuperable handicap was lack of democracy, it is an open question whether in the long run free marketeers or their critics will benefit more from the disappearance of the USSR. But it would come as no surprise if the removal of the incubus of association with the Soviet 'plan' were to contribute to a resurgence in optimism about non-market collective choice – and if the twenty-first century were to witness a flowering of debate, East and West, over varieties of democratic planning, from indicative planning, industrial policy and market socialism, to the total reconstituting of a participatory polity.[23]

Notes

1. See P. Boettke, *Why Perestroika Failed: The Politics and Economics of Socialist Transformation* (London, 1993).
2. Francis Fukuyama, *The End of History and the Last Man* (London, 1992).
3. Alfred R. Wallace, *The Wonderful Century: The Age of New Ideas in Science and Invention* (London, 1903), pp.506–17.
4. S. G. Wheatcroft and R. W. Davies, 'Population', in R. W. Davies, Mark Harrison and S. G. Wheatcroft (eds), *The Economic Transformation of the Soviet Union, 1913–1945* (Cambridge, 1994), pp.62–4.
5. 'Some interesting experiments may be the result,' wrote Beatrice Webb in July 1924 commenting on the prospects for the Soviet system, 'though I am afraid the conclusions will be more negative than positive.' See *The Letters of Sidney and Beatrice Webb*, ed. Norman Mackenzie (Cambridge, 1978), p.207.
6. Wheatcroft and Davies: 'Population', pp.67–79.
7. Friedrich A. Hayek, *The Road to Serfdom* (Chicago, 1944), p.64.
8. Alec Nove, *An Economic History of the USSR* (London, 1992); Eugene Zaleski, *Stalinist Planning for Economic Growth, 1933–1952* (London, 1980), esp. pp.260–68; R. W. Davies, 'Economic and social policy in the USSR 1917–1941', in P. Mathias and S. Pollard (eds), *The Cambridge Economic History of Europe*, viii (Cambridge, 1989); R. W. Davies, *The Soviet Economy in Turmoil, 1929–1930* (London, 1989).
9. Lynne Viola, *The Best Sons of the Fatherland: Workers in the Vanguard of Soviet Collectivization* (Oxford, 1987).
10. Lewis H. Siegelbaum, *Stakhanovism and the Politics of Productivity in the USSR, 1935–1941* (Cambridge, 1988).

11 See especially Gabor T. Rittersporn, *Stalinist Simplifications and Soviet Complications: Social Tensions and Political Conflicts in the USSR, 1933–1953* (London, 1991), and the articles by Rittersporn, Manning, Thurston and Hoffman in J. Arch Getty and Roberta T. Manning (eds), *Stalinist Terror: New Perspectives* (Cambridge, 1993).
12 Nursultan Nazarbaev, *Without Right & Left* (London, 1992), p.69.
13 See in particular R. W. Davies, *The Industrialization of Soviet Russia*, i: *The Socialist Offensive. The Collectivization of Soviet Agriculture 1929–1930*, ii: *The Soviet Collective Farm 1929–1930* (London, 1980–81); Viola, *Best Sons of the Fatherland*; and Moshe Lewin, *The Making of the Soviet System: Essays on the Social History of Inter-War Russia* (London, 1985).
14 G. A. E. Smith, 'Agriculture', in Martin McCauley (ed.), *Khrushchev and Khrushchevism* (London, 1987), pp.95–117.
15 Donald Filtzer, *Soviet Workers and Stalinist Industrialization: The Formation of Modern Soviet Production Relations, 1928–1941* (London, 1986); D. Filtzer, *Soviet Workers and De-Stalinization: The Consolidation of the Modern System of Soviet Production Relations, 1953–1964* (Cambridge, 1992).
16 For differing views over the issue, see Zaleski, *Stalinist Planning*, pp.482–512; H. Ticktin, 'Towards a political economy of the USSR', *Critique*, i (1973), pp.20–41; A. Nove, *The Economics of Feasible Socialism Revisited* (London, 1991), p.86–7.
17 Peter Rutland, *The Myth of the Plan: Lessons of Soviet Planning Experience* (London, 1985).
18 Hayek, *Road to Serfdom*, pp.56–71.
19 See the discussion in *Russian Review*, xlv/4 (1986), pp.357–400 and xlvi/4 (1987), pp.382–431.
20 See Hiroaki Kuromiya, *Stalin's Industrial Revolution: Politics and Workers 1928–1932* (Cambridge, 1988) and Sheila Fitzpatrick, *Education and Social Mobility in the Soviet Union 1921–1934* (Cambridge, 1979).
21 For the best-known elaboration see W. Brus, *The Economics and Politics of Socialism* (London, 1973).
22 For an excellent treatment, see John Barber and Mark Harrison, *The Soviet Home Front, 1941–1945: A Social and Economic History of the USSR in World War II* (London, 1991).
23 For a lively contribution directly engaging Eastern European democrats, see H. Wainwright, *Arguments for a New Left: Answering the Free-Market Right* (Oxford, 1994); an exceptionally crisp straw in the wind is Pat Devine, *Democracy and Economic Planning: The Political Economy of a Self-Governing Society* (Oxford, 1988).

4. JAPAN

Ian Nish

In 1900 Japan was a country of some 45 million people. By reason of her overwhelming victory over China in 1895, she had acquired an indemnity of £30 million payable in London. This had enabled her to build a fleet (largely in British yards) of five battleships and 11 cruisers to add to her experienced army. Meanwhile her industry was developing strongly and the gigantic government steelworks at Yawata in Kyushu island was opened in 1900. On the political front, Japan had a constitution (1889), parliamentary institutions in the form of a Diet (1890) and a cabinet system of government. She had already thrown off the restraints of extraterritoriality, associated with the treaty port system (1899), and was on the way to fixing her own tariffs on imports and exports (which she was to accomplish by the Anglo-Japanese treaty of 1911). She might reasonably claim by the turn of the century to be an independent, 'modernized' country on the verge of economic take-off.[1]

Japan, however, recognized the limitations of her strength. An interesting test-case arose in June 1900 when Britain asked Japan to send a force to China in the midst of the Boxer Uprising in order to join the expedition to relieve the siege of the Peking Legations. The foreign minister replied significantly: 'although Japan has made great progress, she was not yet in a position to take an independent line of action in so grave a crisis, and it was imperative for her to work in line with other powers'.[2] But eventually, having established an international consensus that she might take part in a multinational force alongside European armies, Japan sent a large number of troops who played a conspicuous part in rescuing those who had been trapped in the legations at Peking.

This hesitation to act alone was modified when Japan entered into her alliance with Britain in 1902. However one views the Anglo-Japanese alliance, it was a remarkable recognition of Japan as an up-and-coming country by a front-rank power. But one should bear in mind two factors. First, Japan as a proud nation-state had not gone down on bended knee to become the ally of a European power; indeed, she claimed that Britain had been the true initiator of the negotiations. Second, the Japanese recognized that her British alliance was not an alliance of peoples and that its terms, if not exactly secret, were hardly known outside a limited circle. Indeed, they seem to have concluded that the generality of British people was ignorant about its new ally, and the government seems to have subsidized the publication of volumes about Japan from British publishers. At the end of the decade, Japan made a supreme effort to increase the British awareness of Japan's achievements through the Japan–Britain exhibition at White City, Shepherd's Bush, London, held between May and October 1910. While Britain exhibited her wares, Japan played the more prominent part, regarding it as a national undertaking to promote the knowledge of Japanese society, geography and agricultural and industrial products, and pulled out all the stops to educate the British people about her institutions and her colonies.[3]

Six years earlier Japan had been so confident that she was bold enough to declare war on Russia. Although she exhausted herself in the fighting, she scored decisive victories on land and at sea, so that she was able to emerge from the war as the naval master of the west Pacific. By 1910 she had acquired a substantial colonial empire, including Formosa (Taiwan), Korea and a toe-hold in north-eastern China (Manchuria). The British alliance was revised in 1905, revised radically in 1911 and was to continue into the 1920s. Over these decades Japan established herself in the international community, while her industrial, commercial and banking efforts made her a force to be reckoned with in East Asia and beyond.

In 1920 Japan became a founder-member of the League of Nations and thus accepted a global role rather than one confined to the East. It was a symbol of the new status she had acquired in the world by the time of the Paris Peace Conference of 1919. She claimed to be one of the major victors in the First World War and the third largest naval power. Her diplomats had to play their part in the international conferences of the 1920s and to work towards the resolution of some of the intractable European issues of the day. When at the Washington Conference (1921–2) Japan was deprived of some of her earlier gains at the expense of China and had to agree to the ending of her British alliance, it was her membership of the League which continued to give her a foothold in international affairs. Japan remained an enthusiastic member so long as the League's rulings did not conflict with her national interests. But first in 1927 and later in 1931, she was taken aback by the 'interference' of the League in her disputes with Nationalist China.

The 1920s were harsh times for Japan. She had done well out of the First World War with her expanding exports. New companies were created in great numbers, many of them, the 'narikin' (*nouveaux riches*), on a shallow economic base. At the end of the European war there was a wild speculative boom which was soon overtaken by a severe postwar panic in 1920, the first of several cyclical depressions. This was soon followed by the Great Earthquake of September 1923 which laid waste the area around Tokyo and Yokohama. With the help of generous foreign aid, government assistance and private charity, the country was quickly restored. But the disaster damaged Japanese confidence and held back economic growth, creating great unemployment. By 1925 the population had grown to 59,700,000; by 1930 to 64,500,000. It was a turbulent time also for the foreign exchanges which led to the financial panic of 1926 when many famous banks went to the wall. Despite complaints about corrupt politics, over-population and exclusion from markets overseas, Japan scraped through the world depression rather better than other countries. The yen, which had been put back on to the gold standard in 1930, had to be taken off again in December 1931.

To add to these domestic problems, there were the problems created by the emergence of Manchukuo in the spring of 1932 and its recognition by Japan in September. When in February of the following year, the League passed a resolution which was offensive to Japan's stance over Manchukuo, she gave notice of leaving the League.[4] In this the government was responding to the pressure of the army and its civilian collaborators. In spite of financial difficulties, it held on to Manchukuo and its monopolistic position there until 1945.

The feeling was gaining ground among Japanese that the League was the symbol of an international order which was increasingly unjust to Japan, a country with few natural resources and therefore needing foreign trade in order to survive. The World Economic Conference of

1933 only confirmed the protectionist trend which was becoming evident in world trade. Japan's civilian leaders recognized (what her soldiers probably did not) the fragility of Japan's economic position in a hostile financial world. Thus Japan in 1936 complained to Britain that 'Japan's credit in this country was unhappily low. ... Japan had never defaulted on her obligations, whereas China, who had defaulted, had now better credit in London than Japan.'[5] Resentful as Japan was of this and other hostility she encountered, she had to accept it as she could barely afford the greatly increased budgets for the development of Manchukuo and later the war with China.

Japan's isolation in the world was ended with the completion of the anti-Comintern pact with Germany in November 1936. While there was a widespread fear in Japan of the Soviet Union and of the steps which she was taking to build up her armed forces in Siberia and the Maritime Territory, there were many in Japan who felt that a binding commitment to Nazi Germany was a high price to pay for security. This accounts for the reluctance of the Japanese leadership to take the next step, a formal alliance with Germany and Italy. This came in September 1940.

From the spring of 1941 Japan had been engaged in talks with Washington for a general settlement. While there were various hiccoughs on the way, these continued until the very moment of the bombing of Pearl Harbor itself on 7–8 December. They carried on against the background of the Soviet agreement which Matsuoka had entered into in April and the Nazi attack on the Soviet Union in May. Both sides were unyielding; and indeed the conditions for a possible settlement (namely Japan's withdrawal from Indochina) do not seem even now to be a basis for fruitful negotiations.[6]

Understandably, therefore, the Japanese were anxious to secure firm guarantees from their allies, Germany and Italy. They asked that her European allies would stand by her, in the event of Japan being at war. Germany would rather have had Japan creating a second front on the Soviet eastern flank but did indeed present on 5 December the draft of a treaty offering to join with all available means and promising not to make a separate peace, provided Japan joined Germany in war with Russia. Japan refused to accept this proviso, thereby risking the German offer. In fact, however, Hitler decided to stand on the side of Japan in case the Tripartite Pact was seen to be dead. Convinced that the United States would use the Pearl Harbor attack to declare war on the Axis countries in Europe, he decided to jump the gun and declare war on Washington. On 11 December Germany, following Japan's plea, declared war on the USA in company with the other ally in the European war, Italy. Five days later the three issued an undertaking that they had made to build a new world order and entered into fresh understandings about conducting the war in common and not entering into a separate peace. Later, on 18 January 1942, after a month of military-naval talks, the representatives on the tripartite military commission in Berlin signed an agreement defining their spheres of operation, the dividing line being 70° east longitude.[7]

Important as Pearl Harbor was as the spark which ignited the Second World War in the East, it was the event which slightly preceded it which has greater historical significance. At 2 a.m. on 8 September, Japanese armies landed at Kota Bahru in Malaya. This was evidence of the Southern Thrust which had for five years been the adopted policy of the navy and, through the revised Imperial Defence Policy of 1936, of the army. There were various aspects to it. On the ground there were logistic factors, linked to the war in China. If Japan was to plug the supply-routes for military supplies reaching the Nationalist Chinese, she had, she felt, to close the access to China through Indochina and the Burma Road. It was moreover necessary for industrial reasons to get access to the raw materials from which she had, she claimed, been excluded by the ABCD powers (America, Britain, China and the Dutch). In addition to her need for rubber from Malaya, she needed greater quantities of oil from the Netherlands East Indies. In spite of two diplomatic missions, agreement was not reached on supplies and price to suit Japan's requirements.[8]

There was also the ideological need for rhetoric which would articulate Japan's sense of leadership and mission in East and South-east Asia and bring it into line with Hitler's claims of a new order in Europe. This was articulated in the statement of the prime minister, Prince Konoe, in November 1937, containing his proposals for a New Order in East Asia. It mushroomed in the 1940s into the proposals for a Great East Asia Co-prosperity Sphere. On 12 December 1941 the Japanese cabinet announced that it would describe the hostilities as the 'Great East Asian War' and include within it 'the China incident'. This was intended to convey the message that it was to be a war of decolonization and Asian liberation. Following that, Prime Minister Tojo confirmed in January that Japan's actions were based on coexistence and co-prosperity, with herself as the core of the Asian sphere. By 1942 Japan was professing to play on an Asian, if not a world, stage.

In the first few months of rapid conquest, the Japanese had a natural feeling of exhilaration. For a resource-poor country which had for decades been complaining of the lack of raw materials available to it, Japan became understandably punch-drunk. Of course there was still an urgent job to be done to repair assets like the oil wells in Sumatra and Borneo; but there was tremendous optimism about the natural resources of the Co-prosperity Sphere, both there and in Malaya (tin and iron ore) and Burma (tungsten and copper).

Japan's good fortune in due course created new problems that can best be illustrated in the case of rubber. Before the war Japan, without rubber resources, had developed her production of synthetic rubber. She could not therefore absorb the output of the important areas of rubber production which she had occupied by virtue of her wartime conquests. In a government report of 1943, she speculated about what could be done with her rubber surplus in the 'South Seas region'. She cannot consume it herself; she cannot greatly expand the consumption of the countries of the Co-prosperity Sphere; and, she concludes rather limply, 'the problem of supplying the Axis powers with rubber must be considered'. Her problem was compounded by the lack of a mercantile marine adequate for her newly expanded resources and before long by the losses which her ships were suffering. The battle of Midway (June 1942) and the allied landings at Guadalcanal (August 1942) deprived Japan of her command of the sea and disrupted her supply routes.[9]

In January 1943, before the Allies began to fight back, the Tojo cabinet tried to rally Japan's partners in the Co-prosperity Sphere. To this end Tojo visited the capitals of Japan's various allies and persuaded their leaders to visit Tokyo. On 5–6 November was held the Great East Asian Conference, attended by representatives of the Nanking government, Thailand, Manchukuo, the Philippines and Burma (the last two having been given their independence during the year). It was to be the fulfilment Japan's Great East Asia ideology; but the tide of war had already turned.

Japan's surrender came after the entry of the Soviet Union into the war and the dropping of the atomic bomb on Hiroshima and Nagasaki. The first was traumatic enough since Russia had been regarded for over half a century as Japan's primary enemy. But the dropping of the bombs on Hiroshima (6 August), an important provincial capital of some 350,000 people, and on Nagasaki (9 August), with a population of some 270,000 and the centre of Roman Catholicism in Japan, brought the war home to every Japanese. Of course, there had previously been 'carpet-bombing' which had had its impact on most of Japan's prefectural cities and brought the threat of destruction close to all Japanese regions. But the destructive power of the atomic bombs was more awesome. The sheer horror of the attack and the casualties inflicted numbed the people. It was estimated that the deaths by the end of 1945 were 130,000 to 140,000 in Hiroshima and 60,000 to 70,000 in Nagasaki.

There is little doubt that the atomic bomb played its part in the ending of the war. True, many things about Japanese industry, communications and the war effort had broken down; and surrender was inevitable in the long term. But the events of Hiroshima and Nagasaki offered a threat of horrendous consequences. It was no longer possible for the politicians to prevaricate and delay.

Japan had faced this unique and exceptional experience of total war in the twentieth century, nuclear warfare against a civilian population. The death rate by 1950 in both cities had risen to 50 per cent of the population. How far this affected the thinking of the Japanese people is hard to judge. It certainly seems to have had the long-term effect of discrediting pre-war militarism and encouraging pacifist causes. It has also led Japanese governments to oppose atomic testing in the south Pacific and to declare Japan as a non-nuclear state. The events of August 1945 also had their effect in reducing the rigours of the military occupation that followed.

The period after 1945 is often described by Japanese as the era of the New Japan, thereby implying a disjunction with what had gone before. On the surface there was a disjunction: much of the power resided in the hands of General MacArthur as SCAP (Supreme Commander of the Allied Powers). Japan of the 1930s had been characterized by relative economic stability, by the excessive influence of the military in the body politic and by territorial expansion. Now she faced a time of disorder and devastation with the virtual collapse of her industrial infrastructure and hyperinflation as she confronted the tasks of reconstruction. The power of the military was gone; her forces were repatriated from overseas. Japan accepted a new constitution in 1946 which laid down (Article 9) that 'the Japanese people forever renounce war as a sovereign right of the nation' and, until the creation of her own self-defence forces, was dependent on the protection of the United States. Her industries too were demilitarized. The days of expansion were over; and she lost her colonial and occupied territories and had to absorb a large number of repatriates. These were grim times. But thanks to American aid, the success of the economic stabilization policies and the stimulus given by the Allies' procurement policies during the

Korean War, industrial production recovered and returned to the level of 1934–6 by about 1955.[10]

Political independence returned only in April 1952. Japan made peace with the wartime allies by the San Francisco peace treaty of September 1951 and signed simultaneously with the United States a security treaty permitting the USA to keep military, naval and air bases on Japanese soil. A complicated administrative agreement (1952) spelt out the American rights. The security treaty was revised in favour of Japan in January 1960. In the Diet ratification proved difficult because of Socialist opposition but was eventually achieved in May. A proposed visit by President Eisenhower had to be called off because of the unpopularity of the government's tactics.

During the period between 1956 and 1974 the Japanese economy enjoyed annual growth rates generally around 10 per cent, although there were severe cyclical fluctuations. Under pressure from the USA, the Japanese government in 1960 announced the liberalization of its 'import trade and foreign exchange dealings'. Hence in 1964 she was admitted to membership of the IMF and OECD. Following the international success of the Olympic Games in Tokyo in 1964, there was a period of successful industrial policy during which the skilful administrative guidance of the bureaucracy sought to steer the country towards modern, high-productivity industries. But these successes coincided with an estrangement between the USA and Japan caused by trade disputes on the one hand and the American initiative towards China in 1971–2. Japan spoke of her need for a 'more diversified foreign policy', less tied than before to the wishes of the USA. This became more vital with the coming of the oil crisis of the mid-1970s when it was essential to cultivate the goodwill of the oil-producing countries of the Middle East.

The third stage of Japan's postwar development began in 1975 with the oil crisis. The postwar reconstruction of Japan's industry had largely been dependent on imported oil as an energy source. Japan had as a matter of urgency to adopt a series of comprehensive conservation measures, requiring (for example) all companies to develop a mechanism to oversee energy policy. By various laws and by increasing the range of oil-supply sources, Japanese industries came through the emergency remarkably well, though it did lead to sharp declines in the rates of economic growth. Meanwhile they became world leaders in the production of goods like cars, semi-conductors and electronic devices. Japan began to enjoy large trade surpluses and found herself involved in 'trade friction' with the USA and Europe. This led to arrangements for limiting exports of specified products and to considerable overseas investment.[11]

Japan's international stature had also changed. For most of the 1970s Japan was remoulding her relationships with the People's Republic of China through a cluster of agreements and considerable private investment. As tension was relaxed on the China front, however, it intensified in relations with the Soviet Union, especially over the sensitive issue of the Northern Territories, the islands to the north of Hokkaido. There was no let-up in this tension until Gorbachev's coming to power but even his visit to Japan in spring 1991 did not resolve the issue. With the coming of the Russian Republic, the bargaining on this issue has become, if anything, more difficult. During the 1980s steps were taken to prevent the deterioration of relations with the USA, with whom the security treaty was maintained, having been revised in 1960.

Both domestically and internationally there have been calls for Japan to take a role commensurate with her economic success. Naturally Japan has been an active member of the G7 summits of industrialized powers, although she often occupies a position of isolation. The question of a political role turned on the degree to which the Japanese were prepared to take part militarily in United Nations actions and on their interpretation of their constitution. After Iraq's invasion of Kuwait, Japan eventually announced a package of measures which were primarily financial and in the main ignored the problem of military involvement. The crisis led to much heart-searching but eventually to a consensus which allowed her to take part in UN operations under certain conditions. Thus Japan sent troops for the UN peacekeeping operations in Kampuchea in 1992 'provided that a ceasefire agreement was in place'. Moreover, the director of UN operations there was a Japanese, Yasushi Akashi, who was later transferred to a similar role in Bosnia. At the end of a protracted and bitter debate in the Diet and among the general public, the Peace Keeping Operations (PKO) Bill was passed in June 1992, giving the government the mandate to send overseas 1800 members of the Jieitai (Self-Defence Forces) which had hitherto been used only within Japan. By a strange irony, some nine decades after Japan sent a strong expedition to join the international troops in China in 1900, she also sent the largest force to take part in the international operations in Kampuchea. In each case, the other nations invited her to do so; in each case, she would not act without a consensus of the powers involved. But the experience was an unfamiliar one for Japan; and the casualties sustained played into the hands of the doubters. Still the Social Democratic Party, which has hitherto been most sensitive to the provisions of the constitution over defence commitments overseas, has redefined its position, saying that the Self-Defence Forces are constitutional provided they are kept to a minimum and are used for 'defence' only. Japan, which has gradually become the largest spender on defence in the world after the USA, may therefore be more active in UN-sponsored operations in the future.

Japan's international reputation has been tarnished by major domestic scandals since the 1970s. The Liberal Democratic Party, which governed from 1948 for 45 years, consisted of a number of competing factions which required formidable funds to fight elections. This led to various instances where senior politicians were found to have accepted money from dubious sources. There have been many attempts at introducing political reforms in order to overcome this practice but they have not had much impact. Reformists from several dissident groups managed to form a coalition government in July 1993 which displaced the Liberal Democrats and held power for a year. It was succeeded by an administration shared between the Social Democratic Party and the remnant of the Liberal Democratic Party. These recent happenings suggest that there are no certainties left in Japanese politics. Whether the future rests with the large parties or with small parties forming multi-party coalitions is hard to predict.

The twentieth century was hardly Japan's century. For her it was a period of peaks and troughs. In the first half of the century she rose from comparative obscurity to great power status. She revealed remarkable powers of growth and qualities of political creativity and commercial acumen. She came to be recognized as one of the strongest military-naval powers in the world. But she found herself opposed and subject to restrictions which were inconsistent with her sense of mission. She embarked on a war which was more exhausting and protracted than she expected and more exacting than her slender resources could bear. Initially she was very successful; ultimately she failed disastrously. She lost the war at three levels: the guerrilla war in China; the American island-hopping campaign in the Pacific; and the protracted struggle in South-east Asia. After 1945 she suffered from a period of individual poverty, severe disruption and national trauma. Thereafter in the second half of the century Japan emerged with great determination and the people showed a remarkable capacity for recovery. She avoided military expenditure for some decades and concentrated on economic development. As a result of her export achievement and industrial management, Japan will see herself at the end of the century on an upward path, unquestionably one of the great powers. There is an 'unspoken assumption' that the twenty-first century will be the Pacific century, and possibly Japan's century.

Throughout the twentieth century Japan remained an independent nation-state. Throughout the peaks and troughs – in spite of the successful expansion, the failed war and effective rehabilitation – her emperors, her cabinets and her parliament have been in continuous existence. She has had a relatively free press and a people who are well educated and relatively sophisticated politically. She has always been conscious of being a strong contender for the role of the most successful state in Asia. This led her in the 1930s to seek for a leadership role on the subcontinent. At its most extreme this culminated in claims for creating a New Order in East Asia and the Great East Asia Co-prosperity Sphere. In the postwar period Japan promoted the idea of Pacific Rim solidarity, most notably the concept of Prime Minister Ohira at the end of the 1970s.[12] Certainly Japan has been very successful in the markets of the Pacific Rim. It is also true that many of the leaders of South-east Asia have expressed their admiration for Japan and may in effect have admitted a leadership role for Tokyo. But it is too early to predict whether some multinational or supranational union will emerge out of the wide diversity of states in the region .

In conclusion, one has to say that, in spite of a century of economic success, Japan has not been similarly successful on the political front. She has had a century of conservative government which has on the whole given remarkable stability without a whiff of left-wing revolution. But, both in the pre-war and postwar periods, Japan has had serious problems in making her parliamentary institutions work. Before the war she was weakened by the encroachment of the military in the political process.[13] Parliamentary institutions have been dogged by serious nationwide scandals over the last two decades. While the apparatus of democratic institutions, political parties and regular elections exists, it is open to complaints on the grounds of faction fighting, money politics, corrupt practice and financial irregularities. In spite of frequent promises of political reform – and the elimination of factions especially – nothing positive has so far been done. Though Japan's international image is otherwise high, it has been damaged by shortcomings in the political field.

Lest this analysis of Japan's experience appear too non-Japanese and too judgmental, we should say that Japanese intellectuals are very much concerned by these issues. In 1984 the Japan Foundation published a selection of conference papers entitled 'Experiencing the Twentieth Century'. They confronted the central themes of the century but naturally reflected the special characteristic of the host country. Considering Japan's future role in the world, a Japanese author, Hagihara Nobutoshi, identified two alternative courses open:

> to refrain consciously from meaning anything positive to the twentieth century while Japan places itself in a modest position on the periphery, always keeping some distance from the center. This posture accords with Japan's traditional role. ... The other alternative is simply that of responding to history rather than creating it. More crudely, just drifting.[14]

One might call these the alternatives of abstention. Twenty-first century Japanese will have to determine just how abstemious they wish to be.

Notes

1 Japan's *fin-de-siècle* achievement is illustrated by Okuma Shigenobu (ed.), *Fifty Years of New Japan* (London, 1910) and Suematsu Kencho, *The Risen Sun* (London, 1905).
2 Whitehead to Salisbury, 25 June 1900, in British Foreign Office Papers, Public Records Office, Kew, FO 95/405
3 Ayako Hotta, 'The Japan–Britain Exhibition of 1910', in Ian Nish (ed.), *Britain and Japan: Biographical Portraits* (Folkestone, 1994), pp.146–58.
4 Ian Nish, *Japan's Struggle with Internationalism, 1931–3* (London, 1993), pp.230–4.
5 Eden to Clive, 6 November 1936, in W. N. Medlicott (ed.), *Documents on British Foreign Policy 1919–39*, 2nd series, xxi/1, p.3.
6 Akira Iriye, *Power and Culture: The Japanese–American War, 1941–5* (Cambridge, MA, 1981), pp.30–5.
7 (Sir) Nicholas Henderson, 'Hitler's biggest blunder', *History Today*, xliii (1993), pp.35–43.
8 J. W. Morley (ed.), *The Fateful Choice, 1939–41* (New York, 1980), articles by Nagaoka Shinjiro, Hata Ikuhiko and Tsunoda Jun.
9 Ian Nish, 'The Greater East Asian Co-prosperity Sphere', in K. Neilson and R. Prete (eds), *Coalition Warfare* (Waterloo, Canada, 1983), pp.125–42.
10 Iokibe Makoto, 'Japan meets the United States for the second time', in C. Gluck and S. R. Graubard (eds), *Showa* (New York, 1992), pp.91–106.
11 A. Graham and A. Seldon (eds), *Government and Economies in the*

Postwar World, 1945–85 (London, 1990), pp.253–70.
12 S. Sato, K. Koyama and S. Kumon, *Postwar Politician* (Tokyo, 1990), chap. 37.
13 Ian Nish, *JapaneseForeign Policy, 1869–1942* (London, 1977).
14 N. Hagihara, A. Iriye, G. Nivat and P. Windsor (eds), *Experiencing the Twentieth Century* (Tokyo, 1985), pp.27–8.

5. EUROPE

William Wallace and Piers Ludlow

The nineteenth century was the European century. European history since the Great War of 1914–18 has been a story of confusion and renewed war, and of postwar recovery masking a shrinking of horizons. Our great-grandparents lived at the centre of world power and civilization. We live in a subcontinental region, uncertain of our relations with a changing North America and a dynamic East Asia; and uncertain too of the boundaries or guiding principles of a 'Europe' within which nation-states proliferate but in which the centrality of the nation-state is undermined by developments above and below the state level. Echoes of European disorders a century ago have returned to haunt us, while the structure and geographical reach of a future European order still escapes us.

Geography is not an exact science. Countries and international regions emerge, expand, move across the map and disappear, while experts propound 'natural' boundaries and communication links. The Mediterranean – as its name implies – was at the heart of the civilized world of the Roman Empire. The expansion of Islam transformed it into the contested frontier between Europe and the Muslim world; to become instead a European sea in the late nineteenth century, as France, Britain and (later) Italy took control of North Africa, while European tourists and archaeologists swarmed across the Ottoman Levant.[1] The Danube, the Baltic, the Black Sea, have all passed from centres of trade and dominion to backwaters – and back again.

So too with 'Europe': a geographical label which first distinguished those parts of ancient Greece west of the Hellespont from the colonies in 'Asia' to the east, and which has moved gradually west and north over the centuries. Medieval Europe was defined by the limits of Western Christendom, and by the struggles to resist Moors and Mongols, and later Turks. Byzantine and orthodox territories – the 'eastern' Empire and the 'eastern' church – were outside the boundaries of this half-organized and half-violent feudal European community: tolerated or pillaged during the Crusades, with Byzantine territories as well as Saracen divided into dukedoms and petty kingdoms 'outremer' during the southern and eastward expansion of Frankish and Norman Europe.

Eastward expansion of this Europe of the West was followed by contraction, as the Ottoman Empire pushed north from the Balkans through Hungary to the gates of Vienna. Seventeeth-century Europe was western Europe, with Austria as its eastern kingdom, and Sweden and Poland holding its north-eastern borders against half-civilized and half-Asiatic Russia. Renewed expansion began in the eighteenth century, as Ottoman Turkey entered its long decline. The modernizing rulers of Russia made their state into a European power: its capital moved west to St Petersburg, its borders moving further west with each partition of Poland, with French as its court language, Scots in its armies and Germans in its commerce and civil service. The maritime North Sea states carried European expansion and settlement across the seas, following and partly supplanting earlier Spanish and Portuguese colonization.

But it was the nineteenth century which witnessed the rise of 'Europe' to world domination: fuelled by technological and industrial advance, and by the ideologies of progress and of Western civilization. In the half-century before 1900 over 40 million people emigrated from Europe to North and South America, Australasia, northern and southern Africa. In the last three decades of the century competitive imperialism brought most of Africa and South-east Asia under European rule. China remained nominally independent, but with Europeans running its customs service and dominating its trade, and with privileged European settlements along its coast. The Middle East became a more informal protectorate, with German influence reaching through Istanbul to Baghdad and British influence pushing up the Nile and the Persian Gulf. In 1900 Europe *was* the civilized world; Europeans ran the world, secure in the conviction of their own moral, intellectual and racial superiority. Modernizing elites in Japan – and later in Turkey – sought to make their countries European, in manners and in dress as well as in education and state and military structures, seeing acceptance as 'honorary Europeans' as the symbol of sovereignty and security.

For Europe was an idea – or rather, a collection of ideas – as much as a geographical region. Late nineteenth-century Europe had absorbed Charles Darwin's 'survival of the fittest' and applied it to international relations, seeing in the rapid expansion of European population, wealth and political domination a self-justifying rationale for disregarding the interests of the 'degenerate' non-European races. Social Darwinism added an extra layer to the loose collection of ideas which constituted the 'West': a term interchangeable with 'Europe' throughout the eighteenth and nineteenth centuries, as 'Asia' was interchangeable with the 'East', the mysterious, exotic but uncivilized Orient.[2] The Renaissance had rediscovered the intellectual heritage of classical Greece; preserved in Alexandria, passed on through Muslim and Jewish scholars in Cairo, Baghdad and Almaravid Spain, now firmly claimed for Western Christendom by enlightened men in Florence, Amsterdam, Paris and Geneva. The eighteenth-century Enlightenment had added the idea of progress through rational understanding, in contradistinction to the cyclical and mystical world-views of ancient and Asian civilizations. The French Revolution drew from the Enlightenment the ideas of citizenship and of the nation as a community of citizens, to which Napoleon's reforms, and Prussian reaction to them, added the idea of the mobilizing and modernizing administrative state. The Industrial Revolution, as it spread across Europe from west to east, brought with it a further mixture of ideas and ideologies: of economic rationality and technological progress.

Europe may plausibly be defined as the region which has inherited the ideas and assumptions of Western Christendom; or those of Western Christendom as filtered through the experience of the Renaissance, the Enlightenment and the (French) Revolution.[3] From the Westphalian settlement on, a certain sense of community – of shared culture, of conflict and competition within acceptable limits – held this region together, even through repeated limited wars. The shock of the French Revolution roused competing nationalist movements while at the same time spreading French ideas and administrative practices across Europe. A small number of European thinkers harked back to the medieval ideal of European political and Christian unity, or community; reacting to the carnage of the Thirty Years' War, to the revolutionary and Napoleonic wars, or to the contradictions between the nineteenth-century liberalism and nationalism by formulating schemes for perpetual peace or for a European confederation of free nations. But these were of little influence in a nineteenth-century European system built around confident states and empires, cooperating through a European concert to manage their limited conflicts and to settle the affairs of less fortunate peoples and continents.

Europe at the beginning of the twentieth century: the proud tower

The high point of European self-confidence – and of the identification of 'Europe' with modernity and civilization – came during the first decade of the twentieth century. The gap in living standards between European and non-European countries, relatively modest in 1800, had grown through industrialization and empire to a gulf. The surge in European population had brought its share of world population to an estimated 30–35 per cent. European emigrants were creating new European societies in other continents; European officials were carrying the message of civilization and good government across their recently expanded empires and protected territories; European missionaries were spreading education, godliness and cleanliness around the globe.

The Europe of 1900, linked from Paris to St Petersburg, from Calais to Istanbul, by train, was a broad continent at the centre of the global political and economic order. But those who lived there knew that it had a political, economic and cultural core, and a wider dependent periphery. Paris remained unchallenged as the cultural capital of European civilization, the city to which intellectuals in Poland, Russia and Hungary were instinctively drawn, while Berlin and Vienna, and to a lesser extent London, also provided focal points for artistic and intellectual ferment. Western Europe – then defined as the North Sea countries of Britain, France, Belgium and the Netherlands – had led the continent both in industrialization and in liberalism through the first half of the century. Central Europe – the German Empire (as *it* became in 1871) and the Austro-Hungarian Empire (as it became from the historic compromise of 1867) – had pulled the balance of European politics and economics some distance east of the North Sea. The unification of Italy, and the expansion of France into North Africa, had to a more limited degree brought the western Mediterranean back into the European balance. The rapid growth of the German economy, and the mercantilist and military ends to which its newly acquired industrial base was applied by the efficiently administered German state, shifted the core of the European economy east and north of the Rhine.

If Berlin and Vienna were clearly part of the core of Europe in 1900, their eastern territories shaded into its dependent periphery. Hungary, Pomerania and Germany's Polish lands fed the cities and industrial towns to the west; the Ruhr and the North Sea ports were Germany's industrial heartland. Germans looked down on Slavs, and Hungarians clung to their claims to be superior to Slavs. Slavs in their turn looked west to 'Europe' with mingled envy and suspicion – of wealthy sophisticates offering industrial progress, but determined to take advantage of peasant innocence and goodwill. The rich, and largely Protestant, north-western Europeans also looked down on their Latin and Catholic neighbours to the south. They travelled down to the Mediterranean for their health, or as tourists fascinated by the relics of an old civilization which they had now surpassed – rather as Japanese tourists visit Western Europe today.

Outside Europe, European solidarity in the face of non-European challenges limited imperial conflict among the European powers – most evidently in China, where British, French, American and Russian troops operated jointly in occupying Peking after the Boxer Uprising and in policing the treaty ports. As also did Japanese: accepted, like their Russian counterparts, as quasi-European because of their determined drive for 'European' modernization. Within Western Europe a degree of stability had been reached in territorial conflict and the consolidation of nation-states – with the single exception of Alsace and Lorraine, reclaimed for a united Germany in 1871 but bitterly regretted by France. Europe's south-eastern periphery was far more difficult to manage. Ottoman Turkey, outside the ideological boundaries of 'Europe', was half-supported by France and Britain in order to contain competitive expansion by Eastern Europe's two multinational empires, Austria-Hungary and Russia. Western romanticism and classicism accepted the Greeks (on highly questionable grounds) as fully European – as Western European governments were again to accept Greece uncritically into the European Community in 1981. Bulgarians and Serbs, Romanians and Albanians were less evidently to be accepted as full members of a European 'concert': provided with surplus German or Danish royalty, their boundaries drawn and redrawn in conferences in Berlin and consultations among the major 'powers'.

In the first decade of the twentieth century (as in the nineteenth) wealth, population, prestige and regional power were concentrated in Europe's north and west, spreading gradually more thinly as one moved further east and south through the eastern borderlands into Asia. Western Europe had settled and centralizing nation-states. Germany and Austria began as states but extended eastwards as empires, to meet Eurasian Russia and Eurasian Turkey. The contradiction between nationalism as the legitimating principle for European statehood – as it had become, with German and Italian unity, in the 1860s and 1870s – and empire as a continuing claim in Eastern Europe was most acute within Austria-Hungary, with its 18 official languages and overlapping populations and national myths. Modernity and European status meant national self-assertion. But much of Eastern Europe was hardly modern (and only uncertainly European), and its powers were all unstable admixtures of traditional authority and rationalizing administration. Accumulated contradictions between empire and national aspirations, between the national memories and myths which modernizing elites in Bulgaria, Greece and Serbia attempted to harness in building new states on the Western European model out of the former territories of European Turkey, led to Balkan instability. This was enough to ignite a continent where national feelings were running extremely high, and where the concert of Europe had never really come to terms with a united Germany whose military power and fast-growing economic strength alarmed French, Russians and British alike.[4] Europe was plunged into a disastrous war and the 'proud tower' collapsed.

The loss of European self-confidence, 1918–1940

Europe was exhausted by the Great War, militarily and financially. Throughout the conflict, both Britain and France had been forced to draw extensively on manpower from their non-European empire: troops from the dominions, from India and even from China had fought alongside the British, while the French had used North and West African recruits to bolster their ranks. The entry into war of a non-European power – the United States – had, moreover, been a vital factor in the final defeat of the central powers.[5] Similarly, European victors and vanquished alike were economically and financially drained. Between 1914 and 1918 Britain lost its position as the banker of the world, only to become the world's greatest debtor nation. And traditional export markets vanished, as non-European competitors took advantage of the war to establish themselves in areas previously dominated by the British, Germans or French.[6]

Yet if the First World War highlighted the dwindling strength of some of Europe's leading powers, the conflict also appeared to vindicate the nation-state as an organizational unit. In 1914 national feeling had everywhere triumphed over both 'European' and class solidarity; by the end of 1918, the Austro-Hungarian Empire – Europe's most complex multinational state – had totally disintegrated. As the peace makers assembled at Versailles in 1919, the concept of national self-determination seemed destined to be one of the conference's guiding principles.[7] The shortcomings of this approach became only too quickly apparent, however. In Central Europe, particularly, new national borders obstructed long-established cultural, commercial and economic links. The Austrian textile industry, for instance, was crippled, with the spindles largely located in Bohemia and Moravia – part of the newly created Czechoslovakia – and the looms concentrated in and around Vienna.[8] As Keynes argued forcefully, a settlement which ignored the high degree of economic interdependence in the region was likely to prove disastrous.[9] Nation-states like Czechoslovakia, Poland, Yugoslavia and Romania were, moreover, characterized by the presence of substantial ethnic minorities and important irredentist claims.

It was the fate of Germany, however, which posed the most intractable problems. When Germany was discussed at Versailles, certain exceptions to the principle of national self-determination were permitted: Alsace and Lorraine were ceded to France; Eupen and Malmédy to Belgium; much of Posen and West Prussia to Poland; and the coal mines of the Saar to the French. But despite these territorial losses, post-Versailles Germany remained dauntingly large, a European state which because of its size and economic potential could scarcely be controlled by traditional balance of power politics. As a result, Germany's neighbours, and France in particular, pushed with partial success for economic and military sanctions, which they hoped would render Germany powerless to press once more for European hegemony. Strict controls were placed upon Germany's military might and financially crippling reparations were demanded by both the British and the French. That a weakened yet resentful Germany might be a still greater threat than the economically prosperous Reich of pre-1914 was overlooked.[10]

French hopes of resolving the European imbalance of power by means of a Carthaginian peace collided at Versailles with the American desire to secure lasting stability in Europe through the creation of an institutional framework within which disputes and tensions could be legally and not militarily settled. President Wilson's faith in a new type of international relations, centred on the League of Nations, proved insufficient to prevent either territorial annexations or punitive sanctions against the central powers. The American leader did succeed, however, in moderating the ferocity of the peace treaty and in securing international approval for the Covenant of the League of Nations. The latter, Wilson hoped, would soon make French and British concerns about strategic balance, or spheres of influence, totally redundant.[11]

Within a year, Wilson's idealistic vision had been badly damaged by the failure of his own country to ratify the Versailles Treaty and to join the League of Nations. The American retreat into isolationism, moreover, was matched by that of the Soviet Union. Ravaged by civil war and economic crisis, the new Communist state withdrew into itself, symbolically moving its capital from the Western-orientated Petrograd to distant Moscow, and deliberately shunning the League.[12] It was thus with a numerically larger but much weaker cast that the attempt to find a viable balance of power in Europe resumed. France, for instance, found itself obliged to multiply alliances with the minor powers of Eastern Europe, in its attempt to surround and contain the German threat.[13] In a continent awash with national grievances and unsatisfied territorial aspirations, this was a fragile basis indeed on which to build.

For five short years at the end of the 1920s it appeared that a more solid arrangement might have been secured. The Treaty of Locarno, signed by the French, British, German and Italians in October 1925, consolidated the postwar settlement in Western Europe,. provided France with a greater sense of security and reduced German resentment.[14] Under Briand and Stresemann, moreover, Franco-German relations became less fraught. Even the new European rhetoric employed by the French foreign minister was encouraging: in May 1930 Briand sent his fellow foreign ministers a memorandum 'on the organization of a European federal union'.[15] But Briand's proposal was widely denounced and the weakness of calls for European solidarity underscored, as the onset of economic crisis provoked a general retreat into protectionism and heightened nationalism.[16]

In the 1930s Italy and Germany were mercilessly to expose the shortcomings of League diplomacy and the fragility of a European status quo to which only two major powers – Britain and France – were committed. Mussolini's and Hitler's drive to regain their 'places in the sun' was countered ineffectively by the British and the French. France was politically unstable, diplomatically isolated, and militarily over-reliant on its defensive Maginot line.[17] Britain meanwhile agonized about any form of 'continental commitment'. Acutely aware that the Dominions opposed too great a British involvement in European affairs and anxious to avoid the financial burden of a large-scale rearmament, the National Government rejected French feelers about an Anglo-French alliance. Likewise, when rearmament did occur, it was concentrated on the Royal Navy – essential for safeguarding the Empire but of limited utility in the event of a European war – and on the largely defensive Royal Air Force, rather than being designed to give Britain the ability to intervene decisively in another European conflict.[18] Neither France nor Britain was able to mount an effective challenge to the dictators; Munich and the policy of appeasement simply reflected the position of weakness into which the two democracies had allowed themselves to be manoeuvred by the late 1930s. More fundamentally, the slide into war emphasized the instability of a European order which lacked both a militarily powerful guarantor and a robust institutional skeleton.

1940–1965 the collapse and the rescue of the European nation-state – or, America's Europe

The Second World War profoundly shook the assumptions upon which historical accounts of the nineteenth and early twentieth centuries were based. Defeat and occupation – the fate of all but a handful of European nations – discredited not only the governments and political parties of the interwar era, but also led many to question the viability of the nation-state. Resistance leaders throughout occupied Europe toyed with internationalist and federalist ideas – to the left of the political spectrum the Italian Altiero Spinelli spoke of a federal Europe in terms not dissimilar to General de Gaulle and his entourage in Algiers.[19] Underground newspapers, whether Catholic or Socialist, also preached the merits of a more unified post-war Europe.[20] Such solutions promised to eradicate the demon of nationalism and so avoid future European conflicts. Furthermore, only through unity could Europe match the power and prosperity of the world's new leaders, the USA and the USSR.

The scale of this last task was underlined by the final stages of the war. To a far greater extent than had been the case in the First World War, it was the economic wealth, military equipment and manpower of North America and the Soviet Union which had defeated Germany. The impact on European confidence and self-esteem was correspondingly greater. Likewise, the attractiveness of the United States as a model, political and economic, for a future united Europe was highlighted. But the USA was much more than simply an example for Europe's postwar leaders to follow. It was a country with very strong views of its own about how Europe should be rebuilt and one determined to use its considerable influence to minimize the likelihood of a further European conflict.

There were two key elements in America's vision of postwar Europe. The first was that it be democratic, capitalist and Western leaning; the second that it should be more united.[21] Neither ambition was completely fulfilled; both, however, were to be of enormous importance in the shaping of the postwar West. The former led inexorably towards disagreement with the Soviet Union. America's vision of Europe proved to be totally incompatible with Soviet ambitions of extending its political control and economic system over the Balkans, Poland, Hungary and Czechoslovakia. With the four-power conferences held between the victors degenerating into ever more intractable disagreement, the *de facto* division of Europe between East and West hardened into political reality. In Germany what had been occupied zones became the basis for two separate and antagonistic states.[22] This political reorganization of the continent was accompanied by massive population movement and the redrawing of national frontiers. The western zones of Germany alone received an influx of 9.4 million uprooted people, many of them ethnic Germans expelled from Soviet-occupied Eastern Europe – a forcible resolution of some of Europe's minority problems.[23] And both Germany and Poland were moved west, the latter forfeiting to the Soviet Union some of its eastern territory but receiving by way of compensation former German land to the east of the Oder and Neisse rivers.

The principal instrument used by the United States to promote its second objective – European unity – was financial assistance. Aid received through the Marshall Plan was made conditional on the nations of Europe cooperating in order to divide up and disburse American largesse, and strong political pressure was used in an effort to transform the Organization for European Economic Cooperation (OEEC) into the first institutional building block of a united Europe.[24] Such hopes were to founder on the scepticism of both the British and the French.[25] The Marshall plan did, however, facilitate subsequent moves towards European integration. The fact that American assistance was limited to 16 European nations underlined and reinforced the division of Europe into two blocks and set clear limits on the geographical extent of European cooperation. Still more important, the lure of Marshall funds proved vital in obliging the French to accept both the East/West division of Europe and the infeasibility of their own Carthaginian plans for postwar Germany. This dual volte-face paved the way for a total reorientation of French foreign policy strategy – a reorientation which was to see France initiate and lead the first moves to integrate the continent.[26]

Before France could take any initiative in reorganizing the western half of Europe, however, a further US contribution proved necessary. The American military guarantee to Europe that underpinned the North Atlantic Treaty, signed in 1949, introduced an element of stability and security into the continent which had been lacking since 1918. In the aftermath of the Second World War, there was to be no repetition of the American withdrawal of 1919. The knowledge that American might was constantly at hand bolstered the confidence of European states faced by the new Soviet threat and helped quell residual anxiety about the military aspect of the German problem. It also lessened the very real fear of internal Communist subversion which afflicted France and Italy in particular. Furthermore, NATO represented the central element of an over-arching Atlantic framework of institutions and relationships within the security of which the nation-states of Europe felt able to experiment with an increasing variety of forms of integration.

The first significant move in this direction came in May 1950, with the French announcement of the Schuman Plan. This in turn led to the establishment of the European Coal and Steel Community (ECSC), a body designed to manage jointly the coal and steel industries of the six founder-members. But the significance of this move extended far beyond the reorganization of a vital but limited sector. For the launch of the ECSC had at least three novel aspects which were to be of great importance for the subsequent development of the continent. The first of these was the institutional shape of the new body and in particular the degree of supranationality which its high authority introduced. Although the subsequent Treaties of Rome were to modify these arrangements, the fundamental departure from traditional international cooperative arrangements signalled by the ECSC was not to be reversed. Second, the Schuman Plan and its aftermath underlined the centrality of Franco-German cooperation. In launching his idea in May 1950, Robert Schuman, the French Foreign Minister, made clear his readiness to press ahead with Germany alone should it prove necessary.

This did not in fact happen, as Italy and the Benelux states quickly rallied to the Plan. Nevertheless, the extent to which French thinking was focussed on Germany had been demonstrated. Third, 1950 marked a further geographical limitation of 'Europe'. Neither Britain nor the countries of Scandinavia were willing to commit themselves to the ECSC, and the decision of France and her five partners to forge ahead regardless constituted an important step towards the 20-year separation between the inner Six and the outer Seven.[27] 'Europe' had shrunk to its medieval, or Carolingian, core.

The prosperity of the 1950s and 1960s meanwhile helped restore a degree of confidence in the nation-state model. Indeed, in the years after 1945, unlike those that had followed the First World War, there was no concerted effort to cut back the role of the state; the postwar years were the great period of state-centred welfare and national economic strategies. The nation-state also provided a framework for democratic corporatism. Paradoxically, however, this 'rescue of the nation-state' was highly dependent on international cooperation: in the immediate postwar years American financial assistance enabled the nation-states of Western Europe to deliver the economic and welfare benefits which their electorates demanded, while in the 1950s and 1960s state intervention was made possible by the booming international and especially intra-European trade. One of the key purposes of European integration was to safeguard this new-found prosperity from any repetition of the economic nationalism of the 1930s.[28] Economic necessity thus dovetailed well with the political imperative of constructing a stable West European system, within which Franco-German relations in particular could be repaired.

European revival raised important questions for both the United States and those countries like the United Kingdom which had chosen to exclude themselves from the European core. Under Kennedy, the American government sought to adapt the Atlantic partnership in order to take account both of Europe's growing economic strength and the moves to provide the Six with a coherent political voice. By so doing, the Americans hoped to head off de Gaulle's planned loosening of the Atlantic ties. Central to the US President's vision was the acceptance by Europe of a very limited and tightly controlled multinational nuclear capability – in exchange for a renunciation of national nuclear ambitions – and the widening of the European Community to include Great Britain.[29] The latter – a move designed to guarantee that any further progress towards European political union would not undermine the

Atlantic Alliance – had become more feasible as Britain gradually appreciated the economic and (still more importantly) the political costs of exclusion from the EEC.[30] De Gaulle, however, had rather different ambitions. He hoped that a more politically unified Western Europe would be able to distance itself from the United States and strike out on a more independent course. This in turn might allow a lessening of East-West tension, thus opening up the prospect of a wider Europe, stretching from the Atlantic to the Urals. Britain's entry into the Community – a key plank in Kennedy's strategy – was, for de Gaulle, to be avoided at all costs.[31]

By mid-1963 both projects had collapsed. Kennedy's Grand Design was derailed in January, when de Gaulle skilfully exploited British hesitations about EEC membership and his own strengthened domestic position to rule out both Community enlargement and French participation in a NATO-centred nuclear force. France, the General made clear, would develop her own nuclear deterrent.[32] De Gaulle's own ambitions, however, already dented by the failure of the political union discussions among the Six, were further damaged when in May 1963 the Bundestag seriously weakened the Franco-German Treaty which de Gaulle had negotiated with Chancellor Adenauer by adding a highly Atlanticist preamble.[33] The Elysée Treaty was to live on as a symbol of Franco-German reconciliation and as a basis for a highly effective partnership; but its potential as the corner-stone of the new Europe, free from American leadership, had been destroyed. Despite French misgivings, European integration continued to take place within a secure Atlantic framework.

1965–1989: widening, recession and transatlantic difficulty

Three themes characterize the period between the mid-1960s and the collapse of the Berlin Wall. The first of these was the widening of 'Europe' from the inner core of the six countries to which it had shrunk. Part of this change reflected the re-emergence of Germany as a central actor on the European stage, and the resultant renewal of attention towards Eastern Europe. Secure in its membership of the West – the legacy of German diplomacy in the Adenauer era – the Federal Republic felt able to turn once more towards its eastern neighbours and try to mitigate, if not end, a division of Europe which, since the construction of the Berlin Wall in 1961, appeared more permanent than ever before. *Ostpolitik* and the conclusion of economic and other agreements with countries on the Council for Mutual Economic Assistance

(CMEA) represented a major new step, but one which had become possible only as West Germany no longer feared being abandoned by the its partners in a neutralist limbo between East and West. The whole Helsinki process, the proliferation of contact groups and the intellectual rediscovery of 'Mitteleuropa' were all signs of this new trend.[34] After the contraction of the early Cold War years, the mental horizons of Europe were once more expanding to encompass all of Western Christendom. Appropriately, in 1979 a Polish Pope was elected.

Alongside this intellectual widening, the long delayed expansion of Community membership had finally occurred in 1973. The Six had become the Nine, with Britain, Ireland and Denmark joining the EEC. Enlargement, moreover, had been accompanied by the conclusion of economic agreements with the remaining members of the European Free Trade Association (EFTA); there was thus the prospect of free trade over most of Western Europe.[35] Further confirmation of the Community's economic and political magnetism was provided by the countries of the Mediterranean. By 1979 three countries in the region – Greece, Spain and Portugal – had applied for membership, while several others had negotiated association agreements with the EEC.[36] Population movements anticipated this widening of Europe, with immigrants from the Mediterranean pouring into Northern Europe. 'Klein Europa' – the derisive term coined by those who had resisted the decision to press ahead with integration among just six European states – became an outdated concept.

The second theme was economic recession. *'Les trentes glorieuses'*, the three decades of postwar recovery and boom, petered out in the early 1970s. In their place came widespread economic crisis, characterized by high inflation and declining intra-European trade. This both undermined the prevalent social democratic consensus – the first signs of popular resentment at ever-rising public expenditure were shown during the late 1970s – and called into question the economic integration which had occurred in the preceding 20 years: economic divergence in policy as much as in results, severe exchange-rate fluctuation and the proliferation of non-tariff barriers threatened to undermine the EEC customs union. Of great future significance, however, was West Germany's conspicuous success in avoiding many of these economic woes. This further altered the balance of power within Western Europe – the move to set up the European Monetary System (EMS) in the late 1970s was the first major example of German leadership – and encouraged the emergence of a European consensus on the need for low inflation, exchange rate stability and trade liberalization.[37] The Single Market project and the revival of European fortunes in the second half of the 1980s was a fruit of this consensus. In Eastern Europe, by contrast, the stagnation of the 1970s continued throughout the 1980s, with the technological and wealth gap between the two halves of Europe growing progressively.

The third theme was growing tension and rivalry between Europe and the United States. Problems had started to appear in the Johnson era, but it was under Richard Nixon that transatlantic relations seriously deteriorated. Western European leaders were angered and dismayed by Nixon's decision to withdraw from the Bretton Woods system and by the placing of a surcharge on US imports; the 'year of Europe' initiative, designed to restore relations, succeeded only in aggravating matters further. Policy disagreements with the Americans – notably about East–West relations and the Middle East – were a significant factor in persuading the Community member states to experiment once more with limited foreign policy cooperation. Under Carter, European irritation was succeeded by alarm at the Democrat President's apparent vacillation, particularly over monetary policy. Once again the European response was to seek greater control for themselves; discontent at US policy was an important element in the genesis of the EMS.[37]

This trend accelerated during Reagan's presidency. A succession of foreign policy disputes – over the Middle East, Poland, Nicaragua, the Strategic Defense Initiative (SDI) and the gas-pipeline project – in which the US President's confrontational attitude towards East–West relations had been at odds with the European desire for détente, was abruptly followed by his apparent willingness at the Reykjavik meeting with Gorbachev in 1986 to bargain away all of Europe's nuclear shield. All of these tensions underlined Europe's need to extend cooperation into fields where American leadership had previously been unchallenged. Transatlantic commercial disputes also multiplied in the early 1980s – the GATT was inundated by US and EC complaints about each other's behaviour – while hi-tech rivalry with the USA (as well as with Japan) increased European industry's appetite for an effective internal market.[38] Disputes with America thus proved an important element in widening the agenda of European integration, from the narrow confines of commercial and agricultural policy, to the range of economic, monetary and even political affairs discussed among the Twelve in the late 1980s.

After 1990: Eastern Europe and the West

The transformation of Central and Eastern Europe in 1989-90, followed as it was by the disintegration of the Soviet Union, raised a whole variety of new questions about the geographical and cultural limits of Europe, and about the viability of its political organization.[39] The debate about a wider Europe and about the extension of the Community structures could no longer centre upon the Scandinavian and Alpine members of EFTA, or the Mediterranean 'orphans' Malta and Cyprus. Instead, the whole Western European attitude to the former Communist states needed to be reviewed. Could and should Europe extend up to the former Soviet border? Or would this constitute an unnecessary and unwise assault on Russian sensibilities? Or was the answer to incorporate the Soviet successor states also? The questions were myriad; the answers equally numerous. Different European organizations adopted widely differing criteria for eligibility. Thus the North Atlantic Cooperation Council established by NATO adopted a maximalist approach, extending membership deep into the former Soviet Union, while the Western European Union (WEU) Forum balked at admitting any territory which had formed part of the USSR. The EC meanwhile signed full Association agreements with some of the new democracies, and mere commercial accords with others. A Europe of gradations of privilege, of concentric circles, appeared likely.

Faced with this confusion, some commentators turned to cultural and historical factors in an effort to draw the borders of the new 'Europe'. Could those parts of the Balkans once controlled by the Ottoman Empire be incorporated into the same 'Europe' as the Protestant Nordics? And did religion matter? Could Muslim Bosnia fit comfortably into a predominantly Christian Europe? Could the cultural and political idea of a European Community, already uncertain in Western Europe, be made to stretch deep into Eastern and South-eastern Europe? Others preferred to concentrate on the stage of economic reform reached, although given the diverse economic strategies adopted by the states of Eastern and Central Europe this too has proved highly subjective.

In the former Communist states themselves, there was a degree of ambivalence. Membership of European organizations, and in particular the ultimate prize of EU membership, was regarded by many of the governments as a promise of future prosperity, political stability and security. Acceptance into Europe or even the secure promise of future acceptance would consolidate the reform process, provide an incentive for short-term sacrifice and render less likely a relapse into Communist or authoritarian rule. But alongside such optimism there were also fears about the loss of national identity, about the imposed alteration of national economic and social priorities, about the threat to a newly rediscovered sense of nationhood. Popular uncertainty about the desirability of European integration appeared in the former Eastern bloc, just as it was also gaining strength in those nations firmly within the Western European core.

Finally there were questions about the adaptability of European integration as hitherto pursued.[40] Some queries focussed on the complications that large-scale enlargement would inevitably bring: predictions of institutional paralysis were rife as the prospect of a 30-member Community emerged. Could the institutions, already under strain in a Community of 12, possibly cope with more than twice as many members? Would any agreement be possible in so large a grouping? Was it likely that the policies and legislation suitable for Finland would also meet the needs of Albania? A second category of questions re-examined the fundamental motives of the drive to European Union. Western European integration, some suggested, had been a child of the Cold War and in part at least the product of extensive American sponsorship. Could it and should it survive the ending of the East–West divide and the gradual American disengagement from Europe? Alternatively, if one of the central purposes of European integration had been to find a framework within which the diversity in power and strength of the European powers, and in particular the economic and political pre-eminence of Germany, could be accommodated, did not German reunification and the new centrality which the transformation of Central and Eastern Europe gave to the Federal Republic increase rather than diminish the need for some form of European unity? In 1989 it was not just the Berlin Wall that had fallen; with it had vanished many of the certainties upon which Western Europe had thrived in the preceding decades. As the search for their replacements begins, one consequence of the twentieth century is unlikely to be challenged. Europe in 1900 could claim, with justification, to be at the centre of international affairs; in the 1990s, by contrast, it has become just one reasonably prosperous region in a much more genuinely global system.

Notes
1   Fernand Braudel, *The Mediterranean and the Mediterranean World in the Age of Philip II*, 2 vols (London, 1972–3).

2 Edward W. Said, *Orientalism* (London, 1978), pp.49–73.
3 Richard Hoggart and Douglas Johnson, *An Idea of Europe* (London, 1987), pp.5–27.
4 Paul Kennedy, *The Rise of Anglo-German Antagonism* (London, 1980), pp.441 ff.
5 J. M. Roberts, *Europe 1880–1945* (London, 1967), pp.263–303.
6 Derek Aldcroft, *The European Economy 1914–1970* (London, 1978), p.25.
7 Alan Sharp, *The Versailles Settlement: Peacemaking in Paris 1919* (London, 1991).
8 Aldcroft, *The European Economy*, p.31.
9 John Maynard Keynes, *The Economic Consequences of the Peace* (London, 1919).
10 Sharp, *The Versailles Settlement*, pp.102–29.
11 Thomas J. Knock, *To End All Wars: Woodrow Wilson and the Quest for a New World Order* (Oxford, 1992), p.210 ff.
12 Roberts, *Europe*, pp.328–30.
13 Nicole Jordan, *The Popular Front and Central Europe: The Dilemmas of French Impotence 1918–1940* (Cambridge, 1992), pp.5–92.
14 Jon Jacobson, *Locarno Diplomacy: Germany and the West 1925–29*, (Princeton, NJ, 1972), pp.13–35.
15 Walter Lipgens, *A History of European Integration* (Oxford, 1982), pp.41–2.
16 Charles P. Kindleberger, *The World in Depression 1929–39* (London, 1973), pp.131–5.
17 Robert Young, *In Command of France: French Foreign Policy and Military Planning 1933–40*, (Cambridge, MA, 1978), pp.62–3.
18 Michael Howard, *The Continental Commitment* (London, 1972), pp.97–122.
19 John W. Young, *Britain, France and the Unity of Europe* (Leicester, 1984), p.6.
20 Lipgens, *A History*, pp.44–62.
21 Jeffry Diefendorf, Axel Frohn and Hermann-Josef Rupieper (eds), *American Policy and the Reconstruction of West Germany, 1945–55* (Cambridge, 1993), pp.45–134.
22 Anton DePorte: *Europe between the Superpowers* (New Haven, 1986), pp.42–57.
23 *The Integration of Refugees into German Life*, A Report of the ECA Technical Assistance Commission on the Integration of Refugees in the German Republic, March 1951, p.1.
24 Michael Hogan, *The Marshall Plan: America, Britain and the Reconstruction of Western Europe 1947–52* (Cambridge, 1987), pp.26–87.
25 Ian Milward, *The Reconstruction of Western Europe 1945–51* (London, 1984), pp.68–211.
26 Gérard Bossuat, *La France, l'aide américaine et la construction européenne 1944–54* (Paris, 1992), pp.253–94.
27 Raymond Poidevin and Dirk Spierenburg, *Histoire de la Haute Autorité*

      de la Communauté Européenne du Charbon et de l'Acier (Paris, 1993), pp.9–52.
28 Alan Milward, *The European Rescue of the Nation-State* (London, 1992), pp.119–223.
29 Pascaline Winand, *Eisenhower, Kennedy and the United States of Europe* (London, 1993), pp.161 ff.
30 Miriam Camps, *Britain and the European Community 1955–1963* (Oxford, 1964), pp.274–366.
31 Edmond Jouve: *Le Générale de Gaulle et la construction de l'Europe* (Paris, 1967), pp.178–88, 718–25.
32 Charles de Gaulle: *Discours et messages*, iv (Paris, 1970), pp.66–71.
33 Hans-Peter Schwarz: *Adenauer: Der Staatsmann, 1952–1967* (Stuttgart, 1991), p.825.
34 Timothy Garton-Ash, *In Europe's Name: Germany and the Division of the Continent* (London, 1993), pp.48–83.
35 Thomas Pedersen, 'EC–EFTA relations: a historical outline', in H. Wallace (ed.), *The Wider Western Europe* (London, 1991), pp.18–19.
36 Loukas Tsoukalis argues that political motives outweighed economic factors. *The European Community and its Mediterranean Enlargement* (London, 1981), p.145.
37 Peter Ludlow, *The Making of the European Monetary System* (London, 1982), pp.63–87.
38 R. Ginsberg: 'US–EC relations', in Juliet Lodge (ed.) *The European Community and the Challenge of the Future* (London, 1989), pp.256–78
39 John Peterson, *Europe and America in the 1990s* (London, 1993), pp.44–8.
40 See for instance Michel Foucher, *The Next Europe: An Essay on Alternatives and Strategies towards a New Vision of Europe* (Bilbao, 1993).

6. THE NUCLEAR REVOLUTION

Richard Wyn Jones

The exploding of an atomic bomb over the Japanese city of Hiroshima on 6 August 1945, will surely be seen as one of the defining moments of the twentieth century. The instantaneous slaughter of 68,000 civilians by a bomb known incongruously by the diminutive 'Little Boy', and dropped from the equally homely 'Enola Gay', is an event firmly etched on humanity's collective memory.

While the material effects of the bombs on the populations of Hiroshima and Nagasaki was, and indeed remains, painfully apparent, their wider resonances and effects remain deeply contested.[1] For example, the questions of why the American government decided to use its nuclear weapons, and whether their use had any influence on Japan's decision to capitulate, are some of the most controversial of all issues in the study of contemporary international history.[2] However, what is incontrovertible is the strength and the global extent of the psychological shock-waves caused by news of the awesome destructive power unleashed on the unsuspecting Japanese cities. Even after the first successful testing of a nuclear weapon, but before their deployment against human beings, Churchill is said to have exclaimed: 'What was gunpowder? Trivial. What was electricity? Meaningless. This Atomic Bomb is the Second Coming in Wrath.'[3]

According to the Book of Revelation, the Second Coming is to be accompanied by a final battle at Armageddon on the Day of Judgment.

This is the battle to end all battles, in which, according to the Apocalyptic vision, the world would be shaken by 'flashes of lightning and peals of thunder, and a violent earthquake, like none before in human history, so violent it was. Since Hiroshima, Armageddon has been routinely invoked as a means of conveying the unimaginable horrors that would ensue from an all-out nuclear war. The use of religious or quasi-religious imagery is suggestive. It indicates the way in which the harnessing of the tremendous energy unlocked during nuclear fission, the physical process initiated by the detonation of an atomic bomb, and the even greater amounts of energy unleashed during nuclear fusion, utilized in hydrogen bombs, has given some human beings an almost divine power over both nature and their fellow humans.[4] Certainly, in the Western world at least, there has been a prevalent assumption that the advent of nuclear weapons has revolutionized such social activities as warfare and international relations.

This assumption seems to have extended right across those societies. Among political elites, and their military advisers, the implications of nuclear weapons have – until very recently at least – been a source of constant vexation. Some have agonized about the burden of responsibility that the control of nuclear arsenals has placed upon their shoulders. Almost all have felt it necessary systematically to deceive their publics, succumbing to the obsessive secrecy that has characterized the 'nuclear states'.[5] In Western academia, Strategic Studies was developed as a field of enquiry mainly concerned with thinking through the political and military implications of nuclear weapons. A rival discourse, Peace Studies, also developed in the shadow of 'nuclear fear'. This tradition eschewed the spurious value-neutrality so characteristic of Strategic Studies by making a normative commitment to the abolition of nuclear weapons.

On the popular level, Western Europe, Australia, New Zealand and North America all at different times saw massive mobilization against their deployment and testing. Nuclear weapons, and nuclear technology more generally, have also permeated into popular consciousness through their influence on modern culture where they have proven to be an apparently endless source of fascination and inspiration. This popular interest predates the Second World War but rather seems to have been a recurrent theme throughout the century. When the Museum of Natural History in New York put a speck of radium on exhibition in 1903, it was inundated by the biggest crowd in its history who proceeded to elbow and push each other in their eagerness to view the 'dull pinch of powder' on display.⁶ Of course, since Hiroshima, the image of the nuclear mushroom cloud has been ubiquitous in popular culture: following a familiar pattern, the horrors that the image represents have been made psychologically managable through trivialization. In his introduction to his book *Knowing Nukes*, William Chaloupka relates the tale of a high school near a nuclear weapons base in Richland, Washington State, which adopted the mushroom cloud as the mascot for its sports teams.⁷

Efforts to think through the implications of the nuclear revolution have tended to concentrate on one of these levels. There are numerous historical studies of how nuclear weapons have been incorporated into military strategies and how they may have affected behaviour in international crises.⁸ Others have focussed on how nuclear weapons have permeated every level of our culture, even into our very language.⁹ An alternative approach might be to study the horrendous human and environmental impact of the nuclear weapons tested since 1945. According to the most recent estimates there have been 2031 nuclear tests worldwide since we entered the nuclear age. About a quarter of these tests were conducted in the atmosphere generating a yield of approximately 438 megatons: the equivalent of 29,000 Hiroshima-sized bombs.¹⁰ Although one may baulk at fully accepting Masahide Kato's claim that these tests represent an undeclared nuclear war against the 'fourth world and indigenous peoples', there can be no doubting that all the nuclear powers have been at best cavalier in their attitude to the indigenous people living on or near the test sites.¹¹ Moreover, this disregard towards the human toll of testing has also extended to the service personnel of the nuclear states themselves as well as to their civilian populations. With the end of the Cold War, a new spirit of openness has led the US Energy Department to reveal information on a series of horrific secret experiments in which sections of the American public were used as unwitting human guinea pigs in radiation tests.¹² However, rather than pursue these issues, this chapter will follow a different track.

Implicit in most reactions to the nuclear revolution is an assumption that nuclear weapons technology has in some way fundamentally altered the human species' relationship with technology *per se*. Raymond Aron, for example, lamented that we now live in an age of 'virile weapons and impotent men'.¹³ Indeed, the assumption that something fundamental has changed is, of course, inherent in the term 'nuclear revolution' itself. It is on this implicit assumption that we will focus here. By first outlining some of the possible models of the relationship between humans and technology, and then surveying some of the theory and practice of nuclear weapons, we shall attempt to shed some light on the deeper, often unquestioned, assumptions which underlie our thinking about this particular revolution. Those uninitiated in the study of military strategy might expect that such an approach is hardly novel. Sadly, this is far from the case. Although technology is of central concern to strategists – Barry Buzan has even argued that Strategic Studies should be designed as the study of the military-technological variable in International Relations – the strategists' conception of technology remains curiously underdeveloped.[14] Athough many strategy texts discuss the relationship between strategy and technology, these discussions tend not to move beyond rather superficial comments about the pace of technological change; for example, how technology complicates, or alternatively complements, arms control.[15] The deeper issues concerning the nature of the relationship between technology and society are hardly ever addressed. This chapter is concerned with precisely those issues. It is confined to one particular application of the technological harnessing of the processes of nuclear fission and nuclear fusion, that is their military application. Clearly, one could also dwell upon the utilisation of nuclear fission as a source of energy, and its medical-scientific usage. Yet, while accepting the utility and efficacy of nuclear technology in medical treatment, it seems highly improbable that nuclear fission would ever have been developed as a source of energy were it not for the fact that the by-products of the power-production process are militarily useful. Nuclear power plants are ultimately unthinkable without nuclear weapons.

The question of technology

Beyond the bounds of traditional Strategic Studies, the question of how developments in modern technology have affected the relationship between 'men and machines' has recently received much attention, especially from poststructuralist philosophers and a range of cultural theorists. They have been particularly concerned with the implications of developments in communications and computer technology – which some have argued augurs the start of a 'third industrial revolution'. The common usage of terms such as 'hyper-reality' and 'virtual reality', as well as the rapid development of relatively new fields of study such as cybernetics, reflect this interest. Additionally, feminist scholars and activists have done much to expose the gendered and engendering nature of technology. The approach adopted here, however, is that of another, possibly less fashionable, tradition of social theory, that of the Critical Theory of the so-called Frankfurt School.[16]

There are two main justifications for viewing the nuclear revolution through the lenses of Critical Theory. The first is the nature of the scientific discoveries that made the development of nuclear weapons possible. These discoveries formed part of a paradigm shift away from the previous Newtonian understanding of the physical world to an Einsteinian model. The Newtonian paradigm posited a rigid distinction between subject and object: between the scientist and that which she or he was studying. The physical world was seen as governed by cast-iron laws, which even if not presently understood, were potentially discoverable. By contrast, the new quantum physics, pioneered by Einstein, rejected the Newtonian view that there is a world 'out there' existing independently of our observation. Rather, following Heisenberg's Uncertainty Principle, scientists realized that by the very act of observation, the observer affects the behaviour of the object being observed. This realization fatally undermined the model of the natural sciences which most social scientists have hoped to emulate in their own work. All the familiar distinctions between subject and object, fact and value, which most social scientists saw (and often still see) as characterizing 'scientific understanding' were rendered deeply problematic. Critical Theorists, however, never accepted this positivistic model of social science.[17] Indeed one of the fundamental claims of Critical Theory is that the observer and observed are inextricably intertwined. As such it would seem to provide a particularly apposite position from which to view the nuclear revolution.

The evolutionary trajectory of Critical Theory itself provides the second reason for adopting it as a framework for exploring some of the implications of that revolution. For Critical Theorists, the question of technology, and in particular the form of rationality utilized in the development of modern technology, has always been of central concern. However, their views have not remained constant: rather those working within the Critical Theory tradition have, at various times, embraced very different conceptions of the relationship between humans and technology. By reviewing these contradictory conceptions we can build up a picture of the range of positions that theorists have taken on this issue and thus view the nuclear revolution from a number of different angles.

Continuing a familiar tradition in progressive thought during the nineteenth century, the first works of the Critical Theorists, written in the 1930s, exhibited a sanguine attitude towards technological progress. New technology was equated fairly simplistically with progress. Even if that technology were not always utilized for progressive purposes – if it were for example used in order to further domination – this was not because of any inherent failing in the technology itself. Rather it was because of failings in *human* relations: class bias, imperialism and the like. If only modern technology were placed in the framework of an emancipated society, then its liberating potentialities could be released.

The coming of the Second World War, and especially the extermination of European Jewry, shattered the Critical Theorists' faith in the traditional Enlightenment equation of science and technology with progress. The establishment of death camps such as the one at Auschwitz – another defining event in this century's tragic history – was particularly important. Here the Nazis marshalled the power of technological rationality systematically to slaughter a whole people. Mass murder was placed on a scientific basis. Adorno's and Horkheimer's joint work *Dialectic of Enlightenment* was written in the shadow of Auschwitz, and exhibits a wholesale loss of faith in the familiar nostrums of the Enlightenment. In the introduction the authors set themselves the task of discovering 'why mankind, instead of entering into a truly human condition is sinking into a new kind of barbarism.'[18] Their conclusion was that:

> The fallen nature of modern man cannot be separated from social progress. On the one hand the growth of economic productivity furnishes the conditions for a world of greater justice; on the other hand it allows the technical apparatus and the social group which administers it a disproportionate superiority to the rest of the population. The individual is wholly devalued in relation to the economic powers, which at the same time press the control of society over nature to hitherto unsuspecting heights.[19]

The problem identified by the authors is that the type of rationality necessary for the gradual subjugation of nature – necessary, in other words, for the development of civilization – tends to dispense with any rational consideration of ends, simply concentrating on questions of means. For Adorno and Horkheimer, Auschwitz represented the nadir in this process of the atrophy of reason and, in their subsequent work, was used as a motif representing the catastrophic degeneration of civilization. Hiroshima and the subsequent nuclear arms race between the superpower blocs merely served to confirm their bleak view of contemporary society.

The vast amounts of scientific and technological know-how and economic resources pumped into the Manhattan project and subsequent nuclear weapons research and development – in the United States and elsewhere – produced weapons which, if used in large enough numbers, could destroy the human species itself. One could hardly devise a clearer illustration of the atrophy of reason than an application of rationality which produces a potentially species-destroying device, and then contrives strategies for bringing this about in some circumstances. Adorno himself berated the atrophy of reason in these terms, arguing that 'no universal history leads from savagery to humanitarianism, but there is one leading from the slingshot to the megaton bomb'.

The conclusions drawn by Adorno and Horkheimer were deeply pessimistic. Technology and technological rationality had structured the world in a particular way, and they could see no escape from this dystopia. They regarded society as being 'totally administered'. This was a society in which technology had an autonomous logic beyond human control; a society in which the effects of technology and technological rationality – the form of reason necessary for producing technology, and then embodied within it – are so all-pervasive that humans cannot help but be implicated in them. In *Dialectic of Enlightenment*, Adorno and Horkheimer seem to be positing the end of the autonomous human subject: an end of the individual if not an end of history.

It is hard to overstate the shift in attitudes towards technology from the Critical Theory of the 1930s to that of the 1940s. Unsurprisingly perhaps, much postwar Critical Theory seems to have been an attempt to deal with the implications of Adorno's and Horkheimer's thesis. For, if they are right, and we do inhabit a 'totally administered society' from which there appears to be no escape, then obviously the Critical Theory project of aiding and abetting the development of an emancipated society is itself fatally wounded. One of those who grappled most assiduously with the issues raised by Adorno and Horkheimer was their Frankfurt School colleague Herbert Marcuse. He is perhaps best remembered as one of the inspirations of the student movement of the 1960s and the rather improbable guru of 'free love': a man who managed the remarkable feat of attracting the condemnation of the American right, American liberals, *Pravda,* the French Communist

Party, and the Pope, all at the same time![20] However, one suspects that one of his most lasting contributions will be to the development of a Critical Theory of technology.

Marcuse tried to uphold a dialectical tension between the two contradictory conceptions of technology expounded by Critical Theorists. The first view, propounded in the 1930s, conceived of technology as a 'vehicle of liberation', to use a typically Marcusean turn of phrase. The second view, developed in response to Auschwitz and Hiroshima, conceived of technology as a form of domination, a 'vehicle of reification'. Marcuse regarded both positions as valid – neither could simply be collapsed into the other. While he never really developed these insights systematically, Marcuse nevertheless laid the foundations for the subsequent development of a more complete Critical Theory of technology by a generation of American Critical Theorists, in particular by Andrew Feenberg.

Conceptualizing technology

In order to construct his Critical Theory of technology Feenberg first develops a taxonomy of the usual approaches to technology. He discusses, and subsequently dismisses, two main views: the *instrumental* and the *substantive*. The instrumental view of technology is the more usual one. It sees technology as neutral: 'as subservient to values established in other social spheres i.e. politics and culture'.[21] That is, technology can serve a 'plurality of ends' depending on the particular circumstances of its use.[22] A simple illustration of this view is the National Rifle Association (NRA) position encapsulated in the slogan 'it's not the gun, it's the person holding the gun'. The implication is that the gun itself is neutral; it can be used for 'good' purposes – defending family and home – or for nefarious ones – robbery and extortion. Another example, this time in the field of military strategy proper, is the recurrent controversy over the banning of 'offensive' weapons. The argument here is that weapons are not inherently offensive or defensive, rather it depends on the attitudes and outlooks of those controlling their use. 'What is not a weapon in the wrong hands?' is a question which vexed those involved in the interminable debates on disarmament in the League of Nations during the 1920s. Thus the instrumental view is predicated on the 'common-sense' notion that the subject of action is independent from the means of action, and that those means are neutral.[23]

The substantive view of technology, on the other hand, may be regarded as a deterministic attitude which 'attributes an autonomous cultural force to technology that overrides all traditional or competing values. Substantive theory claims that what the very employment of technology does to humanity and nature is more consequential than its ostensible goals.'[24] The argument here is that no matter what the intentions of those inventing or introducing a new technology, it will determine social and cultural relations in a particular way. For a military example one might use the invention of the conoidal bullet. This was first developed for hunting and duelling and for many years military chiefs opposed its introduction into warfare. However, they were eventually forced to accept its deployment and this ultimately precipitated a radical change in military tactics. Units on the battlefield could no longer be arranged in centrally controlled massed ranks as these became simply too vulnerable; rather troops had to be dispersed into small units and given operational autonomy.[25] This example fits particularly well with Feenberg's description of technological determinism which he sees as based on two theses:

> 1. The pattern of technical progress is fixed, moving along one and the same track in all societies. Although political, cultural, and other factors may influence the pace of change, they cannot alter the general line of development, which reflects the autonomous logic of discovery.
> 2. Social organisation must adapt to technical progress at each stage of development according to the 'imperative' of technology. This adaptation executes an underlying technical necessity.[26]

Despite their best efforts, military leaders could not resist the introduction of the conoidal bullet, and once this occurred military organization was eventually forced to adapt to the 'imperatives' of the new technology. In one of his more deterministic moments Marx once wrote to Engels asking the rhetorical question: 'Is our theory that the organisation of labour is determined by the means of production confirmed anywhere more splendidly than in the man-slaughtering industry?'[27] Despite the fact that Marxists have regularly succumbed to technological determinism, the substantive approach is more usually associated with such figures as Heidegger and Ellul. Thus the substantive view is predicated on a deterministic, even fatalistic attitude to technology.

Technology is autonomous and as such, it is a destiny which cannot be avoided or escaped.

Feenberg, developing a Critical Theory approach, rejects both these views of technology.[28] The instrumental view is too simplistic. To revert to previous examples, 'the army is not merely accidentally related to its weapons, but it is structured around the activities they support'.[29] It is not merely a coincidence that military organizations tend to change their operational structures and even tactics when new technologies are introduced. Similarly, the number of violent deaths in a society, despite the NRA's arguments to the contrary, are not somehow accidentally related to the ease of access to firearms within that society. Easy access to firearms undermines prevalent social and cultural values. In reality, subjects and means are related. But this does not mean that Feenberg accepts the substantive position that technology is autonomous and that a particular set of social values or social relations is embodied within a given technology: that the means of action ultimately controls the subject of action. Rather, Feenberg regards means and subject as 'dialectically intertwined'.[30] He provides a succinct explanation of this position:

> Critical theory argues that technology is not a thing in the ordinary sense of the term, but an 'ambivalent' process of development suspended between different possibilities. This 'ambivalence' of technology is distinguished from neutrality by the role it attributes to social values in the design, and not merely the use, of technical systems. On this view, technology is not a destiny but a scene of struggle.[31]

The important term here is 'ambivalence'. Technology *does* have a logic in that it simultaneously creates and constrains the choices available to society, yet technology *does not* predetermine which of those particular choices is made. That decision is a social one, and as such reflects a whole series of social, cultural and power relations. The fact that these relations are contestable leads to the argument that technology is a 'scene of struggle'.

Feenberg reformulates this argument in a slightly more sophisticated way. Each technology, he says, contains within it a number of neutral 'technical elements', be they springs, pumps or whatever, but the way in which these particular elements are configured reflects certain values. These values arise from the pattern of power relations in society. It follows that the values embodied in the technology often serve the function of supporting or legitimating the position of the most powerful elements. Thus the Critical Theory position developed by Feenberg rejects the instrumental view that technology is simply a neutral means. It also rejects the substantive view of technology as destiny: such technological determinism is, in the words of Raymond Williams, a 'form of intellectual closure of the complexities of social process'.[32] Rather Critical Theory views technology as an ambivalent process which contains within it a number of possibilities. The decision as to which of these possibilities is ultimately realized is a social one and as such reflects a whole complex of (contestable) social, cultural and power relations.

Nuclear weapons as technology

The discussion at the start of this chapter might lead one to expect that most views of nuclear weapons would have been consistent with either the substantive or critical approaches to technology. After all, these are the ones that view technology as non-neutral, and the implication was that something fundamental had changed with the advent of nuclear weapons. Surprisingly, however, despite the rhetoric, many of those writing and thinking about nuclear weapons have perceived them in what can be described as instrumental terms.

As we have seen, the instrumental approach argues that technology does not affect the social, political and cultural fundamentals in either domestic or international politics. From this viewpoint one discovers that a rather unlikely collection of individuals share the the same 'deep' assumptions about the role of nuclear weapons technology in society. For example, it seems that Colin Gray, the arch proponent of a 'nuclear warfighting' strategy, John Mueller, the proclaimer of the 'essential irrelevance' of nuclear weapons, as well as Mao Zedong, all share the same broad assumptions about nuclear weapons technology. While they all hold highly dissimilar views as to the nature and trajectory of global social and political relationships, they would all agree that nuclear weapons do not significantly alter those relationships.

Gray and the nuclear warfighters have seen nuclear weapons very much in what we might call NRA terms. To paraphrase: 'it's not the nuke, it's the person (state) holding the nuke'. That is, in the hands of the 'free', 'civilized' and democratic Western powers, nuclear weapons could be deployed in such a way as to deter a potential aggressor, or if deterrence was unsuccessful, to defeat an adversary. Yet, those very same weapons in the hands of the 'aggressive', 'expansionist', 'evil' Soviets, were inevitably dangerous and provocative. Nuclear weapons did not alter what were seen as the fundamental traits of Soviet behaviour nor their basic goals, but simply gave them a new (and dangerous) means of pursuing them. Gray contemptuously dismissed those who argued that 'all weapons are created equal and have equivalent consequences according to their technical qualities but regardless of their political ownership'.[33] For Gray and the other warfighters close to the Reagan administration in the early 1980s, the possibility that the Soviets might acquire a 'first-strike' capability was intensely worrying, but in the hands of the United States such a capability could be viewed benignly. Similarly, the development and deployment of the Soviet SS18 missile was regarded as a highly dangerous development, while the technically similar American MX was dubbed 'the peace maker'. It isn't the gun ...; or as Gray titled one of his works, *Weapons Don't Make War.*

John Mueller's view of the nature of the Soviet Union and the essence of the East–West relationship since 1945, advanced in his influential article 'The essential irrelevance of nuclear weapons', differs fundamentally from that of Gray and the warfighters.[34] He argues that a 'general stability' existed in East–West relations, a stability created by a complex of sociopolitical, economic factors, and – interestingly – a stability upon which nuclear weapons had no effect. Thus despite their different interpretations of the nature of the Soviet Union, Gray and Mueller share the same conception of the role of technology in the superpower relationship. Both reject what Gray has dubbed 'the fallacious idea that weapons or technologies move history along'.[35] According to Mueller, 'nuclear weapons have changed little except our way of talking, gesturing, and spending money'.[36]

Another proponent of the instrumental approach to technology in relation to nuclear weapons was Mao Zedong. He often stated his belief that no weapons system, no matter how sophisticated the technology incorporated within it, could alter the fundamental political and economic 'correlation of forces', most famously in 1968:

> The atom bomb is a paper tiger which the U.S. reactionaries use to scare people. It looks terrible but in fact it isn't. Of course, the atom bomb is a weapon of mass slaughter, but the outcome of a war is decided by the people, not by one or two new types of weapon.[37]

Mao was convinced that the 'correlation of forces' favoured the socialist bloc and was concerned that those ensconced in the Kremlin would squander the historic opportunity offered by such apparently propitious circumstances because of their fear of these 'paper tigers'. Indeed he seems to have been convinced that not even a nuclear war could derail the global advance of Marxism–Leninism. In a discussion entitled 'We must not fear nuclear war', Mao remarked that 'if the worst came to the worst and half of mankind died, the other half would remain while imperialism would be razed to the ground and the whole world would become socialist'.[38] Again, Mao's argument was that technology, even nuclear technology, could not affect the fundamental patterns of political and social relations, which in this case were seen as heralding the inevitable triumph of socialism.

In this way, questioning assumptions about technology, we find that those who rang alarm bells about 'windows of opportunity' seem to have shared, and indeed continue to share, the same 'deep' assumptions as those who were sanguine about the intentions of the Soviet leadership. Similarly, we find an avowed anti-communist like Colin Gray in the same camp as the author of the famous little red book. A similar phenomenon can be observed with respect to the substantive approach.

The substantive approach argues that technology has an autonomous logic of its own which determines a particular form of social organization. When we assemble those who share a substantive approach to nuclear technology we find some strange bedfellows: McGeorge Bundy, the exponent of 'existential deterrence'; Kenneth Waltz, a supporter of (gradual) nuclear proliferation; and the late E. P. Thompson, the charismatic and indefatigable anti-nuclear campaigner.

According to Bundy and other proponents of existential deterrence, the very fact that a state possesses nuclear weapons is enough to ensure that other states will be deterred from threatening its vital interests, no matter how hostile their political relationship. The 'existentialists' believe that numbers, force postures and targetting, in short all those issues which have exercised generations of strategists and policy makers, are irrelevant. Possession is enough: 'I exist; therefore I deter.'[39] Bundy argues that nuclear weapons are so destructive that their mere presence will moderate state behaviour because of the fear and uncertainty they introduce into any crisis situation.

> A decision that would bring even one hydrogen bomb on
> one city of one's country would be recognised in advance

as a catastrophic blunder; ten bombs on ten cities would be a disaster beyond history; and a hundred bombs on a hundred cities are unthinkable.[40]

Quite simply, 'existentialists' believe that nuclear weapons technology is so devastating that its potential effect overrides all other political, social and cultural considerations in the calculations of decision makers.

Kenneth Waltz's well-known argument in favour of gradual nuclear proliferation is based on the same kind of assumptions as those underlying the 'existential deterrence' position: he merely pushes the argument to its logical conclusion. Like Bundy, Waltz believes that the presence of nuclear weapons inevitably moderates the behaviour of states, arguing that 'the probability of major war among states having nuclear weapons approaches zero'.[41] He emphasizes that this benefit accrues whatever the political hue of the states in question: 'One need not become preoccupied with the characteristics of the state that is to be deterred or scrutunize its leaders.'[42] Because of the technologically determined, pacifying nature of nuclear weapons, Waltz argues that their benefits should be spread throughout the international system. He summarily dismisses the 'ethnocentric views' of those wary of allowing nuclear weapons to fall into the hands of the leaders of unstable Southern states: 'Many Westerners who write fearfully about a future in which third-world countries have nuclear weapons seem to view their people in the once familiar imperial manner as "lesser breeds without the law".'[43] Clearly, Waltz views nuclear technology as an autonomous force which determines a particular pattern of state behaviour, thereby overriding all other social and political factors.

The arguments put forward both by the proponents of existential deterrence and of proliferation suggest that the autonomous logic of nuclear weapons technology is benign. Others who share a substantive understanding of the nature of nuclear technology have developed a diametrically opposed analysis of the direction in which their autonomous logic is pushing society. In particular many in the peace movement have argued, in Frank Barnaby's words, 'we are being driven toward nuclear world war by the sheer momentum of military technology'.[44] The most eloquent exponent of this view was E. P. Thompson. In a celebrated essay on exterminism, first published in 1980, Thompson argued that the nuclear arms race had an autonomous, 'exterminist' logic which would lead to the extermination of the human race. Nuclear weapons and their attendant support systems, 'seem to grow of their own accord, as if possessed by an independent will'.[45] Although he called for, and indeed participated in, a movement of concerned citizens dedicated to checking exterminism, such is the autonomous power that he ascribed to nuclear weapons that it is hard to see how their deadly logic could be checked. Thompson's anti-nuclear activism seems to have been based on a Gramscian 'pessimism of intellect and optimism of will'.

Despite the very different conclusions arrived at in their work, the common thread in the thinking of Bundy, Waltz and Thompson is a similar, substantive approach to the relationship between human beings and nuclear technology. They all saw technology as an autonomous force shaping social relations, a universal destiny which overrides cultural particularity.

Most contributions to the vast literature on the implications of nuclear weapons seem to have been based on either instrumental or substantive conceptions of technology. For example, the recurrent debate in the USA between nuclear-use theorists and proponents of mutually assured destruction was essentially an argument between instrumentalists and substantivists respectively. However, it is those studies that have utilized a critical approach to technology that have offered most insights into the actual behaviour of nuclear-armed states.

The critical approach stresses the ambivalent nature of technology: technology opens up a range of options or choices for society; the options chosen depend, in part, on the configuration of power relations within that society; the choices made almost invariably serve to reinforce the position of the hegemonic group. Some of the studies that have adopted this approach fall into the broad category of 'arms race literature'. These studies have placed issues like procurement decisions in the context of domestic political disputes. They have exposed the way that these decisions reflect bureaucratic and political power struggles rather than any rational threat. Others have analyzed the role played by nuclear weapons in the construction and legitimation of the 'national security states' on both sides of the Cold War divide.[46] Such work undermines both instrumental and substantive understandings of nuclear technology, while simultaneously exploring the familiar Critical Theory theme of the relationship between technology and power.

Bruce Blair's recent comparative study of American and Soviet nuclear forces provides powerful support for proponents of a critical approach to technology.[47] Blair demonstrates the technological constraints within which both states had to operate. Developments in rocket technology reduced both the time needed to prepare missiles for firing, and the flight time en route to their targets. This forced both countries to develop command and control systems which could react rapidly in times of crisis. However, the force structures developed by the two sides to deal with this problem were very different and reflected their wider strategic and political cultures. The USSR, sceptical about the possibility of fighting a nuclear war, was obsessed with retaining full political control over nuclear weapons and thus adopted a highly centralized command and control system. The USA, on the other hand, was deeply concerned with the possibility of not being able to retaliate in the case of a Soviet first-strike because of paralysis in decision-making structures; and with ensuring that its forces could destroy the wide range of targets allotted to them under the 'single integrated operations plan' (SIOP) for nuclear war. Thus US politicians and planners adopted a highly decentralized command and control system in which authority to launch nuclear weapons was pre-delegated down the chain of command in time of crisis. This led to the development of a highly unstable system in which each side's mix of hardware and doctrine seem to have been almost custom-built to arouse its enemy's worst fears. The Soviets' highly centralized system made it difficult for the Americans to 'read', while any American moves towards pre-delegation were certain to fuel Soviet fears that an American surprise attack was in the offing Blair's analysis strongly suggests that the human race was extremely fortunate not to see the whole system break down disastrously.

The compatibility of Blair's thesis with the critical approach to technology lies in the fact that both the USA and USSR were faced with technologically constrained choices and chose particular solutions which reflected the values and interests of the ruling elites in each state. This compatibility hints at another potential strength of the Critical Theory view of technology. Emphasizing the importance of politics and culture on the decisions surrounding nuclear weapons technology allows space for the effects of 'strategic culture' to be considered.[48]

In his path-breaking study, Jack Snyder defined strategic culture as the outcome of a 'socialisation process' through which 'a set of general beliefs, attitudes and behavioral patterns' achieve 'a state of semipermanence that places them on the level of "culture" rather than mere "policy"'.[49] The concept has since been utilized to provide insight into different 'national styles' in war and peace. While an instrumental approach to nuclear weapons technology might well allow us to absorb those insights, the critical approach, by stressing the ambivalent nature of technology, focusses our attention on the way in which technology and strategic culture interact dialectically. So rather than concentrating exclusively on the way in which strategic culture influences decisions pertaining to technology, Critical Theory also invites us to explore the way in which technological developments affect strategic culture.

Technology at the fin de siècle

During the twentieth century technology has developed at a bewilderingly rapid pace, a trend which seems certain to persist into the next millennium. These developments have had, and will continue to have, massive social implications. However, neither the direction of these developments nor their implications are predetermined. Rather this will depend on a process of bargaining and struggle within and between societies: in short, it will be the result of a political process. Critical Theorists and concerned citizens must seek to intervene in this process in order to try to ensure that new technologies are not developed and imposed in ways which simply re-create and reinforce present patterns of domination and injustice. More positively, they must try to ensure that the liberating potential of technology is fulfilled.

As for the nuclear revolution itself, Blair's revaluation of the Cold War relationship between East and West should alert us to the dangers of any complacency in a world which many seem to regard as being further away from nuclear war than at any time since 1945. We have survived so far without a nuclear exchange more through luck than judgment. With further proliferation almost certain in the twenty-first century, we may not be so lucky in future.[50] Meanwhile, despite the end of the Cold War, the national security state is still alive and well. It is still characterized by secrecy and, at best, suspicion of democracy. As intellectuals and concerned citizens, we surely have a role to play in exposing the inflated threat-assessments which masquerade as rational justification for a large, unaccountable, and grossly expensive security apparatus. By helping to nail the half-truths and distortions by which governments perpetuate the national security state, we can help ensure the continuation of human society after the nuclear revolution.

Notes

I should like to acknowledge the assistance of Ken Booth, who made detailed comments on an early draft, and Susie Carruthers, Timothy Dunne and Nicholas J. Wheeler who commented on a later version. I am grateful to David Steeds for guiding me through the labyrinthine thoughts of Chairman Mao. Those attending the Cambrian Discussion Group at Aberystwyth and the International Seminar at Keele also contributed a number of useful comments and suggestions.

1. For the American government's assessments of the casualty figures in both cities, as well as a detailed description of the physical effects of nuclear explosions, see Samuel Glasstone and Philip J. Dolan (eds), *The Effects of Nuclear Weapons* (Washington, DC, 1977), pp.541–74.
2. The literature on this subject-area is vast. For a broad, though far from comprehensive survey of the literature, see J. Samuel Walker, 'The decision to use the bomb: a historiographical update', *Diplomatic History*, xiv, No.1 (1990), pp.97–114.
3. Cited in Lawrence Freedman, *The Evolution of Nuclear Strategy* (London, 1987), p.16.
4. For an accessible scientific and political history of the development of the first nuclear weapons see Richard Rhodes, *The Making of the Atomic Bomb* (Harmondsworth, 1988).
5. Robert Jungk, *The Nuclear State*, trans. Eric Mosbacher (London, 1979).
6. Cited in Daniel Pick, *War Machine: The Rationalisation of Slaughter in the Modern Age* (London, 1993), p.176, n. 28.
7. William Chaloupka, *Knowing Nukes: The Politics and Culture of the Atom* (Minneapolis, 1992), pp.xi–xii.
8. The following are among the most useful: Robert Jervis, *The Meaning of the Nuclear Revolution: Statecraft and the Prospect of Armageddon* (Ithaca, NY, 1990); John Newhouse, *The Nuclear Age: From Hiroshima to Star Wars* (London, 1989); Freedman, *The Evolution of Nuclear Strategy.*
9. See, for example, Chaloupka, *Knowing Nukes* and Alan M. Winkler, *Life under a Cloud: American Anxiety about the Atom* (Oxford, 1993).
10. 'Known nuclear tests worldwide, 1945–1993', *Bulletin of the Atomic Scientists* (May–June 1994), pp.62–3.
11. Masahide Kato, 'Nuclear globalism: traversing rockets, satellites, and nuclear war', *Alternatives*, xviii/3 (1993), p.348. See also Jane Dibblin, *The Day of Two Suns: US Nuclear Testing and the Pacific Islanders* (London, 1988).
12. Arjun Makhijani, 'Energy enters guilty plea, *Bulletin of the Atomic Scientists* (March–April 1994), pp.18–28.
13. Cited in Gregg Herken, *Counsels of War* (New York, 1985), p.343.
14. Barry Buzan, *An Introduction to Strategic Studies: Military Technology and International Relations* (London, 1991).
15. See, for example, John Garnett, 'Technology and strategy', in John Baylis et al. (eds) *Contemporary Strategy*, i (London, 2/1987), pp.91–109.

16 There are now many excellent English-language introductions to Critical Theory. Among the best are: Rolf Wiggershaus, *The Frankfurt School*, trans. Michael Robertson (London, 1994); Helmut Dubiel, *Theory and Politics: Studies in the Development of Critical Theory*, trans. Benjamin Gregg (Cambridge, MA, 1985); Martin Jay, *The Dialectical Imagination: A History of the Frankfurt School and the Institute of Social Research. 1923–1950* (Boston, 1973); Peter Uwe Hohendahl, *Reappraisals: Shifting Alignments in Postwar Critical Theory* (Ithaca, NY, 1991).
17 On the philosophy of the social sciences see Richard Bernstein, *The Restructuring of Social and Political Theory* (London, 1979).
18 Theodor Adorno and Max Horkheimer, *Dialectic of Enlightenment*, (1994), trans. John Cumming (London, 1989), p.xi.
19 Adorno and Horkheimer, *Dialectic of Enlightenment*, p.xiv.
20 Douglas Kellner, *Herbert Marcuse and the Crisis of Marxism* (London, 1984), p.1.
21 Andrew Feenberg, *Critical Theory of Technology* (New York, 1991), p.5.
22 Ibid., p.12.
23 Ibid., p.65.
24 Ibid., p.5.
25 See Manuel De Landa, *War in the Age of Intelligent Machines* (New York, 1991).
26 Feenberg, *Critical Theory of Technology*, pp.122–3.
27 Cited in David Holloway, *The Soviet Union and the Arms Race* (London, 1983), p.131.
28 It should perhaps be noted that perhaps the best-known of all contemporary Critical Theorists, Jürgen Habermas, has adopted a neutral, instrumental view of technology. See, for example, his critique of Marcuse in *Towards a Rational Society: Student Protest, Science and Politics*, trans. Jeremy J. Shapiro (London, 1971).
29 Feenberg, *Critical Theory of Technology*, p.65.
30 Ibid.
31 Ibid., p.14.
32 Raymond Williams, 'The politics of nuclear deterrence', in Edward P. Thompson *et al.*, *Exterminism and Cold War* (London, 1982), pp.67–8.
33 Colin S. Gray, *Weapons Don't Make War: Politics, Strategy, and Military Technology* (Lawrence, KS, 1993), p.155.
34 John Mueller, 'The essential irrelevance of nuclear weapons: stability in the postwar world', *International Security*, xiii/2 (1988), pp.55–79. See also John Mueller, *Retreat from Doomsday: The Obsolescence of Major War* (New York, 1990).
35 Gray, *Weapons Don't Make War*, p.155.
36 Mueller, 'The essential irrelevance of nuclear weapons', p.68.
37 Mao Tse-Tung, *Talk with American Correspondent Anna Louise Strong* (Peking, 1968), p.8.
38 Stuart R. Schram, *The Political Thought of Mao Tse Tung* (London, 1969), p.409. See also Mao Tse-tung, 'The Chinese people cannot be cowed by the atom bomb', *Selected Works of Mao Tsetung*, v (Peking, 1977), pp.152–3.

39 Lawrence Freedman, 'I exist; therefore I deter', *International Security*, xiii/1 (1988), pp.177–95. The classic statement of the 'Existential deterrence' case is McGeorge Bundy, 'Existential deterrence and its consequences', in Douglas McClean (ed.), *The Security Gamble: Deterrence Dilemmas in the Nuclear Age* (Totowa, NJ, 1984), pp.3–13. Interestingly, one of the main proponents of existential philosophy, Jean-Paul Sartre, viewed nuclear weapons in instrumental terms. He shared Mao's view that fear of these 'paper tigers' should not be allowed to deflect the forward march of international soclalism. See Nigel Young, *An Infantile Disorder?: The Crisis and Decline of the New Left* (London, 1977), p.317.
40 McGeorge Bundy, 'To cap the volcano', *Foreign Affairs*, xlviii/1 (1969), p.10.
41 Kenneth N. Waltz, 'Nuclear myths and political realities', *American Political Science Review*, lxxxiv/3 (1990), p.740.
42 Ibid., pp.737–8.
43 Kenneth N. Waltz, 'The spread of nuclear weapons: more may be better', *Adelphi Paper No 171* (London, 1981), p.11.
44 Frank Barnaby, 'Nuclear conflict: a global prospect?', in Frank Barnaby and Geoffrey Thomas, *The Nuclear Arms Race – Control or Catastrophe* (London, 1982), p.35.
45 Edward P. Thompson, 'Notes on exterminism, the last stage of civilization', in Edward P. Thompson et al., *Exterminism and Cold War*, p.5. See also Edward P. Thompson, 'Sources of exterminism: The last stage of civilization', *New Left Review*, 121 (1980), pp.3–31.
46 See, for example, the following works by Michael Cox: 'Western capitalism and the Cold War system', in Martin Shaw (ed.), *War, State and Society* (London, 1984), pp.136–94; 'The Cold War as a system', *Critique*, 17 (1986), pp.17–82; and 'From the Truman doctrine to the second superpower detente: the rise and fall of the Cold War', *Journal of Peace Research*, xxvii/1 (1990), pp.25–41.
47 Bruce G. Blair, *The Logic of Accidental Nuclear War* (Washington, DC, 1993).
48 On strategic culture see Ken Booth, 'The concept of strategic culture affirmed', in Carl G. Jacobsen (ed.), *Strategic Power: USA/USSR* (New York, 1990).
49 Jack Snyder, *The Soviet Strategic Culture: Implications for Limited Nuclear Operations* (Santa Monica, CA, 1977), p.v.
50 For a sobering assessment of the dangers see Scott Sagan, 'The perils of proliferation: organization theory, deterrence theory, and the spread of nuclear weapons', *International Security*, xviii/4 (1994), pp.66–107.

7. Economism

Patricia Clavin

In the summer of 1899 a group of Russian Social Democrats, in a dispute with their orthodox Marxist comrades, argued that the party should pay more attention to the workers' economic demands. The movement, known as 'economism', determined that the hardships endured by the Russian working classes were so pressing as to relegate the political battle for workers' 'freedom' under the tsars to an auxiliary role. The 'economist' view was vigorously condemned by respected Marxist theorists like Georgii Plekhanov and Lenin, and after 1903 the movement had only a limited influence on Russian Marxism.[1] Yet, despite its short life-span, the economist *Credo* (the name given to their published statement) illustrated the centrality of 'bread and butter' issues to the politics of many Russian workers. It also highlighted the ever-present tension between political and economic goals, and, in this instance, the victory of politics over economics. The interaction between politics and economics is a dominant theme in this chapter, which takes the term economism, like many of the other 'isms' that help to define the meaning of the twentieth century – imperialism, nationalism, socialism – to denote the pervasiveness of economics in almost all aspects of the modern polity.

One of the principal characteristics of the twentieth century undoubtedly has been the changing relationship between political and economic life. It is a truism to say that individuals, whether citizens, subjects, clan-members or serfs, have always been interested in their material welfare, but a defining feature of the twentieth century is that government has been assigned responsibility for maintaining a continuing level of economic activity.[2] In what follows I attempt first to paint a broad picture of the relationship between national economic success and political legitimacy, the new role of particular social groups in the national economy, and the changing character of the international economy. The second part of the chapter is devoted to two brief case studies – Britain's membership of the gold standard (1925–31) and the Exchange Rate Mechanism (ERM) in the 1990s – designed to illustrate and to compare how the modern political economy operates in specific instances. The case studies also explore how successful the world's large economies have become at balancing sensitive national economic and political needs with their international commitments, and, more particularly, the primacy of politics in the formulation of economic policy.

State and economy

By the end of the nineteenth century there had emerged a modified notion of the nation-state with a more complex network of mutual political obligations between rulers and ruled. The trend was accelerated in the twentieth century by two world wars which required government to organize its resources on an unprecedented scale. The wars also forced the nation-state to demand new sacrifices of all its citizens in the name of loyalty. Allegiance to the nation at war now entailed possible death, injury, bereavement and upheaval. The state, in return, was prompted to extend its obligations to its people and make changes to the political system which such promises implied.

During the interwar period, however, it proved easier for government to fulfil its promises of greater political representation than its pledges of economic growth and social improvement. The story of political development in the interwar period became one of frustrated expectation. Those who stood to benefit from greater democracy and industrialization – the working class, newly demobilized soldiers, women, agricultural labourers – discovered that most traditional political parties failed to address their needs. The frustrations of this group were matched by the mounting apprehensions of the more established elements of political life – the landowners, businessmen, military authorities, artisans, and many white-collar workers – who were fearful of potential working class radicalism and, in some instances, of losing their status in the industrialized twentieth century.

The failure of liberal democracy to manage the global agricultural depression and the subsequent Great Depression (1929–33) clearly indicated that, more than ever before, the state was expected to generate employment opportunities, promote relative price stability and nurture continuous economic growth. As the deafening clatter of collapsing democratic regimes in the 1930s testified, when politicians failed to provide effective answers to 'bread and butter' demands, they quickly lost popularity and, ultimately, legitimacy. The Great Depression ushered in greater state intervention in many economies – exemplified by Roosevelt's New Deal in the USA and the introduction of the four-year plan in National Socialist Germany.

One of the many possible 'meanings of the twentieth century' can be uncovered by exploring the emergence of this intimate connection between economic success (however it is defined) and political legitimacy. An obvious measure of the rise of the popular expectation that the state was to manage the domestic economy to the collective advantage of its electorate (or at least its participating majority) is to chart the progress of state intervention in the economy. Certainly until the 1960s historians and contemporary commentators who wrote of the relationship between government and the economy were able to chronicle the rise and rise of state intervention in times of peace and war.[3] Only the 1920s, a period characterized by a marked determination to abandon the structures of wartime planning and return to the pre-First World War freedom of unregulated business transactions, was the exception that appeared to prove the rule: the identification of this decade with the origins of the world's greatest economic crisis only seemed to confirm that the era of *laissez-faire* economics was past.[4]

The experience of Western Europe after the Second World War, of course, offers the best example of the widespread rejection of the belief that capitalism, if left to its own devices, would be able to generate a 'good society'. From 1950 to 1968 Western Europeans acquired and consumed more cars, washing-machines, houses and toasters than ever. (In Western Europe growth averaged 5.5 per cent per annum against world rates of 3.0 per cent.) It was also a period in which government increased its income and levels of expenditure on welfare, education and health soared. For the first time the powerful package of economic interventionist policies which national governments had introduced in wartime were modified and extended in peacetime to assert the economic and social role of the nation-state. The tools of Keynesian economics, particularly the modification of the national budget into the key economic regulator of the domestic economy, transformed the role of government in the economy. With the election of the postwar British Labour government, for the first time the state explicitly declared its responsibility for the 'success' of the economy as defined by its election pledges of 'full employment' and 'economic growth'.

During this period Western governments, in particular, were able to claim that they had secured far greater social stability than during the interwar period, although by the late 1960s young people began to reject the consumerism of their parents and experiment with new political ideas. Nonetheless, the social conflict which characterized politics in the first half of the century eased. Governments believed they no longer needed to concentrate their energies on redistributing national wealth – an important preoccupation in the nineteenth century and the first part of the twentieth – because higher levels of economic growth meant that they were able to deliver on wartime promises of 'fair shares' for all.

But how far did the phenomena of increased state involvement in the economy, and society's propensity to consume and invest interrelate? Contemporary politicians and commentators were united in the belief that unprecedented levels of growth were largely due to the behaviour of the state. But it was not long before some scholars began to contest that the state's 'management' of the economy had merely interacted with other unique characteristics of the period to promote economic growth – the novel integration of Western Europe, the impact of the Korean War, the creation of NATO, new patterns of international trade and investment, a managed system of fixed exchange rates.[5] (A similar debate continues over the efficacy of state intervention in the 1930s, notably with regard to the 'depression-busting' policies of Roosevelt's New Deal and National Socialist Germany.)[6]

The happy confidence in the growth and competence of state intervention in the domestic economy dissipated rapidly during the 'stagflation' crisis of the 1970s. During the next decade rising global inflation – an average of 3.4 per cent per annum – was regarded by most developed countries as an undesirable, but arguably unavoidable, accompaniment to continued economic growth and the widely accepted economic and social goal of full employment.[7] But President Nixon's dramatic devaluation of the dollar in August 1971, coupled with the quadrupling of oil prices in 1973, boosted existing levels of inflation to staggering new heights. Tremendous inflationary pressure now quickly ate away at the developed world's levels of economic growth and, more importantly, the easy confidence of government that the determinants of economic activity could be managed readily by the state.

The impact of inflation on economic prosperity and social stability is a further defining feature of the twentieth century. The magnitude and direction of inflationary episodes ranged from breathtaking hyperinflation in Weimar Germany, Austria and the Soviet Union in 1922, 'Latin' inflation (ranging from double-digit inflation beyond 100 per cent per annum) typified by the experience of postwar Latin America and Britain in the 1970s, and the 'creeping' inflation which characterized the economies of postwar Western Europe. The impact of inflation poses important questions of the state regarding the allocation of resources and welfare. Inflation, like depression, revives social conflict between different interest groups. On the whole, the unlikely bedfellows of workers (concerned to secure high levels of employment) and industrialists with large export markets have the most to gain from inflation, while lower middle class groups on fixed incomes and with limited assets have the most to lose.

In the wake of the 1970s inflationary crisis the spectre of inflation appeared to pose a far greater threat than depression to the future prosperity and stability of the developed world. This trend was reflected in popular music. Louis Armstrong's *S.O.L. Blues*, recorded during the depression, reflected the desire of poor, black Americans for work. By the 1970s B. B. King, another legendary American jazz musician, complained, not of unemployment, but of *The Inflation Blues*.[8] The crisis also laid bare the mechanics of state bargaining between different social groups in order to preserve social peace. West Germany, for example, fared better than Britain or France as good labour relations between government, employers and employees enabled Chancellor Helmut Schmidt to keep wage demands down and thus help to control inflation. The experience underlined that the state in the twentieth century was 'no longer an umpire' but a 'player deeply enmeshed in a game of social and economic bargaining'.[9]

Indeed, not only does rampant inflation destroy governments unable to resolve the social and political conflict generated by such crises, like those of British Prime Ministers Edward Heath and James Callaghan in the 1970s, it can undermine national sovereignty more profoundly. After all, the symbols of sovereignty are depicted on every national currency. During a severe inflationary crisis just as the value of each note declines, so the sovereignty of the state is visibly devalued and eroded.

During Weimar's hyperinflation, local government authorities and German industrialists printed over 2000 different 'currencies' to pay their workforce. The political life of the Weimar Republic never fully recovered from the impact of the hyperinflation. But it would be simplistic to characterize the experience of inflation in the twentieth century as all bad. The 'creeping' inflation which accompanied postwar European growth was all-important in facilitating harmonious labour relations. When levels of postwar growth did not rise quickly enough to fulfil popular expectations, inflation often disguised the lag, acting as an effective 'social lubricant'.[10]

An important political consequence of the 1970s inflationary crisis was the emergence of monetarist and free market ideas which soon came to influence the economic policies of Conservative and Christian Democrat dominated Western Europe and the Republican Administration of the USA.[11] In some instances, monetarism was heralded as the new economic credo, but even when it was rejected, the ideas of *laissez-faire* economics found a ready audience. This trend also affected the economic philosophy of many to the left of the political spectrum, and was awarded a specious validity by the stagnation and subsequent collapse of the centrally planned economies of Eastern Europe. (This despite the fact that the 1980s was hardly a decade of unqualified economic success for capitalism.) The crucial importance of monetarism in helping to define the economic meaning of the twentieth century was its apparent simplification of the task of economic management and the revival of nineteenth century notions that the market economy was a 'quasi-natural system' best left untampered by man or woman.[12]

The most extreme example of monetarist application was in Britain in the 1980s where the overriding objective of the government's economic policy was to reduce inflation, and the sole means by which this was to be achieved was the control of the money supply. Gone were hallowed policy objectives like full employment; gone were traditional instruments of economic policy like the official regulation of credit and incomes. In their place, Margaret Thatcher and her first Chancellor of the Exchequer, Geoffrey Howe, brought back the principles of orthodox economic policy which had prevailed in the 1920s. The state was no longer interested in managing demand or unemployment in the economy – growth and employment, it was argued, were sure to sprout from sound money and lower rates of direct taxation.[13] The recipe for economic success now lay in 'the greatest practicable market freedom within an overall framework of financial discipline'.[14]

In the post-inflationary era of the 1980s, like the mid-1920s, the emphasis was placed on 'new' rules of economic growth. During the 1980s and 1990s the 'old' industrialized world revived many aspects of *laissez-faire* economics, notably the determination to achieve sound money. In Western Europe governments which followed deflationary policies were re-elected (British Conservatives in 1983 and the German centre-right coalition under Chancellor Helmut Kohl in 1986) and those who were tolerant of inflation in the quest for lower levels of unemployment were defeated, like the Socialists in France in 1985. Politicians who stressed the importance of liberating 'market forces' to drive and direct the economy appeared to be asserting the 'primacy of economics' in the struggle to secure economic growth.

Yet, despite the claims of politicians that the rules of *laissez-faire* economics help to liberate the economy from the confines of ideology (a type of 'economic truth'), market forces generate their own political outcomes. The political economy of the 'Brash Eighties', like the 'Roaring Twenties', favoured some social groups over others – bankers and stockbrokers were obvious 'winners', the unemployed obvious 'losers'. During both deflationary periods, the potentially inflationary battle to redistribute wealth among different social groups was abandoned in an effort to promote economic growth. But *laissez-faire* economics brought only limited growth during the 1980s and 1990s, and persistently high levels of unemployment increasingly menaced social and political stability in the developed world. Moreover, while the world's oldest industrialized economies claimed to have abandoned government intervention, the newly industrialized countries (NICs) of the Pacific rim, all with highly interventionist states, rose to challenge the economic dominance of the West.

The West's recourse to *laissez-faire* in the 1920s and 1980s followed the dictum that 'politics is always confronted with the necessity of dealing with the consequences of previous policies'.[15] The appeal of 'market economics' must, first and foremost, be explained within the context of the political and economic prognosis of the immediate postwar period and the 1970s. In this way government economic policy falls into the trap of 'fighting the last war' regardless of the current economic context. The state's primary objective to stamp out inflation persisted throughout the 1980s, regardless of deep-seated structural economic difficulties and the changing character of national and international economies. This pattern helps to explain the swings between *laissez-faire* and interventionism which have characterized the twentieth century. But it would be a mistake to suggest that just because governments claim that economic policy is governed by economic, not political priorities, it is necessarily so. As the case studies of Britain's membership of the gold standard and the ERM will demonstrate, domestic, regional and international political concerns continued to play an important role in formulating economic policy in two periods of *laissez-faire* economics. Similarly, the globalization of the world's capital and, to a lesser extent, trade markets is offered increasingly as an explanation of the inability of government to pursue nationally determined economic objectives. It is true that, as the case study of the ERM illustrates, globalization has taken the world economy in fundamentally new directions. Nevertheless, at the end of the century the political responsibility for the health of a national economies continues to rest with nationally elected (or imposed) governments, regardless of their economic 'philosophy', and governments continue to use economic policy for political ends.

Class and economy

During the European 'Century of Revolution', the uprisings of 1848, above all, dramatically demonstrated to the traditional arbiters of power that they would no longer be able to preserve social peace by simply restricting, redefining or even extending the vote. Thereafter, autocratic and democratic governments alike began to take limited measures to prevent excessive suffering among chosen groups which, in turn, prompted greater state involvement in the economy. By the end of the nineteenth century, economic protection which government had awarded to the wealthy upper and middle classes (in Bismarckian Germany the landed gentry received tariff protection for rye production, hard-pressed businessmen were permitted to form cartels and monopolies) was extended to the rising numbers of working class people offering limited protection from illness, accident, unemployment and old age in a strategy which, in the case of Germany, was designed to preserve Prussian ascendancy and the conservative order of the Reich.

The novel contribution of the twentieth century was the incorporation of the working class into the policy-making elite. Working class representation became an essential component of public policy in all democratic, industrial societies. So just as the major political transformation of the nineteenth century was to co-opt bourgeois representatives alongside landed ones in the formation of public policy, the major change in the twentieth century has been the absorption of spokesmen (and latterly spokeswomen) for the non-revolutionary working class into selected areas of decision making. The degree of working class representation varied from country to country and was dependent upon such variables as the health of the economy and the political ethos of the government.[16]

On the level of 'managing' or 'planning' the national economy, then, the big challenge for the state in the twentieth century has been to reconcile the aspirations of different groups in society to preserve social peace. During the first half of the twentieth century small farmers and landless peasants were largely excluded from these efforts, despite the fact that around 65 per cent of the world's population made their living from agriculture which was blighted by a deep and lengthy depression in primary prices.[17] Their frustration with interest group politics encouraged many of them to support fascist parties which claimed that conflicts of interest could be overcome and that all groups in society, no matter how divergent their interests, could work together in, as Hitler claimed, 'not a class party, but a party of honest producers'.[18] The isolation and vulnerability of Europe's small farmers found a remedy of sorts in many countries after the Second World War when state support for agriculture became a universal practice on a large scale. In Western Europe national protection of agricultural income was even enshrined in the European Economic Community's adoption of an integrated Common Agricultural Policy (CAP) which subsidized production, guaranteed domestic markets, and restricted imports. Nonetheless, despite greater state intervention in primary production, agricultural surpluses continue to be a serious difficulty in the world economy – a problem exacerbated by the instability in the world's financial markets since 1971.[19]

For many scholars of political economy, the explanation as to why one economic policy is adopted in preference to another lies in analysing the political behaviour of conflicting interest groups or classes to secure particular economic policies. For most of the century the social hierarchy of class or occupation has been sufficient to delineate conflicting interest groups. But as the economy of the developed world has moved away from traditional manufacturing industries in favour of service industries, and societies, in some respects, have grown more diverse, dividing society into industrial classes no longer sufficiently explains interest group politics. Ethnic loyalties, feminism, the environment and disarmament have also become important 'classes' in the political economy.[20]

Nevertheless, at the end of the twentieth century the main issue for most countries remains the same as it was at the beginning of the century: how far should capitalism be administered and regulated by the state? The notion that there are viable alternatives to a capitalist society and an open world economy – the communist and nationalist models that were energetically touted during this century – has almost completely disappeared.[21] The pragmatic vision of the German industrialist and financier-cum-philosopher Walther Rathenau, drawn up at the beginning of the century, now appears more resilient than that of Karl Marx and his successors. Rathenau's original contribution was to assign industry a particular role in his vision of a more 'equal' society: to manage the economy and to take a lead in the cultural and educational life of the nation by establishing foundations accessible to all social classes.[22] It was a system which upheld the values of free enterprise and drew upon the special skills of the business community, presaging aspects of state corporatism which surfaced later in the twentieth century.[23]

Today the state is often depicted as cooperating and encouraging the activities of business for the good of all society – the best examples are the well-documented cooperative relationships between state and industrialists in postwar West Germany and Japan – rather than controlling the activities of greedy capitalists. Government is also increasingly presented in the guise of a management corporation, partly, of course, to avoid the characterization of the state as a lumbering, complex and inefficient bureaucracy. Although, as J. K. Galbraith has recently pointed out, there is compelling evidence to suggest that large corporations, too, are burdened by 'the bureaucratic tendency' as they seem able to shed large numbers of personnel to achieve lower costs and higher efficiency whenever the need arises.

What is clear is that the evolution of twentieth-century capitalism has greatly enhanced the power of the nation-state, particularly after 1945, while political developments have worked to emphasize the national economic responsibilities of nation-states. These developments have been assisted, not necessarily contradicted, by the growth and evolution of the international economy. On an international level, the task for policy makers has been to reconcile the state's national, usually competitive, aspirations with the growing recognition that all nations depend upon a flourishing, cooperative international economy for their long-term prosperity.[24]

National and international economy

During the nineteenth century technological innovation had a profound impact upon the manufacture and transportation of goods and this, alongside considerable levels of migration, fostered the growth of a vibrant international economy. The huge growth of international trade in primary and manufactured goods was possible only through the increase of international capital flows and the establishment of international financial services – commercial banks, insurance and investment houses. From the end of the Napoleonic Wars until the mid-1850s about £420 million was invested abroad. By 1914 this figure had risen to £9500 million.

In the twentieth century the importance of foreign investment in the international economy has increased greatly, in part because levels of migration have fallen drastically, but also because manufacturing has been replaced in leading developed economies by the service sector. This development, and the near collapse of the capitalist system during the 1930s, made most politicians aware of the dependence of the long-term prosperity of their national economy on the economic health of other nations and the international economy as a whole. This recognition permeated the creation of such international institutions as the Bretton Woods System, the General Agreement on Tariffs and Trade and the European Economic Community, designed to safeguard international economic cooperation.

So at the same time as the state's involvement in the national economy has grown, and the interaction of state and industry in the domestic economy has worked to obscure the boundaries of the public and the private domains, the blurring of national and international boundaries in economic relations and their impact upon national and international politics is, arguably, a more novel feature of the twentieth century.[25] Some economic historians argue that there is little inevitability about the growing interdependence of nation-states in the world economy.[26] Economic interdependence, they claim, is a product of national choices and priorities, even though these national priorities are sometimes powerful enough to induce nation-states to give up some of their sovereignty to a supranational authority – an assertion typified by the incremental approach towards European Union.[27]

In practice, however, national and international economic policies are not easily separated. In both the international and domestic spheres of economic relations the determinant of power is the ability to invest. Marx was right to focus on the control of 'capital as the defining aspect' of industrial society.[28] Money affords tremendous national and international influence. For Hjalamar Schacht, best known as Hitler's Minister of Finance and one of the most politically astute financiers of the twentieth century, 'the magic of money lies in its protean nature, which enables it to be used at all times, in all directions and for all purposes. This constitutes its wizardry, its secret, its mystery, its magic.'[29]

But nation-states have found it much more difficult to regulate the movement of capital and services across their frontiers than the movement of commodities – the tradition of territorial boundaries and trading duties is centuries old, the exchange of capital and investment is not. At the end of the twentieth century there are also large corporations (dubbed transnational corporations), which do not share the obligations and priorities of nation-states. Governments have limited authority over these organizations which have the power to spend and invest equivalent to that of small countries. Despite the fact that these firms trade under a national flag, their investments and profits are difficult for national governments to monitor and tax. Furthermore, highly sophisticated money markets and large corporations increasingly threaten governments' domestic and international economic policies, a development which is complicated by the desire of the world's more powerful countries to manipulate their economic power for diplomatic ends – as witness the popularity of economic appeasement in the 1930s, the political conditions attached to loans in the developing world, and the path of economic incrementalism as the means to achieve European Union.

It is this messy interaction between domestic and international economic and political objectives that can be explored further by examining how the world's large liberal economies balance sensitive national economic and political needs against their international commitments and interests; to assess whether they have grown more successful at it; and to investigate how far the growth of important non-governmental economic agencies, in this instance the world's currency speculators, influence international cooperation.

Britain and the gold standard

For Susan Strange, the process by which democratic states define their economic policies emerges out of the constant struggle to balance four conflicting political goals: to preserve individual, group or national security; to create or maintain wealth; to provide economic, social or legal justice for individuals or groups; and to offer freedom of choice or action for individuals or groups.[30] But, of course, the reality of policy making is neither so ordered nor so explicit. In the case of Britain's momentous decision to return to the gold standard in 1925, for example, the Conservative government and its advisers never attempted to formulate a coherent rationale for their preferred policy.[31] In large part, the decision to rejoin the gold standard simply reflected a powerful urge to recapture the growth, prosperity and international dominance the British economy had enjoyed in the nineteenth century. It was an ambition reflected in the decision to return sterling to the gold standard at the same parity as it had been traded in 1913: $4.86.

The decision became infamous. At the time, John Maynard Keynes (one of the few critics of the return to gold) argued that this price overvalued the pound by around 10 per cent, and economic historians have since estimated a 20 to 25 per cent overvaluation.[32] For the six years Britain remained on the gold standard its exports of manufactures and invisibles were uncompetitive – a problem which was exacerbated by the fact that important competitors, notably France, Germany and the USA, returned to or remained on the gold standard at an undervalued exchange rate. So why did the British government choose to shackle its industry in manacles of gold?

It is always important to remember that the politics of currency and money are not an exact science but an applied art. That said, the failure of the British government to formulate clear domestic and international political objectives also led them to underestimate the perils of stabilizing sterling at an exchange rate which took no account of the changing character of the British economy and its altered role in the world economy as a whole. Like other fixed exchange rate mechanisms, the gold standard was perceived by its supporters as an important means to facilitate trade because prices could be guaranteed. Its operation also helped to remove uncertainty from the world's money markets and to limit inflation – its reputation sealed by the tremendous growth of the international economy during the nineteenth century. Every political party in Britain during the 1920s accepted that a strong British economic revival depended upon international trade. According to the Bank of England official Sir Otto Niemeyer, 'no one believes that unemployment can be cured by the dole, and palliatives like road digging. Every party – not least Labour – has preached that unemployment can only be dealt with ... by measures directed at the economic restoration of trade.'[33] This was the gold standard flaunted as an employment policy. And indeed an implicit goal was to restore pre-war levels of employment at, say, 95 per cent of the labour force.

Further international and imperial considerations were also powerful influences on the British government and its economic advisers. At its height there were 54 countries on gold (promoting the utility of the gold standard). This promised to create a healthy market for gold producers in the British Empire (each member of the gold standard required considerable reserves of gold), and to safeguard the position of the City of London as a leading market for investment and financial services from the further encroachment of New York.[34] The City of London and the Bank of England were powerful champions of the gold standard and a loud voice for Winston Churchill, then Chancellor of the Exchequer, to hear. As the senior Treasury official Sir Frederick Leith-Ross put it, Churchill chose to return sterling to gold because the Bank of England and the City had given him 'irrefutable arguments to support it, whereas if he refused to adopt it he would be faced with criticisms from the City authorities against which he would not have any effective answer.'[35] From across the Atlantic the vigorous advocacy of the gold standard by the administrations of Presidents Harding and Coolidge, and the leading role taken by the Director of the Federal Reserve Board, Benjamin Strong, also encouraged the British to take this bold step.[36] The prospect of improved Anglo-American relations, and the widespread identification of the gold standard with Britain's status as the pre-eminent global power in the nineteenth century, helped popularize the rush for gold in 1925. Being a member of the gold standard club, so the government believed, would afford Britain greater opportunity to influence the economic and diplomatic policies of, for example, Germany and France.

Put bluntly, the dominant motivation for Britain's return to gold was international influence, and the issue was given a new urgency by the election of a Conservative government in October 1924. The pound sterling had gained strength considerably on the international market as expectations grew that the new Conservative government would act to restore the pre-war parity of the pound. This market expectation, in turn, made it easier for the government to do precisely that.[37]

Were they right? The British government was certainly right to recognize the importance of a vibrant international economy for their domestic economy, but they were unquestionably wrong to restabilize the pound at $4.86. So why did they do it? The answer lies, in part, but only in part, in the importance of 'credibility' to the British government in international political and economic policy. The financial and political authorities in Britain shared the conviction that for their commitment to convertibility to be credible to the international exchange market, they had to retain sterling's pre-war parity for, so the argument went, any government which tampered with its exchange rate would be treated with suspicion.[38]

A more serious indictment of the policy, however, was the fact that all the policy makers failed to consider, in any detail, the implications of this monetary policy for the domestic economy and British society. Churchill and his colleagues recognized that the pound was overvalued at $4.86 and that this would have serious consequences for, in Churchill's words, 'the merchant, the manufacturer, the workman and the consumer ... (whose interests) do not by any means coincide either with each other or with the financial and currency interests'. The overvaluation of sterling and the high bank (interest) rates required to sustain it imposed a severe deflationary burden on the British economy and its people. But this vague appreciation was as close as the government came to any systematic investigation of the political and economic implications of sterling's overvaluation on the British economy.

The government had set its society an almost impossible task as the stabilization of sterling demanded a reduction in wages and overall production costs of around 5 to 10 per cent. British industrialists and their employees were in an unenviable position. The number of industrial disputes increased as manufacturers struggled to reduce wages, and British goods and invisibles were uncompetitive in overseas markets for the remainder of the decade (the promised rise in American prices to help ameliorate this problem was not forthcoming – American prices did not rise for most of the interwar period).[39] The deflationary pressures triggered by the return to gold impeded economic confidence and threatened political stability at home.

Ultimately, the decision to stabilize sterling at $4.86 was 'an act of faith' – not a blind act of faith, but certainly a myopic one. The failure of the British government to consider the adjustment difficulties posed by this exchange rate for the domestic economy was an important political failure. It was, perhaps, mitigated by the fact that the government was convinced that in the 'long run' the decision would strengthen Britain's role in the international economy and hence its domestic economy, although the British government had not undertaken any serious analysis to support this position.[40]

The political and economic lessons of the recent past, particularly Germany's recent hyperinflation, were also an important influence on policy makers. The gold standard offered a 'solid gold' guarantee against inflation, not only because currencies held fixed values, but because participating nations had to follow orthodox economic policies to keep them there – this called for balanced domestic budgets, bank rates to sustain convertibility, and a positive balance of trade. This was an inflexible, deflationary policy regime which was sensible in a time of plenty, but disastrous in a time of want. After the Wall Street Crash of October 1929, it was this deflationary straitjacket and the persistence of the gold standard orthodoxy in Germany, France and the USA until 1933 which helped to turn the Great Depression into the greatest economic crisis of the twentieth century.

In the summer of 1931 political events and the continued depressed condition of the British economy prompted a currency crisis which forced Britain off the gold standard on 20 September. By this time, many in parliament, the Treasury, and to a lesser extent at the Bank of England, had lost faith in the efficacy of the gold standard and the influence of the international economy as the best means to encourage economic growth. In 1925 the British had forsaken the management of sterling as an instrument of national policy. After September 1931 the British government was determined to foster domestic economic growth and stability as a priority: sterling was depreciated and bank rates were reduced. The primacy of the international economy in the 1920s now became the primacy of the domestic economy.

After 1931 the British were determined to 'get it right' for the national economy. The external value of sterling was now variable and to be adjusted to the needs of domestic policy. The 30 per cent depreciation of sterling and cheap money (reduced base rates) did help to bring some measure of economic recovery to Britain at a time when its leading competitors were still suffering the ravages of the depression. But the new priority given to domestic economic recovery now presented a number of problems for Britain in its international relations.

First, Britain's departure from the gold standard discredited the system's claims to promote stability, particularly as 18 nations which had close links with the British economy also chose to abandon gold in 1931. The diplomatic tensions created by Britain's rejection of the gold standard were heightened by (justified) British protests that there were technical problems in the way that the standard operated.[41] These claims worked to undermine the credibility of the system as a whole and to make life immeasurably more difficult for those countries still committed to the gold standard. Not only were the USA and France smarting from the fact that their large reserves of sterling were worth considerably less once Britain had abandoned gold, the American and French authorities now had to work harder to preserve the credibility of the system. They were also resentful of the trading advantage that the British had secured by devaluation.

Second, these essentially economic considerations also had a powerful impact on other aspects of international relations. After 1931 Britain's monetary policy was in competition with its former allies: the USA and France. By 1933 the USA, too, had devalued. Britain recognized that the floating dollar was 'helpful' to world trade, but also feared that it would lose the competitive advantage it had secured against American manufacturers. The friction in Anglo-American, and to a lesser extent, Anglo-French, monetary relations which had begun during the sterling crisis of 1931 remained a constant source of suspicion between Britain and the USA during the 1930s.[42] American and, to a lesser extent, French pressure on the pound sterling, for example, was an important restraint on the pace and direction of British rearmament.[43]

In the complex, multi-polar world of the 1930s few nation-states successfully managed the intricate interaction of economic, social and political prerogatives in the national and international environment with any success. What emerges from the saga of Britain and the gold standard is the dominance of political considerations in economic policy. The same political issues also dominated the commitment of France, Italy and Germany to the gold standard far into the 1930s at tremendous political and social cost. The experience illustrated the need, above all, for governments and electorates to take full account of the likely political and social cost of economic policy. The misplaced faith of politicians in the gold standard illustrated, too, the dangers of claiming that a single economic tool was a cure for a whole variety of economic and social ills. Perhaps the clearest lesson from the history of the interwar gold standard was that while governments' domestic or international political and social objectives remained relatively constant, the ever-changing nature of economic interaction demanded greater flexibility of government in making economic policy.

Britain and the ERM

Important political objectives and the continued appeal of a single economic policy tool to address a variety of political and economic goals – the features which contributed to the attraction of the gold standard – also emerged as the main attraction of the European Monetary System for Britain in the 1980s. In January 1985 Nigel Lawson, then

Chancellor of the Exchequer, began to press for Britain to join the European Monetary System (increasingly known as the European Rate Mechanism or ERM). In his memoirs Lawson records his rationale as both economic and political.[44] The economic motivation came from his assessment that the ERM, particularly under the leading influence of the German Bundesbank, offered a method of monetary discipline akin to the gold standard: 'not only was the balanced budget the most useful fiscal guide, but an external monetary discipline, such as the gold standard, was the best practicable monetary rule' – this was a selective reading of economic history to justify economic policy.[45] By 1985, after a bumpy start, the EMS had become the most successful version of any European monetary system to date, while free market forces had failed to control British inflation and the pound had faced some trying moments floating on the international exchange (in 1985 it fell to almost $1.00).[46] It proved difficult and costly to manage the floating pound outside the ERM: when trying to shadow the Deutschmark, interest rates had to be kept marginally higher than inside the system; and the Bank of England did not have the automatic commitment of other central banks to intervene on Britain's behalf to defend sterling.[47]

Lawson's attraction to the ERM, however, was not purely guided by the light of 'economic reason'. The well-publicized political appeal of the ERM lay in the desire of 'pro-Europeanists' in the British government to remove some of the tension in Britain's relations with its European partners. Many of the difficulties in Britain's relations with Europe stemmed from Margaret Thatcher's proclaimed determination to protect British sovereignty from the incursion of the EC. But, in reality, the cornerstone of British economic policy in the 1980s – the promotion of the free market – had helped to extend the powers of the EC over British political and economic life.[48] The tension is best exemplified by Britain's commitment to the Intergovernmental Conference resolutions taken at The Hague in 1986 to create a genuine 'single market'. The declaration espoused the ideals of free market forces which had characterized the Conservative government's domestic policies, but it also gave the EC power to intervene in the organization of British industry and economic activity, as well as environmental, technological and social issues, on an unprecedented scale.

By 1990 the disjunction between Thatcher's rhetoric on national sovereignty and the realities of EC membership had become ever more apparent. As in 1925 it was political considerations which determined that it was no longer a question of whether but when Britain would join the mechanism. With Nigel Lawson and Geoffrey Howe, the former monetarist gurus and ERM advocates, no longer in the cabinet, the call for membership was taken up by John Major as Chancellor, and Douglas Hurd as Foreign Secretary. Both men were determined to moderate the jingoistic tone of Thatcher's statements on the EC in time for intergovernmental conferences on monetary and political union scheduled to meet in Rome that year. A further political incentive came from the desire to offer the Tory faithful something to cheer about at the annual party conference due to convene in Bournemouth in the second week of October 1990.

Once again the City of London and the Bank of England were instrumental in taking up the call for exchange rate membership. Sir Robin Leigh-Pemberton at the Bank of England and the City in general were anxious to preserve London's leading role as a financial centre and as a possible site for a European Monetary Institute (or even a European Central Bank).[49] ERM membership also offered the carrot of greater independence for the Bank of England sometime in the future – an independence lost to the Treasury immediately after Britain left the gold standard in 1931. With rumours now circulating that Britain would join the mechanism, market expectations (and the pound) began to rise on the international market. As in 1925 this, too, exerted an important influence on the timing of Britain's decision to join the mechanism, as did continued uncertainty over the situation in the Gulf.

But what of the British economy? In the autumn of 1990 economic indicators were strongly at variance with the new political will in cabinet for ERM membership. Inflation was running at around 10.6 per cent, interest rates stood at 15 per cent, Britain had a severe balance of payments deficit and unemployment of 1.65 million. The inflation figure alone was well above the EC average, a condition which the British government itself had imposed for ERM membership at Madrid in June 1989. Although this problem was resolved by September 1990 the economic rationale for joining the ERM at this time remained unconvincing.[50]

Without access to official documents it is not possible to say for certain, as it is for the 1920s, how far the cabinet explored the implications of a fixed exchange rate (albeit fluctuating within limited bands) for the domestic economy. Like Britain's return to gold in 1925, however, the political emphasis on the need for credibility in exchange rate policy undoubtedly left the British economy vulnerable to currency overvaluation. Moreover, just as the pound sterling had been identified for so long by Thatcher as the symbol of British sovereignty, a strong currency was regarded as a measure of the standard to which the domestic economy had to perform, and the stronger the national economy, the greater its appeal to international investors. The French government pursued a similar policy of a strong franc (*Franc fort*) against the Deutschmark in preparation for the introduction of the single European market in 1992.

Estimates of the overvaluation of sterling after Britain joined the ERM on 8 October 1990 vary. Perhaps the most startling is the assessment that when Britain joined the ERM at a parity of DM 2.78–3.13, within two years the real effective sterling exchange rate was estimated at some 20 per cent above its average in the 1960s and 1970s.[51] Political disquiet in Britain grew after October 1990 with the recognition that sterling was overvalued at its chosen parity. Critics feared not only for the competitiveness of the domestic economy, but for limitations which the rules of ERM membership imposed on the freedom of the domestic government to manage the economy. Opposition in Britain was fuelled also by the radical shift in the ultimate goal of the ERM. When it was created in 1979, the EMS was a system of pegged exchange rates which permitted parity adjustments among its members.[52] The proposal in 1988 by Jacques Delors, President of the Economic Commission, that the EMS be used as a springboard for full monetary union of the EC, however, introduced a new element of rigidity in the systems. Currency parities were to be gradually 'hardened', the discipline required to coordinate the management of EC currencies – low public debts, limits on current-account deficits – was defined explicitly, and a timetable laid down designed to bring about convergence of the EC members' economies and, ultimately, full monetary union. The EMS had lost flexibility and gained a new economic and political agenda.[53]

The growing inflexibility of the EMS coincided with a period of renewed political instability and economic recession. It is well known that the decision of the German government to use higher interest rates to finance German reunification by attracting overseas investment and to control domestic inflation cost its fellow ERM members dear. This 'little local difficulty' was exacerbated by the slow-down in the world economy which began to bite in 1990. In many ways the world of 1990 was beginning to resemble the world of 1930 with the end of the Cold War, global economic recession, nationalists on the streets of Central and Eastern Europe, and a deflationary (or in modern parlance 'disinflationary') mechanism governing Western Europe's monetary policies. Growth in Europe slowed from 3 per cent in 1991 to 1.1 per cent in 1992. In the world's biggest economic crisis since the 1970s, the disinflationary focus of the ERM was rather like 'shouting fire! Fire! In the time of Noah's flood' (Sir Ralph Hawtrey's description of the gold standard).[54]

By the summer of 1992 economic reality had begun to catch up with the ERM. British unemployment had risen to 2,808,000 (seasonally adjusted), an increase of almost a million since 1990, and growing domestic disquiet focussed, in particular, on the continued high level of interest rates to maintain the pound in the ERM.[55] British misgivings over the ERM were soon apparent in the pro- and anti- European wrangling in the Conservative government. Outside Britain, the political commitment to European Union also appeared to waver after the Danish people voted to reject the Maastricht Treaty in June 1992 (a treaty which included a commitment to EMU), and the results of the French referendum on Maastricht looked increasingly uncertain.

By September 1992 the pressure on the ERM had grown irresistible. First, the Italian lira was devalued within the system, and then, in the 'Black Wednesday Massacre' of 16 September 1992, Britain was forced out of the ERM.[56] With sterling floating the British government quickly set about reasserting the primacy of the domestic economy: interest rates were reduced and the pound allowed to depreciate on the international market. Within a matter of days government sources confided that monetary policy had been too tight for some months.[57]

Until the final capitulation of the ERM in August 1993 events continued to echo the gold standard years of 1932–3. It remains unclear whether the ERM could have withstood the speculative attacks of the financial markets, as its architects had argued, if the political commitment of the participants had remained rock solid.[58] Britain's departure certainly increased the vulnerability of the ERM – Britain no longer intervened on the currency markets on behalf of its European partners and, more importantly, had begun to question the viability of EMU. Relations between Britain and its European partners deteriorated rapidly and, as pressure mounted on the French franc, Franco-German relations also became increasingly acrimonious.

Concluding remarks

There are two elements of interest in this pattern of events in the context of the 'meaning of the twentieth century', regardless of the degree of mismanagement by Britain on Black Wednesday as it stands unexplained, and the inevitability of the system's collapse in August 1993. The first, as in the case of Britain's doomed affair with the gold standard, is the primacy of political considerations over economic realities, and the dominance of particular group interests over others for as long as the domestic economy does not threaten grave social unrest. Charles Maier has postulated that the twentieth century has been characterized by a 'recourse to politics'. It is interesting to note how far the British decision in 1925 and 1990 to establish sterling as a strong currency flew in the face of economic reality and this at a time when the government claimed to respect the authority of the market. The Deutschmark is a strong currency on the international exchange, not just because the Bundesbank runs a tight monetary ship, but because of the underlying strength of the German economy.[59]

The ERM débâcle also highlighted a new aspect of international economic relations in the twentieth century: the power and speed of the world's capital markets. The spectacle of Western Europe's central bankers and finance ministers helpless against a tidal wave of global currency speculation is an entirely new historical phenomenon. (Most commentators agree that it would have been possible for Central Bank intervention to have kept sterling on gold in 1931.) It is the globalization of the world's credit markets, far more than the organization of the world's production and trade, which is a defining feature of the final two decades of the twentieth century.

Since the deregulation of credit transactions in the 1980s and the development of information technology, financial transactions are now 25 times larger than world trade in goods and services – a development which helped prompt greater Western European, US and Japanese monetary cooperation in the 1980s in the first place – and the power of the investment market is greater than the power of national governments, as the successive capitulation of ERM currencies to market forces illustrates. According to the free marketeers, of course, the power of the market is 'a good thing' in safeguarding the efficiency of the economy.[60] But of the £560 billion pounds which passes through the world's exchanges every day, the majority of these currency transactions do not relate to trade – estimates suggest that only 10 per cent of present currency deals are made in pursuit of international trade.[61]

The bulk of this money is 'hot money' in search of a quick profit. This development poses a number of important, new questions for economic relations at the end of the twentieth century: are these huge financial markets 'efficient'? Do they facilitate or endanger the smooth operation of the world economy?

The ability of government to manage its domestic and international economic relations is now challenged by the power of the international capital market. To contemporary *laissez-faire* economists, monetary stability and low inflation have become the all-important goals, not tools, of economic policy, yet the power of the capital market threatens precisely this area of policy. For states which believe that their role in the political economy is limited to providing the 'economic backcloth' for growth and which claim to have withdrawn from mediating between different interest groups, the new authority of the capital market is an important challenge. A government which claims to promote *laissez-faire* capitalism and encourage a 'fatalistic acceptance' that there is 'no alternative' among its population will surely find such fatalism more difficult to swallow when it undermines its own political agenda.

Notes

1. Leszek Kolakowski, *Main Currents of Marxism: The Golden Age*, ii (Oxford, 1978), pp.378–9.
2. Charles S. Maier,'The state and economic organisation in the twentieth century', in N. Hagihara *et al., Experiencing the Twentieth Century* (Tokyo, 1985), p.101.
3. See, for example, Angus Maddison, *Dynamic Forces in Capitalist Development: A Long-Run Comparative View* (Oxford, 1991). Andrew Schonfield described and advanced notions of greater institutional management of the economy which, he believed, had contributed to the conversion of capitalism from 'the cataclysmic failure which it appeared to be in the 1930s into the great engine of prosperity of the postwar Western world', in *Modern Capitalism: The Changing Balance of Public and Private Power* (London, 1965), p.3.
4. A. Briggs, 'Economic interdependence and planned economies', in D. Thomson (ed.), *The New Cambridge Modern History*, xii (Cambridge, 1960).
5. See the recent summaries of this debate in Alan Milward, *The European Rescue of the Nation-State* (London, 1992), pp.22-4 and Grahame F. Thompson, *The Economic Emergence of a New Europe?: The Political Economy of Cooperation and Competition in the 1990s* (Aldershot, 1990), p.24.
6. Many of the New Deal policies are now seen by economic and social historians as contradictory and limited in effect – see, for example, Ellis Hawley, *The New Deal and the Problem of Monopolies: A Study in Economic Ambivalence* (Princeton, NJ, 1966). Germany's recovery in the 1930s was presaged on the increasing impoverishment of its working

class and the goal of large-scale, racial war. See Peter Temin, *Lessons of the Great Depression* (Boston, 1989), pp.103–6; Richard Overy, 'Hitler's war plans and the German economy', in R. Boyce and E. M. Robertson, *The Paths to War* (London, 1989), pp.120–1.

7 William Ashworth, *A Short History of the International Economy since 1850* (London, 2/1991), p.295.
8 Its opening verse reflected the widespread, popular perception that it was the responsibility of government to resolve the crisis: 'Hey Mr President/All you Congressmen too/You got me frustrated and I don't know what to do./I'm trying' to make a living'/I can't save a cent/It takes all my money just to eat and pay the rent./I've got the blues/Got those Inflation blues.' *The Inflation Blues*, recorded by B. B. King for MCA records in 1983 and written by L. Jordan, A. Alexander and T. Southern.
9 Charles S. Maier, *In Search of Stability: Explorations in Historical Political Economy* (Cambridge, MA, 1987), pp.189–93.
10 Ibid., p.232. Even Weimar's hyperinflation had some positive effects.
11 Margaret Thatcher has been credited as the pioneer of the application of monetarist doctrines to economic policy. See John Toye, 'Britain, the United States and the world debt crisis', in Jonathan Michie (ed.), *The Economic Legacy, 1979–1992* (London, 1992), p.13.
12 John Goldthorpe, 'Problems of political economy after the postwar period', in Charles Maier (ed.), *Changing Boundaries of the Political* (Cambridge, 1987), p.367.
13 For a critical examination see William Keegan, *Mr Lawson's Gamble* (London, 1989). For the view from the inside consult Nigel Lawson, *The View from No. 11: Memoirs of a Tory Radical* (London, 1992) and Margaret Thatcher, *The Downing Street Years* (London, 1993).
14 Lawson, *View*, p.9.
15 Gustav Schmidt, *The Politics and Economics of Appeasement* (Leamington Spa, 1986), pp.11–12.
16 It was easier for the working classes in West Germany after 1945, for example, to obtain significant extensions of the welfare state than in the USA where the postwar era was marked by a movement away from the achievements of the New Deal. In communist-dominated Eastern Europe and the Soviet Union, of course, all policy allegedly was premised on the needs of the working class, although the reality was quite different.
17 C. H. Lee, 'The effects of the depression on primary producing countries', *Journal of Contemporary History*, iv (1969) p.139.
18 Quoted in J. Noakes and G. Pridham, *Nazism: A History in Documents and Eyewitness Accounts, 1919–1945*, i, (Exeter, 1983) p.17.
19 Robert Gilpin, *The Political Economy of International Relations* (Princeton, NJ, 1987), p.386.
20 Maier, *In Search of Stability*, pp.2–3, 15–16.
21 National-Socialist-dominated Germany, for instance, offered an interesting example of a 'mixed' economy where the cooperation between capitalists and state planners also encompassed the notion of a self-sufficient national economy. Nationalists in the 1990s, on the other hand, now recognize the 'economic value' of international trade and investment, and

attempt to evade the question of how this economic internationalism sits with their political nationalism.

22 Walther Rathenau (ed. Ernst Schulin), *Hauptwerke und Gespräche* (Munich, 1977).

23 Rathenau did not really address the problems of the working class – how they were to be organized and represented – nor did he have much interest in democracy. Political power for Rathenau was best exercised by a select number of enlightened capitalists. See James Joll's introduction to Harmut Pogge von Strandman (ed.), *Walther Rathenau: Tagebuch 1870–1922* (Düsseldorf, 1967).

24 This point is made but not really explored in Briggs, 'Economic Interdependence', p.526.

25 The movement of capital also determines the importance of one economy and hence its nation-state over others in the international economy.

26 Milward, *European Rescue*, pp.11–12.

27 Alan Milward and Vibeke Sorensen, 'Interdependence or integration? A national choice?', in Milward *et al.* (ed.), *The Frontier of National Sovereignty: History and Theory, 1945–1992* (London, 1993), p.11.

28 Maier, 'State and economic organisation', p.115.

29 Hjalamar Schacht, *The Magic of Money* (London, 1955), p.7.

30 Susan Strange, *States and Markets: An Introduction to the International Political Economy* (London, 1988), p.23.

31 The gold standard was a fixed exchange rate mechanism designed to hold currencies to a specific value determined by each currency's value in relation to gold. In 1914 Britain had been on the gold standard with the Bank of England's selling price for gold at 77s 10½d. per standard ounce since Newton had set the price in 1717, with the exception of an interval during and after the Napoleonic Wars. By the 1830s the gold standard had become an article of faith to economists and bankers.

32 John Maynard Keynes, *The Economic Consequences of Mr Churchill* (London, 1925), p.11; Barry Eichengreen, *Golden Fetters: The Gold Standard and the Great Depression, 1919–1939* (New York, 1992), pp.204–5.

33 Quoted in D. E. Moggridge, *The Return to Gold, 1925: The Formulation of Economic Policy and its Critics* (Cambridge, 1969), p.48.

34 The City often secures 'special consideration' in the development of policy because invisible earnings play a large role in the balance of payments. Moggridge, *Return*, p.85.

35 Quoted in Moggridge, *Return*, p.67.

36 Ibid., p.54; Lester V. Chandler, *Benjamin Strong, Central Banker* (Washington, DC, 1958), pp.291–321.

37 The timing of the return was also influenced by the imminent expiration of the wartime gold acts which prohibited all exports of gold from the United Kingdom.

38 Eichengreen, *Golden Fetters*, p.163.

39 Some wage reduction had already been accomplished in the 1920–22 slump, but this had been possible only because many wage agreements were related to the cost of living which had also fallen.

40 Moggridge, *Return*, p.88.
41 The operation of the gold standard was undermined by technical difficulties. Most countries had lacked sufficient gold reserves to stabilize their currencies (gold reserves were also poorly distributed) and used foreign currency reserves as a back-up. This effectively created highly volatile money reserves which moved from financial centre to financial centre with relative shifts in interest rates and confidence. The British had identified some of these problems before 1931, but their efforts to modify the gold standard before its collapse merely looked like Britain trying to compensate for stabilising at the 'wrong rate'.
42 Patricia Clavin, 'The World Economic Conference 1933: the failure of British internationalism', *Journal of European Economic History*, xx/3 (1991), p.524; Diane Kunz, *The Battle for the Gold Standard* (London, 1987), pp.149–51.
43 R. A. C. Parker, 'Economics, rearmament and foreign policy: the United Kingdom before 1939: a preliminary study', *Journal of Contemporary History*, x/4 (1975), p.643. Competition over economic issues in Anglo-American relations was all the more serious because this was one of the few avenues left open to President Roosevelt to improve them.
44 In his memoirs Lawson records that he had favoured the EMS in 1979 and 1981, but Howe had determined the time was not ripe. See Lawson, *View*, pp.111–13. For an introduction to the ERM see Robert Minikin, *The ERM Explained: A Straightforward Guide to ERM and the European Currency Debate* (London, 1993).
45 Lawson, *View*, p.1022.
46 Lawson notes that while Thatcher favoured floating exchange rates, she did not favour a weak pound against a strong dollar: 'She was most definitely not Milton Friedman in drag.'
47 Daniel Gros and Niels Thygesen, *European Monetary Interaction: From the European Monetary System to European Monetary Union* (London, 1992), pp.112–14.
48 See the excellent summary of the ambiguity in British policy in John Young, *Britain and European Unity, 1945–1992* (London, 1993), pp.149–51.
49 Elke Thiel, 'Changing patterns of monetary interdependence', in William Wallace (ed.), *The Dynamics of European Integration* (London, 1990), p.82.
50 At the IMF conference held in Washington in September 1990 Britain announced that what mattered for ERM membership was the 'prospective' rate of inflation.
51 This overvaluation was exacerbated by 1992 by the slump in the value of the dollar and the impact of North Sea oil which worked to strengthen the Deutschmark further. Bank of England calculations published in *The Guardian*, 7 September 1992, p.10.
52 From 1979 until March 1983 there were seven such parity adjustments, but thereafter the system and the global monetary environment stabilized. After 1987 there were no further realignments.
53 One of the interesting political issues unanswered in the Delors report was

that if EMU were achieved, there is no precedent for having a single currency without a central political authority for the currency area. Gros and Thygesen, *European*, p.466.
54   Moggridge, *Return*, p.88.
55   A weak dollar also helped put pressure on the Deutschmark in the summer of 1992.
56   For the best survey of the 'Black Wednesday Massacre', see Will Hutton in *The Guardian*, 1 December 1992, p.15.
57   Norman Lamont announced 'allowing the pound to float is not the outcome I sought, but nor is it the catastrophe some have tried to suggest' (quote of the day in the *Financial Times*, 9 October 1992, p.12). One government economist said that 'Black Wednesday represented the biggest U-turn since Britain left the gold standard.' (*The Guardian*, 23 September 1992, p.1).
58   Gros and Thygesen argued that technical safeguards against currency attacks would have been hard to establish and a poor substitute for 'a firm and credible commitment to subordinate domestic policy goals to the defence of the exchange rate'. See Gros and Thygesen, *European*, p.166.
59   Perhaps, once again, the British government was guilty of masking the 'revolutionary' nature of its commitment to Europe from the British people and, once out of the ERM, succumbed, at least in the short term, to the determination to retain national control over monetary policy. See David Reynolds, *Britannia Overruled* (London, 1991), p.238.
60   See, for example, William Rees-Mogg, 'The market has won, and rightly so', *The Independent*, 17 September 1992.
61   Bank of England figures reported in 1989 estimated around 15 per cent. By 1993 the figure had fallen to around 7–10 per cent.

8. Nationalism

James Mayall

In the twentieth century it became possible, for the first time, to speak intelligibly of world history.[1] Developments in one part of the world had profound, if sometimes delayed, repercussions in other parts. Over the very long term, it was probably always so. After 1900, however, these multiple repercussions were felt increasingly quickly and, from the mid-century, exponentially. More important, the process of interaction began to be understood, however imperfectly. Not everyone was touched equally by the forces of world history. Here and there it was possible to find areas where traditional life lay beyond the reach of modern technologies and tastes, although even these societies were threatened with extinction by contact with the outside world. Elsewhere, people were conscious, however dimly, of their common predicament: how to prosper, or at least survive, the remorseless advance of modernity.

The dawning of world history did not, unhappily, imply the ending of conflict or the triumphant assertion of human solidarity. Indeed, if the story sounded different in different parts of the world, this was because it was almost invariably told – not always consciously – with a national bias. 'Nationalism', in Elie Kedourie's celebrated phrase, 'is a doctrine invented in Europe at the beginning of the nineteenth century.'[2] It asserts that humanity is naturally divided into nations, and on this basis 'pretends to supply a criterion for the determination of the unit of population proper to enjoy a government exclusively its own, for the legitimate exercise of power in the state, and for the right organisation of a society of states'.[3] However, nationalism says nothing about who, or what, constitutes a nation.

For most, the nation is a group which shares a common culture, inhabits an ancestral homeland, has been (or is becoming) shaped by common experiences of peace and war, and can be enjoined to share a vision of its collective destiny. Nationalism can be used as a rallying slogan by any group which feels itself oppressed by an alien power, or betrayed by a home-grown tyranny. By the same token, control of the symbols of national unity has always been jealously guarded by governments as a prop to their own legitimacy. Thus the European origins of nationalism are less important for understanding its impact on twentieth-century history than its ability to mobilize people wherever traditional patterns of life are being eroded. Nationalists habitually appeal to the past, but their appeal is to populations who are being buffeted by forces beyond their control. Thus, while most of the great theorists of the nation – Herder, Fichte, Mazzini, Mill, Renan – died before the nineteenth century ended, their ideas received their apotheosis only in the twentieth.

Despite its universal appeal nationalism betrays its European origins in two ways. Historians distinguish between those who define the nation as a historically framed political and civic community and those who view it as an extended family of kin. For the first interpretation the essential characteristic is citizenship, not social or ethnic determination; for the second it is a predetermined and inescapable ethnic identity.[4]

The second way in which nationalism betrays its European origins is in its inability to stand alone as a self-sufficient political ideology. The strength of nationalism lies in its appeal to deeply embedded even if ultimately invented traditions.[5] Its weakness lies in its almost complete lack of substantive content. Except in colonial situations, it is impossible to derive a programme of action from nationalist thought. And, while nationalism can determine the end of colonialism – i.e. independence – it does not specify the means to be employed. Liberalism, Marxism and fascism, the contending dogmas of the twentieth century, all came from Europe. Unlike nationalism, they could generate large-scale social programmes, but they achieved power only in alliance with nationalism. For this reason the impact of nationalism on history must be understood in conjunction with the other major forces that have shaped the modern world, just as these forces cannot be deciphered without considering how they forged national loyalties, appealed to nationalist sentiment or evoked a nationalist response. People all over the world now identify themselves with nations, and wherever possible, with nation-states. But the nations we inhabit, and the stories we tell each other about them, have been constructed from the more dramatic and far-reaching episodes of twentieth-century history. Let us consider three of them: imperial expansion and anti-colonialism; revolution and ideological conflict; and attempts to fashion a world order based on the principle of national self-determination.

Nationalism and imperialism

Nationalism and imperialism are often seen as opposites, the first a doctrine of self-rule, the second of political domination. However, nation and empire are locked in a complex symbiosis. Nationalists may believe that their homelands have always belonged to them, but the empire-builders drew the political map. On one account there are over 8000 distinct communities in the world; yet in 1994 there were still under 200 independent states. Clearly if political independence is the principle goal of nationalists, their record of success is unimpressive.[6] From the withdrawal of the Spanish and Portuguese from Latin America early in the nineteenth century to the breakup of the Soviet Union at the end of the twentieth, the vast majority of 'nation-states' have been created as the result of imperial withdrawal and within borders determined by the imperial authorities. These were sometimes adjusted to take account of the claims of rival national communities, as in Central Europe after 1919 or the Indian subcontinent after 1947, but more often the successor government simply took over a pre-existing administrative and territorial unit.

The symbiosis operates both at the level of the structures inherited by nationalists and at the deeper level of the ideas on which the modern nation is allegedly founded. During the nineteenth century the values of the French Revolution and of the Enlightenment were initially accepted by European nationalists even though many subsequently rejected them in favour of cultural particularism. Even more paradoxically, the same values – a commitment to liberal democracy, fundamental human rights and self-determination – were spread around the world primarily as a result of British and French imperialism. Both countries had been politically centralized and socially integrated before the rise of nationalism as a political doctrine. Their mercantilist rivalries had also led to the establishment of colonial possessions in Asia and the Caribbean during the seventeenth and eighteenth centuries.[7] But it was as national democracies, i.e. states in which the principle of popular sovereignty was firmly established, that they completed the enclosure of the world during the nineteenth and early twentieth centuries.

Before 1991 there had been two waves of state creation in the twentieth century. First, in the immediate aftermath of the First World War, the political map of Europe and the Levant was redrawn, following the collapse of the Habsburg, Ottoman and Romanov empires; second, the process was extended to Asia, Africa, the Caribbean and the Pacific by European decolonization after 1945. Although the two patterns of anti-imperial nationalism differed, they shared certain structural features.

First, while nationalism is a doctrine of popular sovereignty, twentieth-century nationalist movements were almost invariably led by intellectuals, lawyers or businessmen. In a period when imperial rule was the enemy, the nation proved to be by far the most potent means for conjuring a constituency into existence. Other contenders for political loyalty were associated with internal social divisions, whereas nationalism appealed to a form of solidarity which transcended these divisions. Since empires tend to exploit social and ethnic cleavages as a way of maintaining order, liberals and socialists were at a disadvantage in dealing with imperialism unless they could successfully monopolize the nationalist movement. In this respect, the nationalist opponents of the European dynastic empires had more in common with African and Asian anti-colonial nationalists than is generally supposed.

Second, nationalism alone was seldom strong enough to break the grip of imperial rule. In both 1919 and 1945 war presented nationalists with a window of opportunity. Nationalist agitations had occurred regularly before both World Wars, but they had failed to undermine imperial legitimacy. After each war, nationalists won statehood, even where popular national consciousness barely existed.

Third, nationalism was not merely weak politically, it was also intellectually parasitic. Nationalism provided neither a blueprint for the independence struggle nor a model for the national state once it had been achieved. For this reason nationalists sought allies among those who espoused a programme tailored to the needs and aspirations of modern society. Despite the different contexts in which they operated, both European and Third World nationalists were heirs to the same tradition.

Despite such similarities, there were two major contrasts in the nationalist response to European overseas enterprises. The first concerned the relationship of ethnic to national identity; the second the means by which the transfer of power was effected. Traditional empires were personal or dynastic. They were as strong or weak as their rulers. When they collapsed they disappeared, their lands divided as spoils of war or swallowed up in a new imperial dispensation. Moreover, the dynastic principle was itself a victim of the First World War. No new empire could arise in Europe, claiming title by right of conquest and legitimacy by hereditary descent. The old empires broke up into their constituent ethnic parts, or into unstable federations of related if hostile ethnic communities.

In President Woodrow Wilson's vision of a new world order, the new European states were to be based on democratic principles. Wilson believed that a world made safe for national states would also be safe for democracy. This assumption overlooked the extent to which the peoples of Eastern and Central Europe had become intermingled, so that it was impossible to redraw the map of Europe without leaving ethnic minorities entrapped in virtually every state. Moreover, the political culture was predominantly undemocratic. As early as 1861 John Stuart Mill had noted the difficulty of combining two nations within one state under a democratic constitution.[8] This insight remained valid in the 1920s (as it is still in the 1990s).

Nationalist politicians, therefore, had no alternative but to appeal to ethnic sentiment rather than democratic principle. After 1918 plebiscites were held in regions of mixed national composition, sometimes with surprising results as when Poles voted to stay in Germany rather than live in Poland, or Slovenes preferred Austria to the new Yugoslavia;[9] but the refusal of Britain and France to countenance plebiscites to test national sentiment in Ireland or Alsace robbed the plebiscite of its general validity. In practice, as Alfred Cobban wryly pointed out, no sooner had the principle of national self-determination been elevated to the status of an international norm than it was freely interpreted as a principle of national determinism.[10] Under this reformulation the element of choice was effectively removed from the determination of a person's political identity.

Many European colonies were also ethnically heterogeneous. The territorial division of Africa, for example, had been agreed at the Congress of Berlin in 1884. Borders, mostly straight lines to prevent conflict between competing imperialists, frequently cut through ethnic communities. Yet ethnic, as opposed to racial consciousness, initially played only a minor role in African and Asian nationalism.

The European empires had been constructed by strong national states. When the British and French withdrew from their overseas possessions after 1945 they remained immeasurably more powerful than even the strongest of the successor states. For Asian and African nationalists this was a problem. If, as Isaiah Berlin suggests, the rise of nationalism was an 'automatic psychological accompaniment of foreign rule – a natural reaction ... against oppression or humiliation of a society that possesses national characteristics',[11] the transfer of power was only a partial therapy. The rulers did not vanish, as they had in Europe; they remained influential. Great power attracts as much as it repels. Indeed, the former metropolitan states acted as much as models for emulation as targets for nationalist fury or scapegoats for national failings.

Towards the end of the century, ethnic conflicts had proliferated over much of Asia, Africa and Oceania, and returned with a vengeance to Europe. It is difficult in the 1990s to recapture the optimism that was associated with decolonization and the nearly universal conviction in Asia and Africa that nationalism was a doctrine of liberation. A few movements had supported the Third Reich, but few anti-colonial nationalist parties shared the cultivated irrationalism that was the trademark of nazism and European fascism.

Fascism was the pathological heir of that strand of European romanticism which rejected the universalism of both the French Enlightenment and British classical political economy. After the humiliation of defeat in the First World War, the Germans responded 'by lashing back and refusing to accept their alleged inferiority'.[12] The national socialists were not interested in what they shared with the rest of humanity, but what distinguished them. By contrast most anti-colonial movements accepted the idea of a single humanity and universal values. If they too lashed back against European domination, it was seldom in the name of some pre-colonial ethnic or political identity, but in protest against their exclusion from colonial society.

Once the traditional leadership had been replaced, the second generation elite enthusiastically endorsed the ambitions, life-style and world-view of their conquerors.[13] Their aspirations were cosmopolitan not nationalist. Their political attitudes changed only when they discovered that they could not practise as engineers, teachers, lawyers or doctors on equal terms with the Europeans. Even then their cultural cosmopolitanism often lingered on.

It may be objected that these people had been co-opted by the imperial powers to facilitate their continued control after the formal transfer of power. This was the Soviet view of Third World radicals who wanted to retain the anti-imperial struggle at the centre of the Non-Aligned Movement. But even the radicals were not cultural nationalists; they attacked their political opponents because of their ties with the West, not their cosmopolitanism.

European and Afro-Asian nationalism were both reactions to humiliation at the hands of foreign rulers. However, in Europe this manifested itself in national cultures, most of which were defined by common language, while in many former colonies it was felt at the level of political exclusion on racial rather than ethnic or linguistic grounds. The mass political independence parties accepted the structures and definition of the nation state that had been established by the colonial powers. Ethnicity and religion, of course, were never far below the surface; but awareness of their social diversity reinforced the commitment of most African and Asian governments to the rationalist values of secular modernization and human rights. Whether they had opted for a liberal or a socialist development strategy, the new nationalists needed to 'build' nations, which often had very little or no pre-existing social reality. Anti-colonial nationalists clung to their internationalist and rationalist credentials at least wherever there was no significant European settler population.

European imperial power collapsed so speedily partly because of democratic pressure within metropolitan societies. The British and French were confronted not merely by nationalists in the colonies demanding independence, but by a fifth column of their liberal supporters at home. But in Algeria, which had a population of over a million 'pied-noirs', in Kenya where the settlers had farmed the best land, and in Southern Rhodesia where the settler population had enjoyed *de facto* independence from Britain since 1922, the fifth column operated on the side of the settlers. In each case the transfer of power was preceded by prolonged insurgency. The same was true of the Portuguese empire. In Portugal itself there were no democratic rights until the revolution of April 1974. African nationalists had no realistic opportunity of achieving independence without armed rebellion. Total confrontation between white and black nationalism also took place in South Africa, which had achieved its independence from Britain in 1910, and was governed from 1948 by the National Party under a constitution which disenfranchised the majority non-white population. In 1962 the government drove the African National Congress, the oldest African nationalist organization, into exile.

In all these cases the civic character of anti-colonial nationalism was an early victim. The settler populations defended their interests and suppressed their opponents with a brutality that belied their claims to represent a superior civilization. The African nationalist movements responded in kind, revealing, in their turn, how thin was the dressing of secular rationalism in which their leaders dressed their programmes and pronouncements.

Guerrilla insurgencies depend on morale and discipline. Loyalty is at a premium but often hard to come by. This is why nationalist forces often exploit the 'irrational' superstitions of the local people among whom they operate. In Kenya the aims of the Mau Mau rebellion included the recovery of land, the abolition of Christianity and the restoration of ancient customs. The rebellion was sustained by a secret society whose members were initiated by means of blood-curdling oaths designed to compel obedience. In Rhodesia, the Zimbabwe African National Union (ZANU), the more successful of the two nationalist movements, made extensive use of local witchdoctors. In Algeria, both sides resorted frequently to torture. In these conflicts between settler and indigenous nationalisms the issue of ethnic identity surfaced much earlier than elsewhere. The Mau Mau was a Kikuyu rebellion; no sooner had the Front de Libération Nationale (FLN) secured France's withdrawal from Algeria in 1962 than it faced a rebellion from the Berber population; ZANU was a predominately Shona breakaway from the Ndebele-dominated Zimbabwe African People's Union (ZAPU); the political succession in Angola in 1975 was contested by three largely ethnically based parties.

With the partial and ambiguous exception of Afrikaans-speaking white South Africa, settler nationalisms were defeated by a combination of metropolitan desertion and international pressure. However, despite the excesses to which these conflicts gave rise, the withdrawal of European imperial power was carried out in the name of the civic form of nationalism which the West European states themselves espoused. By 1960 the General Assembly of the United Nations had ruled that all colonial peoples had a right to independence and that lack of preparation for self-rule was no excuse for prolonging colonial government.[14]

The new world order created by decolonization was thus one of nation-states, territorially but not ethnically defined. Indeed, there was a rare East–West and North–South consensus in favour of the territorial status quo. Throughout the four decades of the Cold War, secessionist nationalists found the international environment inhospitable to their aspirations. The collapse of communism in 1991 led to a new wave of state creation in the former Soviet Union and Yugoslavia, although this time, as after 1919, the criteria were largely ethnic. Czechoslovakia split peacefully into its component parts in January 1993. In April 1993 Eritrea, which had fought a 30-year war with Ethiopia, voted in a referendum judged 'free and fair' by international observers for independence. Whether these events will have demonstration effects remains to be seen. Nor is it yet clear whether they will displace official nationalism as the basis of the international order.

Nationalism and ideological conflict

The triumph of an official, theoretically civic, form of nationalism was largely the result of the nationalization of empire and the ideological conflict between the USA and the USSR after 1945.

From the mid-1950s the nation-building projects of the new states were encouraged by the superpowers. Both were anti-imperialist, and the conflict that developed between them was between competing forms of universalism. The founding fathers of liberalism and communism had been profoundly antipathetic to nationalism, liberals regarding it as irrational and romantic, Marxists as the false consciousness which prevented the masses from understanding their true class interest. It was not self-evident, therefore, that the international system over which they presided would be made safe for nationalism, whether of the civic or ethnic variety. This apparently paradoxical outcome was a consequence of the nationalization of socialism and the parallel socialization of liberalism. The former was necessary to defend the Bolshevik revolution against the surrounding capitalist powers, and subsequently against Nazi Germany; the latter was caused by need to defend liberalism during times of economic depression and to adapt it to the needs of a modern war economy.

Soon after the Revolution, Lenin concluded that it would be necessary to appease the nationalists if the Bolshevik victory was to be secured. His solution was a constitution which was federal in form but centralized in practice. He believed that in the end all nationalities would be assimilated into the new socialist society. In the meantime the USSR was defined in terms of national identities even where, as in Central Asia, there was no evidence of nationalist sentiment. The constitution included the right of secession. Nonetheless, the Bolsheviks were able to maintain the Tsarist empire virtually intact for 70 years.

With the collapse of communism in 1989, it became clear that by nationalizing communism, Soviet leaders had offered a dangerous hostage to fortune. Stalin's national policy was far more ruthless than that of Lenin. He deported some, for example, *en masse* to Central Asia and Siberia during the war. Simultaneously he conducted a policy of sustained Soviet indoctrination backed by extensive Russian migration. During the Second World War, Stalin appealed to great Russian nationalism rather than socialism in rallying Soviet citizens to fight for the motherland. In its own terms the nationalities policy was not wholly unsuccessful. Local elites were co-opted and, although peripheral economies were kept dependent on the centre under the system of central economic planning, the non-Russian republics attracted higher levels of investment than they had under the tsars. Had it not been for the catastrophic failure of the Soviet economic system during the 1980s, it is doubtful whether nationalist agitation alone would have made a serious impact on the Soviet state.

Nationalism was not a problem for the Chinese communists in 1949. This is partly because the Han are so dominant in the Chinese population that major challenges to the Chinese state have generally arisen because of internal divisions rather than from the disaffection of ethnic minorities. But the communists pursued their objectives within an unambiguously Chinese cultural framework. They had no internationalist commitments; indeed, they saw social revolution as a solution to the national problem. In 1919 both communists and nationalists had been led by young intellectuals who were attracted to Western liberal ideas of self-determination and impressed by the Bolshevik Revolution. When the united front between the two groups finally split in 1927, the right wing faction under General Chiang Kai-Shek was recognized by the Western powers as China's government and, after the Second World War, it became one of the five permanent members of the Security Council.

However, the communists under Mao Zedong proved more successful both strategically and in mobilizing the Chinese population. During the civil war, Mao, like Lenin, had used national independence to attract ethnic minorities away from the Nationalist government, offering self-determination to districts where the majority population belonged to non-Chinese nationalities. This tolerance did not survive the Revolution. In 1949 Chiang Kai-Shek's government was driven from the mainland to the island of Taiwan. On acquiring power, Mao made his first public speech under the title 'The Chinese people have stood up'.[15] Mao endorsed Sun Yat Sen's doctrine of China's five races: the Han, Tibetans, Uighers, Mongols and Manchus. The communists proceeded to annexe Sinkiang and Tibet.[16] The nationalists harboured irredentist dreams of returning to the mainland until 1972, encouraged by the Americans who continued to insist that the Taiwanese government was the rightful government of China. But to the rest of the world the irredentism of the People's Republic seemed more plausible. In 1979 the People's Republic took China's seat on the Security Council.

The spectre of a successfully nationalized socialism in the Soviet Union and China encouraged the socialization of the civic nationalisms of Western Europe. Before the 1930s Western democratic governments had taken the loyalty of their citizens for granted. Nationalism was a useful resource in war, but in peacetime such enthusiasm might threaten the established order. It apparently did not occur to the French and British governments that their populations, who had so heroically answered the call to arms in 1914, might feel betrayed once peace returned by being treated as mere labour, a commodity like any other traded in a free market. The economist Maynard Keynes sensed the danger that might befall liberal society if it did not reform itself.[17] He saw the problem as essentially technical, the impossibility of operating a harmonious international economy without an adequate supply of credit. Others argued that the breakdown of traditional ties and obligations had confronted European societies with an identity crisis.[18] They believed that the only solution was to educate the mass in the values of liberal civilization. The liberal democracies remained complacent. However, in response to mass unemployment during the 1930s, they gradually edged towards acceptance, in principle, of positive entitlements, the concept which after 1945 was to underpin the welfare state.

In saving liberalism from communism with its sacrifice of individual liberty and human rights to the principle of equality, and from fascism, with its demand that the needs of the state as interpreted through the will of its leader take precedence, Western governments made major concessions to nationalism. They were slower than either communists or fascists in understanding that, to hold on to power, they had to buy the loyalty of the people, but in the end they reached the same conclusion. When the postwar welfare state emerged, it was more nationalist than its founders might have wished. Citizens were now entitled to free secondary education, health care and unemployment benefit. This expensive extension of the state's traditional prerogatives had predictable results: in the second half of the twentieth century all the Western democracies operated restrictive immigration policies. The explanation was straightforward: in deciding who had the right to the new benefits, the easiest principle of discrimination was between nationals and aliens.

The USA, arguably the only successful 'manufactured' nation, was only partly affected by the socialized nationalism that established itself elsewhere in the industrialized world. In 1945 the American economy was so strong and the attachment to free enterprise so deeply embedded that the American government considered it neither necessary nor desirable to construct a welfare state on the European pattern. However, American nationalism had a decisive impact on the second half of the twentieth century. This was partly because the Americans seemed to have devised a uniquely successful formula for 'nation-building', through industrial and technological innovation and the creation of economic opportunity. This perception informed American foreign policy in Asia and Africa. American nationalism was also an active ingredient in sustaining the Cold War. Indeed, anti-communism sometimes seemed virtually synonymous with American ideology. As a result the American government frequently underestimated the nationalist forces arraigned against it. For liberal Americans, the Vietnam War came to symbolize the folly of American triumphalism but also, often with scant regard to the evidence, the legitimacy of nationalism everywhere else. There were many, particularly in the Third World, who agreed. The global reach of the USA, and its zealous attachment to the capitalist free market, ensured that America became the prime target for much anti-Western xenophobia, and therefore the active agent which kept anti-colonial nationalism alive.

The alleged 'artificiality' of many new Asian and African states had more to do with the character and duration of the colonial experience than with their multi-ethnic nature. A short period of authoritarian government – in Africa it was little over 70 years – undermined traditional pre-colonial societies but did not provide the new states with the resources from which to fashion a civic political culture. In this respect India, although deeply divided on religious, ethnic and linguistic grounds, was more fortunate. The Indian business and professional class had grown up over the previous century. By 1947 it was both numerous and committed to liberal values. There was, however, something illusory about this commitment. The Indian National Congress adopted a secular ideology and a modernizing development strategy, but its mass support remained overwhelmingly Hindu and traditional. Moreover, Gandhi successfully adopted traditional cultural and ideological symbolism to nationalist purposes, thus obscuring the extent to which Congress had inherited not merely the administrative structures of the British Raj but many of its attitudes towards government as well. The imperial outlook became evident soon after independence, when the Nagas on the north-eastern frontier rose in revolt. The rebellion was suppressed and its leaders imprisoned, although the government indicated that it would allow a substantial measure of regional and ethnic autonomy. This formula – autonomy within the Union – established the precedent by which the Indian authorities dealt with the numerous centrifugal pressures which emerged. India's success in containing separatism influenced the pattern elsewhere: it established that territory not culture was to determine national identity; and it allowed the government, which alone had access to the international community, to monopolise and propagate an official version of Third World nationalism. This amounted to the continuation of the anti-colonial struggle into the independence period, and by international means.

The international environment thus helped to shape the nationalism of the former colonial world. Except where local enmities dictated otherwise, as in Pakistan, the governments of most new states were determined to stay out of the Cold War. During the second half of the 1950s the Non-Aligned Movement was established under Indian, Egyptian and Yugoslav leadership as an institutionalized expression of Third World solidarity. Non-alignment allowed Afro-Asian nationalists a measure of independence from the Western network of military alliances. At the same time, by accepting economic assistance from both sides in the Cold War, they were able to maximize the economic resources available and to minimize the political costs. Moreover, non-alignment sometimes provided a means of mediating conflicts.

African nationalists found non-alignment particularly useful in this regard.[19] The language of African nationalism was always continental, and at independence all African leaders were committed to unity, a principle which proved elusive in practice. A few governments, under the influence of Kwame Nkrumah of Ghana, maintained that their independence required continental political and economic institutions. A second group of former French colonies argued for a continuation of close economic, military and political links with France, while a third group rejected both the implicit Euro-Africanism of the francophone states and the integrationism of the radicals. On to these arguments were grafted others concerning the nature of African socialism, the appropriate relationship between Africa and the newly formed European Community, and the Pan-African commitment to confrontation with white racism in southern Africa. Between 1960 and 1963 governments engaged in bitter political warfare, in the name of Pan-Africanism. Before long, as opposition politicians fled across the border, governments began to appreciate their common vulnerability to subversion. Beyond the rhetoric of solidarity, they needed an authorized version of African nationalism. The Organization of African Unity (OAU) was created as a consequence of this recognition. Its charter set out the agreed compromise between the three groups: a common commitment to anti-racism and liberation, territorial integrity and non-alignment.

Nationalism and World order

During the 1970s the focus of Africa and Asian nationalism shifted from the East–West to the North–South conflict. For many Third World elites this shift reflected their resentment at continued economic dependence on the industrial North. The enemy thus remained outside the state itself. Ethnic rebellions, of which there were many, had little success in challenging the state authorities or disturbing the established pattern of world politics. The nation- and state-building strategies adopted by Third World governments bore a superficial resemblance to those adopted in Western Europe after 1945. Just as European governments had found it necessary to manage the national economy in the interests of full employment, so Third World governments defined their central task as economic modernization. The difference was that in Europe the socialization of liberalism had been adopted because of popular pressure from below, while the socialization of Third World nationalism was top-down, by political elites on societies, some of which lacked an entrepreneurial middle class and all of which lagged far behind the affluent West in terms of their material standard of living.

The USA, Germany and Japan, by far the most successful twentieth-century economies, during the nineteenth century had used state power to help bring about national unification and economic development. Moreover, Third World governments had previously been encouraged to plan their national economies by the aid policies of the major Western powers, international financial institutions and, for a different ideological purpose, by the Soviet Union. By the 1970s, however, there was little evidence that the strategy was working, except in a few ethnically homogenous and culturally integrated countries, mostly in East Asia.

Official nationalism habitually operates in alliance with some other ideological programme. Since the early 1960s Third World nationalists had attempted to use state power both to promote domestic economic development and, more unusually, to change international trading rules in their own favour.[20] Their campaign failed: the Western powers made token adjustments but rejected any major structural reform. If militant nationalism is often fuelled by a perceived hurt or rebuff, the events of 1973–4 should have been taken as a warning by Third World governments that a price would have to be paid for economic failure. The dramatic quadrupling of world oil prices by the Arab oil-producing countries generated a nationalist reaction, but the wrong lessons were drawn from it.

The drama was played out on the world stage rather than in the relations of governments with their own people. The new oil prices inflicted major damage on the development prospects of most African, Asian and Latin American countries. Very few of them had oil reserves or their own refinery capacity, and most were already facing chronic balance of payment problems. Most Third World leaders failed to understand their own predicament. Most were enthusiastic about the Arab *coup de main*, regarding the success of the Organization of Petroleum-Exporting Countries (OPEC) in apparently effecting a major shift in the world's financial resources as a victory over the West on behalf of the Third World as a whole.[21] The euphoria was short-lived. Recession quickly revealed that oil was a unique commodity. And although the Arab oil producers emerged as major aid donors, they pursued their own national interests and did not make their newly acquired wealth freely available to other developing countries. The idea of a collective Third World solidarity faded in the face of traditional national assertiveness. Most Asian and African countries became even more locked into the Western-dominated international economy. By the end of the decade many were hopelessly in debt, a condition which allowed international financial institutions enormous influence during the 1980s. Even those countries which initially resisted IMF pressures for reform subsequently introduced similar reforms of their own.

The erosion of official nationalism by economic forces was temporarily masked by the international repercussions of the military coup which overthrew the Portuguese dictatorship in 1974. Angola, Mozambique and Guinea Bissau were immediately granted independence. The successor governments in Angola and Mozambique declared themselves to be Marxist-Leninist states and this seemed to indicate the continued possibility of an alternative ideological alliance for African nationalists. However, by the mid-1970s the Soviet authorities were in no position to underwrite the economies of their new allies.[22] Indeed they refused to countenance their membership of the Council for Mutual Economic Assistance (CMEA), instead encouraging them to sign the Lome Convention, thus effectively consigning them to the European Community's sphere of influence.

By the mid-1980s, many former colonial states were in deep trouble. Some were barely functioning as states at all. Others had drifted into disastrous civil wars. The IMF and the World Bank had forced many to adopt structural adjustment policies which reduced the role of the state in direct economic management. These policies also reduced the resources available to the political class, ostensibly for 'nation-building', more often for patronage to secure their own positions. The economic crises of the 1970s and 1980s did not destroy the international economy in the way that the Great Depression of the 1930s had destroyed it. Nor did fascist ideology revive. Nonetheless, the stage was set for an intensification of ethnic and religious conflict.

With hindsight, the Soviet failure to institute a socialist international economy was perhaps an early warning that the Soviet system – always more imperial than truly national – was about to collapse. At the time, however, its failure was a complete surprise.[23] The end of communism resembled the demise of official Third World nationalism in one respect: central government authority and the self-justifying ideology were widely and increasingly openly held in contempt. In few of the threatened Third World states was the opposition genuinely national. Resentment against those in power usually cut across divisions within society without transcending them. By contrast in Eastern Europe and the European parts of the Soviet Union the collapse of the Soviet economy and Soviet political authority was accompanied by the organization of national parties which simultaneously claimed their right of national (by which they usually meant ethnic), self-determination, democratic government and an open market economic system.

These demands threatened to overwhelm the new nationalist politics. In the first half of the twentieth century, liberalism had been salvaged by its socialization, a process which by the 1950s transformed Western politics into a debate about social democracy, that is about the appropriate mix between private and public power. Socialism was saved, and its appeal widened internationally, by nationalization. By such measures, the subversive appeal of popular nationalism was held in check. There were ritual outlets for national sentiment, such as the Olympic Games and the World Cup, but until the mid-1980s it seemed that both the division of the world into two differently organized economic systems, and the political and territorial map, had been fixed once and for all. With the collapse of communism in 1991 these certainties were replaced by confusion and paradox. On the economic side, nationalists regularly professed the values of civil society and the open market. On the political side, the end of the Cold War meant that nationalists could not only operate openly and bid for power, but that territorial questions would inevitably be reopened. If, in the past, states were created out of the debris of empires, how were they to be established in the post-imperial world of the twenty-first century?

Conclusion

There was depressingly little evidence to suggest that international society had devised a satisfactory answer to this question. Historically, states had usually been established as the result of conquest or dynastic marriage. Once the idea of popular sovereignty gained ground, they emerged from the disintegration of empires. Unfortunately, the liberal assumption that demands for national self-determination accurately reflected national realities was false: the number of nationalists always exceeded the supply of nations, however defined. In 1919, when it proved impossible to redraw the political map to coincide with the national map, the peace makers tried to reconcile state to nation by including guarantees of minority rights in the Covenant of the League of Nations. But the concept of minority or group rights fell into disrepute after Hitler had invoked it to justify German aggression in Central and Eastern Europe.

In 1945 the victorious powers faced the same problems as the peace makers of 1919. Again, the obstacles proved insurmountable. Indeed, the Charter of the United Nations represented a retreat, since there was no attempt to provide national or ethnic minorities with legal protection. The Charter rests on the twin principles of sovereignty and inalienable human rights. The issue of human rights articulated in the Universal Declaration of Human Rights, includes the right of all peoples to self-determination. But deciding who could exercise this right proved as problematic as deciding who or what was a nation.

Perhaps we should ask instead, 'when is a nation?'[24] A self-conscious collective sense of national identity emerged much later in Western Europe than is generally imagined and the gap between Europe and the Third World has been exaggerated. If the process of national formation is protracted and incomplete, it is not surprising that governments have been wary of endorsing any substantive criteria for the establishment of nation statehood. Between 1945 and 1991 the conventional interpretation of the principle of national self-determination was based on state practice rather than philosophical or legal argument. It came to be defined, very narrowly, as equivalent to European decolonization and the establishment of black majority rule in South Africa. This equation, not merely of state with nation but of nation-state with colony, was a reasonable compromise from the point of view of those whose primary concern was the preservation of international order. Moreover, this conventional interpretation reflected the political, if not always the cultural, reality at the time of decolonization.

In most post-colonial societies, access to the modern world could be obtained only through a Western education and by mastery of a metropolitan language. Those who saw independence not merely as liberation from alien rule, but as opportunity to widen their experience of the world, had no quarrel with the conventional view of national self-determination, at least so long as they did not perceive themselves to be systematically discriminated against, on racial, ethnic or religious grounds. But the way self-determination had been defined was so obviously a fiction that those groups who lost the battle for state power were bound to challenge it whenever opportunity offered.[25] Nor were the potential national challenges confined to the Third World. By the end of the 1970s there was a general ethnic revival in Europe and North America.[26] Nonetheless, the conventional interpretation survived all but one of the violent challenges that occurred between the partition of India in 1947 and the reunification of Germany in 1990. Secession was proscribed. Thus, Katanga was reincorporated into Zaire by the United Nations in 1964, and, at the end of three years of civil war in Nigeria in 1970, Biafra's surrender was greeted by the UN Secretary-General, U Thant, with the promise that the UN would never preside over the partition of a member state. Although the Secretary-General was proved wrong a year later when Bangladesh was 'liberated' by the Indian army and admitted to the UN, the breakup of Pakistan was an exception.

The end of the Cold War and the collapse of communism reopened the national question. The final implications are impossible to foresee. Western powers resisted recognizing new states until the abortive

Soviet coup in August 1991. They were more concerned to support Soviet reform than to recognize the Baltic Republics whose incorporation in the USSR they had never formally accepted. Similarly, until 1992 they encouraged the Yugoslavs to pursue democratic reform within the Federation despite evidence that it had already disintegrated into ferocious territorial conflicts.

With the collapse of communism, the state monopoly of nationalism has been broken. Since no governments had foreseen the former, they were unprepared for the latter until a series of dramatic events at the beginning of the 1990s forced their hand: the reunification of Germany; the disintegration of the USSR; Germany's insistence on the recognition of Slovenia and Croatia; and the subsequent inevitable recognition of Bosnia, a multinational state whose territory was coveted by Serbs, Croats and Bosnian Muslims.

After the Cold War there was a brief period of triumphalism, particularly in the West.[27] The world, it seemed, was at last safe for democracy, the market and collective security. When President Saddam Hussain of Iraq annexed Kuwait in August 1990, he was repelled by an American-led coalition acting under a Security Council Resolution and with the active participation of most Arab states. Sadly, the vision began to fade with the dual recognition that the costs of policing the new world order were likely to be beyond the will and resources of even the USA, and that nationalism retained its power to destroy as well as to liberate. Sometimes, however, hope overcame despair. In April 1993, 99.8 per cent of the population of Eritrea voted for independence from Ethiopia. Here was nationalism as liberation. The Eritrean referendum also suggested how the question of recognition of new states might be reconciled with the demands of international order. Eritrea had been independent *de facto* for two years before the referendum; but it was agreed when the communist regime in Ethiopia was overthrown that international recognition would depend upon a plebiscite.

In the former Yugoslavia and the Soviet Union, however, hope gave way to despair. As the old system crumbled, communities that had previously coexisted, if not always amicably at least in relative peace, turned on one another. Despite the prevalence of mixed marriages, retreat into ethnic ghettos became common. Nor did the outside world know what to do. While the United Nations could keep a peace that had already been negotiated, or even, on occasion, help to negotiate peace, it had not been designed for peace enforcement in civil and ethnic conflicts. In this respect the Gulf War exposed the limitations of the post-1945 international system. The resolutions under which the coalition acted were carefully drafted to avoid threatening Iraqi sovereignty once Kuwaiti independence had been restored. Western leaders' subsequent call upon the Iraqi people to overthrow Saddam Hussain merely encouraged a Kurdish revolt, which he ruthlessly suppressed. Public opinion, rather than any change in official views of self-determination or minority rights, forced the Western powers to establish safe havens for Iraq's Kurdish and Shi'ite minorities.[28] But they were not prepared to commit ground troops. Similarly, public opinion forced governments to send forces to Croatia and Bosnia to protect humanitarian relief supplies. Inevitably this put the United Nations in the invidious position of presiding over a process of forced population movements which had previously been associated with totalitarian dictatorships.

Will the nationalist politics of the twenty-first century follow the pattern of Eritrea or of Bosnia? The answer will probably vary with time and place. However, one sombre reality must be acknowledged: if states with deep ethnic and religious divisions and no dominant political culture are to survive their internal communal passions and the predations of their neighbours, there will have to be international guarantees, and probably military intervention, of a kind and scale never previously envisaged. One thing seems certain: the need to belong, to locate oneself within a community whose identity can be traced backwards and forwards in time will not easily be transcended, particularly in adversity. Nationalism will continue to dominate world politics into the new century.

Notes

1. See David Thomson, *World History, 1914–1950* (London, 1954), pp.1–11.
2. Elie Kedourie, *Nationalism* (London, 1960), p.9.
3. Ibid.
4. See Hans Kohn, *The Idea of Nationalism* (New York, 1961), pp.572–6, and Hugh Seton-Watson, *Nations and States* (London, 1977).
5. On this theme, see Benedict Anderson, *Imagined Communities: Reflections on the Origin and Spread of Nationalism* (London, 1983) and E. J. Hobsbawm and Terence Ranger (eds), *The Invention of Tradition* (Cambridge, 1983). For a less sceptical view see Anthony D. Smith, *National Identity* (London, 1991).
6. Ernest Gellner, *Nations and Nationalism* (London, 1983), pp.43–50.
7. See, for example, C. A. Bayley, *Imperial Meridian: The British Empire and the World* (London, 1989).

8   J. S. Mill, *Representative Government* (London, 1861; many later editions) chap. XVI.
9   E. J. Hobsbawm, *Nations and Nationalism since 1780* (Cambridge, 1990), p.134.
10 Alfred Cobban, *Nationalism and National Self-Determination* (London, 1969), pp.53–4.
11 Isaiah Berlin, 'The bent twig: on the rise of nationalism', in *The Crooked Timber of Humanity: Chapters in the History of Ideas* (London, 1990), p.251.
12 Ibid.
13 Elie Kedourie, *Nationalism in Asia and Africa* (New York, 1970), pp.71-91.
14 UN General Assembly Resolution 1514 (1960).
15 21 September 1949, printed in *Selected Works of Mao Tse-Tung*, v (Peking, 1977).
16 See Alistair Land, *The China India Border: The Origins of the Disputed Boundaries* (London, 1964), chap.3.
17 See J. M. Keynes, *The Economic Consequences of the Peace* (London, 1920).
18 Ortega Y. Gassett, *The Revolt of the Masses* (London, 1932).
19 See James Mayall, *Africa: The Cold War and After* (London, 1971) and I. W. Zartman, *International Politics in the New Africa* (Englewood Cliffs, NJ, 1966).
20 James Mayall, *Nationalism and International Society* (Cambridge, 1990), chaps 7 and 8.
21 See Kenneth Badzie, 'The United Nations and the problem of economic development', in Adam Roberts and Benedict Kingsbury (eds), *United Nations, Divided World* (Oxford, 1988), p.144.
22 See Margot Light, 'Moscow's retreat from Africa', in Arnold Hughes (ed.), *Marxism's Retreat from Africa* (London, 1992), pp.21–40.
23 Daniel Moynihan and Helen Carrere d'Encausse were notable exceptions. See D. P. Moynihan, *Pandermonium: Ethnicity in International Politics* (Oxford, 1993) and H. Carrère d'Encausse, *Decline of an Empire: The Soviet Socialist Republics in Revolt* (New York, 1979).
24 Walker Connor, 'When is a nation?', *Ethnic and Racial Studies*, xiii/1 (1990), *passim*.
25 Mayall, *Nationalism*, chap. 4.
26 On the links between ethnicity in the politics of multi-cultural states and international politics, see Moynihan, *Pandermonium*.
27 See in particular Francis Fukuyama, 'The end of history?', *The National Interest*, 16 (1989), pp.3–18, and *The End of History and the Last Man* (London, 1992).
28 See James Mayall, 'Non-intervention, self-determination and the new world order', *International Affairs*, lxvii/3 (1991), pp.421–9.

9. Islamism

Maha Azzam

The term Islamism is used here to refer mainly to Islamically orientated political protest in Muslim states, with particular reference to the Middle East. Political protest in this context involves a stress on a particular type of moral order for society and a definition of culture and identity. Islamism has manifested itself during the twentieth century essentially as a political phenomenon based on spiritual resurgence. Although the term Islamism is less emotive than other labels, such as Islamic fundamentalism, it nevertheless conveys an image of a militant and violent political trend that is perceived as posing a threat to the regimes in the Muslim states and to Western interests. Although Islamism's *raison d'être* is its commitment to the implementation of the religion of Islam in society, it is nevertheless not sacred. It is a political movement that attempts to embrace the secular and the religious concerns of contemporary Muslims and has promised to forge a better society for its followers. In the context of the varied, but overall substantial levels of secularization and Westernization that have taken place in Muslim societies, Islam and its particular expression in the form of Islamism has been the main force to stand in the way of this trend and to attempt to reverse or dominate it.

The twentieth century has thrown up various challenges for Muslims, among which has been the dominance of an alternative political and ideological frame of reference backed by superior military and technological power. One of the responses to the demise of Muslim power and the military and ideological penetration of Muslim societies by Western civilization was Islamism, which was partly an attempt at empowerment based on Islam, the central ideological and legal plank of past Muslim power. As a contemporary political response that has translated itself into a popular movement it has had its moments of success but has also fallen prey to the everyday pressures of political reality.

The various Islamist groups have not developed a sufficiently formulated theory with which to establish a radically different political system and entity to that prevalent in Muslim states. However, they have succeeded in becoming the single most important force in a power struggle with existing regimes in the majority of Muslim states.

An important factor in the understanding of Islamism is the question of homogeneity and variety in the different Muslim states of the Middle East, Central Asia and South-east Asia. The once prevalent notion of Islam as monolithic has by and large been replaced by the recognition that there exists a 'variety of Islams'. This newer approach has the advantage of acknowledging the various traditions and interpretations of Islam specific to each society and helps to distinguish between different Islamic strains, such as the traditionalist and modernist or the quietist and activist. While succeeding in steering us away from one conceptual extreme, this latter approach is also flawed insofar as it posits as a substitute another extreme, which admits only of a wide variety of trends and interpretations of Islam. Although it is important to take into account the different political interpretations of Islam, the stress on differences tends to undermine the importance of the shared perception of identity that is essential to understanding contemporary Islamic protest.

The vast majority of Muslims view their religious beliefs as an integrated body of injunctions and teachings that form a unified faith. It is with the nature and interpretation of the political role to be given to Islam that the consensus breaks down and a struggle emerges, primarily between those in power and those in opposition, and between secularists and Islamists.

Islam and politics
The integral link between Islam and politics is one of the main starting-points to most studies on Islamist assertion. It is generally accepted that Islam and politics have been inextricably linked since the origin of

Islam in the seventh century. Islam is considered to have been removed from political power only in the course of the twentieth century, with its major influence remaining primarily in the social sphere especially in relation to family law.

Throughout Islamic history there have been competing schools of thought and political groups legitimizing their right to authority on the basis of a particular reading of Islam.[1] However, in contrast to the twentieth century, Islamic law remained the main source of reference and Islam the over-arching world-view of state and society for the various schools of political thought. With the collapse of the Ottoman empire, the abolition of the Caliphate in 1924 and the spread of colonialism in the Middle East, there emerged more clearly a competing Western-inspired world-view and system of law, which found adherents among the elite that came to power in many of the Muslim states and who believed it to be the route to modernization and progress.

The increasingly widening gap between the developed and lesser-developed world throughout the twentieth century has meant that the majority of Muslim states share, in differing degrees, in the failed promises of Western-inspired ideas of modernization. The Islamists point accusingly not only to this state of decline as a sign of failure of these ideas, but also to their encroachment on Muslim institutions (education, law and religious endowments – *waqf*) and values. The struggle of the Islamists for much of the twentieth century has been an attempt fully to restore Islam into the realm of politics and society and to re-establish it as the core of the drive towards development.

Colonialism and the nation-state

In common with other groups and societies, Islamist attitudes to current politics are often coloured by perceptions of their past and how that past is interpreted in the present. There are a number of key issues that affect the views Muslims have of themselves and their place in the world. There is the belief in a 'golden age of Islam' that existed in seventh-century Arabia when the ideal Islamic state was realized under the Prophet Muhammed and during the era of the Rightly Guided Caliphs. Later, when the Islamically questionable practice of dynastic rule became established, there remained a belief that that period was one of political strength and military expansion.

Past greatness in terms of sciences and philosophy, when the Muslim world was far more developed than the West, is emphasized. Even the Ottoman empire, although weak and disintegrating during its final years, is viewed as a superior state of affairs than the one Muslims find themselves in at present. Current disunity, political and economic weakness and military defeat are juxtaposed against past successes and glories internally and in the face of external challenges. This is not in an attempt to re-create the past and to destroy what aspects of modernity exist in Muslim societies, instead it reflects an attitude of 'look what we once were and what we have become'. Islamists believe that Muslims themselves are responsible for their own demise, insofar as they have turned away from their faith and have embraced what are perceived to be secular and atheistic ideas.[2]

These ideas are believed to have been advanced by colonialism, which is also viewed as responsible for the contemporary setbacks experienced by Muslim societies. The impact of colonialism has of course been varied, yet overall it has been responsible for destroying aspects of Islamic heritage, particularly those related to law and education. Colonialism's cultural onslaught during the latter part of the nineteenth century and into the second half of the twentieth century continues, although now the encroachment is not mainly British, French or Italian but American. This encroachment or 'corruption', as many in Muslim societies would have it, manifests itself in language, media, music, tourism and consumerism.

The independence of Muslim states from direct colonial rule has been one of the most important developments of the twentieth century, the most recent examples of which are the vast expanses of Muslim territories in Central Asia. This has important implications in the growth of a new zone of Muslim adherents linked either to Iran or Turkey. It is a frequently overlooked fact that the majority of Muslims are non-Arab and that in terms of a combination of political power and development (Turkey, Pakistan and Malaysia), they may offer a new and important leadership to Muslims in the future.

Among colonialism's lasting legacies has been its redrawing of territorial boundaries and the creation of nation-states; it is this fragmentation that is seen by Islamists as one of the main reasons for present weakness and disunity. The artificial boundaries imposed by the colonial powers are viewed as a means by which they were able to control a potentially far larger and hence more formidable territorial entity.

Nationalism, although integral to the very nature of contemporary Islamist protest, is nevertheless perceived by Islamists as detrimental and a necessary element in a colonial strategy to strengthen the nation-state and national identities above a common Muslim identity. The emphasis on a national identity based on the boundaries of the new nation-state has constituted an important element in the changing geopolitical and ideological character of the Muslim world.³ Despite the artificiality of many of the boundaries of present-day nation-states in, for example, the Middle East, there has nevertheless been a strong growth, particularly during the second half of the twentieth century, of national identity based on the post-colonial boundaries of these states. Among the factors contributing to this has been the emphasis placed by regimes on national integration and modernization of the state. The authoritarian nature of these regimes dictated a uniform political and national identity, not so much for development but for political control. The forging of a national identity came to fit the general international climate, whereby a national independent state would have its seat in the United Nations, its national flag and airline, some of the emblems that allowed access into the post-Second World War order. This was viewed as the route to recognition, respect and development.

The nation-state as a key structure of the contemporary international order is already undermined by the emergence of economic and security blocs, as well as fragmentation along ethnic and religious lines in different parts of the world. For the majority of Muslims and those in the Islamist movement, the existing structure of the international system forms the parameters of political activity. However, the extent to which the Islamists will affect the idea and strength of the nation-state if they come to power will be influenced by a number of factors: first, the economic and security climate regionally and internationally, which is likely to favour the development of greater cooperation and integration; and second, whether or not there is a change to an Islamic system of government in more than one state, and whether these states have the political will to give up aspects of sovereignty and believe that it is in their mutual interest to unite. There is a current of opinion among the more radical Islamist groups which stresses the religious obligation to re-establish the Caliphate and unite all Muslims within the context of the *Umma* (a united community of Muslims).⁴ There is a rejection of all Western frames of reference, be it the nation-state or democracy, which are considered alien to Islam. Although this view is not representative of the mainstream Islamist movement, the idea of the unity of Muslims is accepted as an ideal to be striven for by the vast majority of Muslims. In contrast, the idea of reinstating the Caliphate is viewed as unrealistic. Belief and commitment to these ideas are being advanced as a necessary prerequisite for being a good Muslim. Gradually they are entering the political discourse of different Islamist groups and individuals.

The spread of ideas about unity and the Caliphate would probably constitute the greatest success for the Islamist message in practical terms. It would involve a break with the political structures of the post-independence era and would allow Muslims a greater sense of independence through the re-establishment and reinterpretation of what are perceived to be Islamic political structures. In general, if notions of unity were to materialize this would not only mean a triumph for Islamism but it would enable Muslim societies to become politically and economically more powerful. They would fall into line with new world trends towards greater cooperation and integration in order to secure common economic and security interests.[5]

The parameters are often far more fluid than is supposed between opinions considered at one moment to be radical and marginal and at another to be mainstream. Many of the ideas promoted by the Muslim Brotherhood in the 1930s and 1940s which were considered extreme at the time – about, for example, the implementation of the *Shari'a* (the divinely revealed Islamic law), prohibition of alcohol and an Islamic mode of dress for women – have gradually become acceptable to the majority in many Muslim states and have been overtaken by more radical ideas, such as the accusation of unbelief (*takfir*) and the legitimization of killing someone so accused.[6] This gradual radicalization of the Islamist movement and the increasing Islamization of many Muslim societies, most notably, Algeria, Egypt, Sudan and Iran, has been an outcome of the persecution of Islamist groups, and of the frustration and disillusionment in society at the general failure of regimes, military defeat (in the case of the Arab states in the Arab–Israeli conflict), the lack of political participation and accountability, and widening economic disparity. Furthermore, regimes in Muslim states have themselves contributed to the islamization process of their societies, particularly during the 1970s and 1980s. In order to enhance their Islamic credentials, partly to gain popular support and partly out of fear, Islamist groups were increasingly becoming the arbiters of what is Islamic and what is not. In an attempt to provide a 'moderate' and non-violent interpretation of Islam, several regimes – particularly those in more secular states such as Algeria and more especially Egypt[7] – saturated the media with Islamic subjects using conservative and pro-government religious figures to promote the faith. In general this resulted in a more visible expression of religiosity in these societies rather than increased support for government. This trend has now been reversed in some countries, such as Algeria, Tunisia and Egypt, where the government has opted for a policy of combining the suppression of active Islamist groups with a retreat from and even the discouragement of the government-sponsored religious campaign. The implication of these developments is that while religion offers a source of legitimacy for those in power and those in opposition, it has also increasingly become the basic criterion of reference over which political polarization is taking place in society. With the Islamists consolidating themselves as the main opposition to the authoritarian regimes in the region, there is increasingly little political alternative for many Muslim states but to move towards greater islamization. However, although this move might express the consensus of the majority, it has inevitably led to a new polarization with the secular, religious and ethnic minorities (Kurds, Berbers and Copts).

Islam, democracy and economic liberalization

At the very heart of this is the issue of the application of the *Shari'a*. For Islamists sovereignty lies with God alone and not with the electorate: the divinely revealed Islamic law is paramount and the sole source of legislation and policy. Government is a trust which an elected Assembly exercises in accordance with the *Shari'a*.[8] The Islamists stress accountability and duty above personal freedom. It is this emphasis on the religion of Islam and on the absoluteness of the word of God as revealed in the Quran that fundamentally differentiates the Islamists' understanding of democracy from that of the West. The Islamist alternative is likely, as is the case in Iran, to allow political expression, albeit within the parameters of Islam, to a greater number of people than is the case in many Muslim countries today. What is generally sought by Islamist opposition groups are political liberties and accountability. There is still a strong sense of religiosity and tradition, acceptance of the traditional family structure and the role of women in these societies (although there have been enormous changes as regards these during the twentieth century, especially in relation to the education of women and their entering the workforce).[9] Whereas for the West the limits of democracy have been pushed much further not only on a political level but also on a social and personal level, in Muslim societies and among Islamists those aspects of democracy that are discussed are related primarily to the political sphere. It is partly this selective understanding of democracy and attempts to combine it with the supremacy of the *Shari'a* that allows the Islamists to be accused by their detractors of seeking the establishment of a theocratic system. Moreover, the Islamists' refusal to accept political pluralism that includes those who do not accept the *Shari'a* as the basis of all authority by definition allows them to be labelled undemocratic.

Besides religious conviction, the Islamists' opposition to secularism emanates from their experience of how it has manifested itself through those in power. Given that there has been little respect for the rule of law under secular regimes in Muslim states and that 'secular law' has done little to protect the basic rights of Muslim citizens, it is argued that there is no substitute for the *Shari'a*. The *Shari'a* would be implemented by believers to serve the interests of the community and above all defend them in the private and public spheres. Islamic values would be upheld by clearly drawing the boundaries between what is religiously permitted and what is prohibited. These boundaries would be guaranteed by the application of Islamic punishments. In the public sphere the *Shari'a* would safeguard the political rights of Muslims and defend them from such abuse as imprisonment without trial and from torture.

Neither during the independence struggle nor in the post-independence political programme was multi-party democracy a primary goal of the majority of the political elite. Along with other emblems of independence, single-party states set up parliaments, assemblies and constitutions which appeared to be partly modelled on Western democratic ones but were essentially instruments of the state. Although some of these parliaments may have had short bursts of democratic activity they were quickly stifled. Nevertheless, lip-service continues to be paid to democracy and many regimes still legitimize their authority by polling impossibly high percentages of popular support in carefully controlled elections.

The attempts during the 1970s and 1980s, in a number of Arab states, at a degree of political and economic liberalization had poor results in the majority of cases. The Camp David Accords and the new era of peace they were meant to herald were seen by the USA and its major new ally in the region, Egypt, as functioning best within an environment of liberalization following the disillusionment with Nasserist Arab socialism. This period marked the beginning of the most apparent and widespread manifestation of Islamic assertion in the majority of Muslim states (reflected in the increasing number of those going to prayers in mosques, the number of mosques being built, the increase in women turning to an 'Islamic' mode of dress, and the growing interest in literature concerned with Islamic subjects). This was a result of factors specific to each Muslim state but sharing some over-arching concerns. There was disillusionment with existing regimes that represented one form of authoritarian system or another and a search for an alternative to what was seen as the bankruptcy of ideologies inspired by the secular, whether in the form of socialism, Ba'athism, or Arab nationalism or eventually the newly emerging economic liberalism coupled with authoritarianism.

Where democratic channels were available they have been used by the Islamists in an attempt to influence government, as in Jordan, or in the hope of coming to power, as in Algeria. The argument justifying military intervention in Algeria to forestall victory for the Front Islamique du Salut (FIS) is that the latter would have reversed the democratic process had it come to power. The methods used against the FIS undermined the idea of democracy even for those who wished to use its channels and heed its principles. It also temporarily holds the Islamists back, while creating further polarization in the political sphere between Islamists, secularists and the regime. It gives greater justification to the Islamists for the use of violence and for the use of force by the government as pre-emptive and punitive measures. For the Islamists the Algerian experiment has shown that even the democratic process can be no guarantee of political participation. It is only a tool used by those in power to co-opt opponents and control a political situation over which they had to take some form of action in order to survive. It is ultimately no less a manipulative use of democracy than its use by the Islamists to further their own ends.

Attempts at economic and political liberalization in a number of Muslim countries (Algeria, Tunisia, Egypt, Jordan) therefore also resulted in an increased demand for an Islamic system of government rather than strengthening the democratic option. This was due to the historical, intellectual and cultural experience and make-up of these societies that still found Islam appealing not only as a private religion but as a philosophical and legal body of learning. This was seen by an ever-increasing number of people throughout the Muslim states as offering a code of behaviour and politics for state and society that was not only valid but superior to any system of a secular or Western provenance.

Given that democracy is by no means the only political or ideological current of the century and that it exists as a political system only in a minority of the world's states, it should not be the only point of reference when looking at Islamist political development. The Islamist movement has absorbed some of the political ideology of Western democracy, but it has also absorbed ideas from other political ideologies and currents. The development of the Muslim Brotherhood (the oldest and probably the most influential Islamist group, also the largest in terms of supporters in the Muslim states) in the 1930s in Egypt coincided with the rise of fascism in Europe, which arguably had some influence on the organizational style of the Brotherhood, but much more so on the Young Egypt movement that combined extreme nationalism with a call for a return to Muslim values.

By the 1950s and 1960s socialism had had some input into aspects of Islamist discourse. The existence of the Soviet Union as a dominant world power and the spread of socialist ideology in many parts of the Third World was bound to influence political currents prevalent in Muslim societies. While the Islamist movement has expressed its enmity to both capitalism and communism, it has been particularly critical of socialism because it was at the hands of socialist regimes that it suffered some of its worst persecution. Socialism is not only seen as bankrupt, a perception now widely shared following the breakup of the Soviet Union, but for the Islamists socialism has the additional negative association with dictatorships whose secular and socialist laws reversed Islamic laws. However, a whole generation of Muslims have grown up under socialist regimes which, while failing to fulfil promises of development, nevertheless succeeded in imbuing socialist values through, for example, the state-controlled media and education. Although socialism has been discredited, not all its principles and values have been erased and are often repeated, couched in the new language of Islamism and Islam's understanding of social justice.[10]

This Islamist message has become more attractive in the context of economic liberalization which has resulted in social and economic dislocation, especially as the gap between rich and poor widened. At the same time, a degree of social mobility produced a new clique of wealthy businessmen. These included some who professed Islamist ideology, but whose ventures were eventually seen as corrupt (including the collapsed Rayyan finance companies). However, there were other Islamist businessmen who participated in the economic liberalization and who found the opportunity to experiment with successful alternative 'Islamic' corporate and financial structures.[11]

Although Islamism's specificity remains apparent, Islamism has nevertheless been influenced by, and has reacted to, the dominant twentieth-century political, economic and social trends. Western civilization and its component ideologies, whether in the form of fascism, socialism or democracy, have in their different ways influenced Muslim societies and their expression of political Islam. This is perhaps an inevitable outcome of being dominated: politically, militarily and economically.

The Western threat

The notion of the threat of Islam is based on the fear of a reversal of the status quo in Muslim states which, on the whole, has served Western interests. The Iranian Revolution in 1979 was a potent symbol of the potential of Islamism in challenging Western interests and world-view. The possibility of a similar success in Algeria brings with it fears of a flood of migrants fleeing an Islamist regime and seeking refuge in the different states of Southern Europe.[12] Change in Egypt is feared because of that country's role as a major ally of American interests in the region, following the fall of the Shah of Iran. An Islamist regime in power is perceived as jeopardizing the peace process, although in reality it is unlikely that there would be an abrogation of agreements already ratified. In addition, an Islamist success in Egypt, a leading regional player, would enhance the power of Islamists throughout the Middle East and beyond, and would undermine the stability and survival of many regimes in the region. The recent successes of the Islamist Rafah party in Turkey, which has become a key player in the political arena, affirms that even Ataturk's secularization of Turkey and its strong legacy has not quelled Turkish society's Islamic identity and the political appeal of Islam.

The changes that have occurred and those likely to occur in favour of the Islamists represent political, economic and social dynamics primarily of domestic significance to the Muslim states and societies concerned. The detrimental implications for Western interests are too frequently exaggerated and are presented as the main concern above those affecting Muslim societies themselves. In practice, economic constraints on many Muslim states are likely to limit greatly any attempts to undermine Western interests. Attacks against Western targets, whether embassies, tourists or investments, is a political act of opposition aimed at destabilizing those in power and defying Western dominance. However, behind expressions of resistance and independence is the desire to reorder relations with the West on a more equitable basis and not to sever relations altogether. The safeguarding of Western interests needs to be balanced against the experience of the West during the twentieth century, in terms of military intervention and support for unpopular and authoritarian regimes.

In general, Muslim disillusionment with the values of the current world order become particularly potent when coupled with military conflicts that have increased Islamist grievances against the West. The question of Palestine, the Gulf War and the suffering of Bosnian Muslims have strengthened Islamist resolve and helped increase their support base.

The Palestine question is a cause over which the Islamists have so far been uncompromising, in that they refuse to accept Israel's right to exist. Arab nationalist and Islamist views on Israel's right to exist and Arab rights to the whole of Palestine were more or less the same, up until Sadat's visit to Jerusalem in 1977. Since then there has been a growing gap between the Islamists and secularists on the question of Israel. While Islamists continue to reject Israel's right to exist, the signing of peace treaties between Israel and its neighbours has made this stance more difficult to sustain. Despite rejecting the principle of peace they have nevertheless not totally committed themselves to resisting the current peace process, partly because the Islamists in Jordan and in the Occupied Territories are not strong enough to mount an effective opposition. The Islamists are biding their time in the belief that 'autonomy' will not meet Palestinians' long-held expectations and that the ensuing discontent will result in greater support for them. The settlement of the Arab-Israeli conflict is one of the main planks of the new world order in the region. Therefore the Islamists believe that any settlement primarily serves Israeli and Western political interests and allows for the cultural penetration of the Middle East. In addition, they see the settlement as a means to further Israeli economic interests by allowing Israel access to Arab markets. The significance of the Islamist position regarding the Palestine question is the emphasis on the religious centrality of Jerusalem, which they claim has been abandoned by the majority of nationalists and secularists.

There is a growing expression of a developing supranationalist identity at a popular level in most Muslim communities which, although unable to change the outcome of political events, rejects their legitimacy and shares a belief that they form part of an anti-Muslim conspiracy. The Gulf War helped increase anti-Western feeling in Muslim countries and focussed grievances against Arab regimes. For the Islamists, it represented yet one more example in a list of devastating blows suffered by Muslims at the hands of their rulers and of the West during the twentieth century. In particular, they came to believe that one of the main outcomes of the war was the destruction of the only Arab military force capable of posing a threat to Israel. This strengthened the Islamists' belief that the West was committed to keeping the Muslims weak. Despite previous opposition to Saddam by Islamists, Iraq's military power, once threatened by the West, became 'Muslim' military power which was being destroyed to serve Israeli and Western interests. Although Iraq's invasion of Kuwait was condemned by Arab and Muslim countries, it did not arouse anywhere near the same anger on the streets of these countries as the attack on Iraq did. Iraq's territorial integrity and military strength came to supersede any sympathy that may have existed for the Kuwaitis. This may be partly explained by the unpopularity of the Gulf states. For Islamists the main issue of the Gulf War was not the occupation of Kuwait, but the defencelessness of the *Umma* or an integral part of it against an attack by a world order that was inimical to Muslim interests. It is as if Kuwait as a nation-state ceased to matter in comparison with the destruction of Iraq's military arsenal.

The Islamists believe that Israeli military capability should be matched by a strong and united *Umma*. The destruction of Iraq as a military power is associated with a broader conspiracy to weaken and neutralize Israel's enemies, Egypt having been formally neutralized with the signing of the Camp David Accords. The dismantling of Iraq's chemical and nuclear programe has given rise to criticism of international bodies and accusations against them of double standards as regards their policies over Israel's nuclear arsenal.

The issue of double standards is frequently raised in relation to the United Nations. From a forum that was seen as representing Third World interests in the 1970s, it now represents for the Islamists, as for many, an arena for the furthering of primarily American interests. The fact that Muslim states had voted in support of United Nations resolutions condemning Iraq and legitimizing the use of force against it did not affect the perception by Muslims of the United Nations as a tool in the hands of the USA. An accusation repeatedly levelled against the United Nations is that it failed to exert a similar degree of pressure on Israel as it did on Iraq with regard to the implementation of its resolutions.

Islamists have an ambiguous view of the West's political morality. On the one hand, they believe that Western powers will pursue their own interests irrespective of what is right or wrong, but on the other, there is shock and accusations are levelled against them when they do so. This is particularly apparent in the case of Bosnia. Islamists in their newspapers, pamphlets and Friday sermons in Muslim countries and among Muslim communities in the West question why sanctions are an adequate tool against the Serbs, while they were not against Iraq. They question the motivation of the West when military intervention is ruled out because of difficult terrain as well as the motivation behind the arms embargo against the Muslim Bosnians. Talk of the 'threat of Islam' makes little sense to Muslims who see themselves as the party under attack, be it in Bosnia or Kashmir.

With the end of the Cold War and with the more active role given to the United Nations, the feeling among Islamists as well as many in the developing world is that whether it is the old or new world order that is being ratified by the United Nations, it is one that will do little to improve their position in the world or defend them. Islamism is an expression of disillusionment with Western policies and international bodies which, as such, constitutes a challenge to Western ideals and influence among Muslims. The West's military and economic superiority over Muslim states and the latter's need to lock into the international system economically, makes the fear of a threat from Muslim states appear unrealistic. However, the lack of accommodation with, and suppression of, Islamists as well as their resort to violence results in the instability that the West fears.

Although the Islamists have failed to change the course of events regarding, for example, the peace process, the Gulf War or Bosnia, they have, nevertheless, succeeded on a number of levels. First, they represent a substantial opposition force in every Muslim country that either actively or passively rejects regime policy and therefore undermines consensus for those in power and for Western interests. Second, despite the fact that the Islamists have failed to come to power except in Iran and Sudan, they have been able to threaten the stability of regimes opposed to them, despite concerted efforts to suppress and control them. This was partly the result of the use of violence by certain factions within the movement who have succeeded in shaking the various authoritarian regimes, which need to be seen to be in control. It is the combination (not necessarily coordinated between the groups) of the work of those groups that justify the use of violence and the gradual educational and welfare approach of the mainstream that has proved that the Islamists as a whole are a force to be reckoned with. Third, the Islamists have succeeded in a way that is not altogether tangible but which has long-term implications and is perhaps the greatest testimony to the fact that they represent a deep-rooted trend in Muslim societies. They have continued to oppose regimes in power and have helped to keep alive various causes in the face of change and compromise. They have therefore helped to instill in a new generation ideas and commitments that were undermined in the second half of the twentieth century, mainly by those in power in Muslim states and by the power and influence of particular Western states.

Economic disparities and social tensions

As the twentieth century approaches its close, the economies of Muslim states vary greatly. Despite success stories such as Malaysia and the wealth of the oil states of the Gulf, the vast majority of Muslim states remain among the poorest in the world (Bangladesh, Sudan, Egypt). There is growing disillusionment with the disparities in global and regional wealth and its uneven distribution. Such a view is not new; expressions of it are inherent in the Non-Aligned Movement and the very idea of a Third World as opposed to a First World or the North–South divide. The Islamists, like others in the developing world, point to this disparity between rich and poor.

It is often argued in the West that economic aid to existing regimes would help solve economic problems and thus remove one of the main reasons for the success of the Islamists. Although Islamist groups have responded to economic problems by providing various welfare programmes and facilities where governments often failed to do so, thus enhancing support for themselves, nevertheless, the argument that the Islamist upsurge is due to economic factors is in some ways too reductionist. It fails to acknowledge the possibility that the Islamist tide is one that would not necessarily be stemmed by improved economic conditions. There are a number of reasons for this, among them the search in Muslim societies for political participation and regime accountability, coupled with the safeguarding of cultural authenticity rooted in Islamic tradition and teaching.

Economic development and aid has been viewed as a possible panacea for Islamic radicalism and not as an investment in the long-term domestic and regional security of Muslim states, even if they opt for an Islamic system of government. When developing countries called for the establishment of a 'New International Economic Order' in the early 1970s they were asking for a change in the way in which the international economic system functions. Among the most fundamental economic concerns of the Islamists and non-Islamists in

Muslim states remain the need for: effective sovereignty by developing countries over the use of their natural resources; the regulation and stabilization of world markets for primary commodities which they produce; the regulation of the activities of transnational corporations; the support of producers' associations; and the promotion of economic cooperation among developing countries.

Islamist attitudes towards free market economies are often contradictory: on one level, the socialist experiment is considered to have been a failure; but on another, free market economics is seen as having caused corruption, excessive consumerism and a widening of the gap between rich and poor in these societies. In addition, tenets of the idea of a welfare state have permeated the political discourse of the Islamists via the nationalist and socialist experience of the post-colonial era, so that a government is seen to have fundamentally failed if it does not provide a basic level of welfare for the poorer part of its population. In this climate the Islamists' call for 'social justice', their attack on the new capitalism and their setting up of welfare projects find many adherents.

The Islamist position is not that the material fruits of capitalism are bad in themselves, but that (like other newly liberalizing economies) the pains, especially for the poor, are acute and that the end is far from clear or promising, especially given the high level of corruption in government and society. The Islamists in a position of power will be judged on the basis of their economic performance and will be susceptible to similar problems as secular parties. For example, the successes of the Islamist Rafah party in Turkey in parliamentary elections in 1992 and its success in gaining control of Ankara and Istanbul in the elections of 1994 have allowed it to be judged on the basis of performance rather than just opposition. The demands and aspirations of people have been shaped by both socialist expectations of welfare and the promise of wealth and luxury through capitalism; the Islamists like any other group in power will confront the challenge of these expectations. The Islamists however have a card that others in power in the Muslim states lack, and that is that they are not tainted with corruption. They can use their Islamic credentials and message to carry out more austere economic programmes which those in power fear instituting in case of a popular uprising.

In the context of Islamist discourse one of the main concerns is modernization without Westernization, i.e. without the cultural and social alienation from Islam. The Islamists offer an alternative to societies whose social fabric is becoming increasingly strained. There is an emphasis on maintaining the solidarity of the family unit, caring for the elderly and safeguarding the position of women as mothers and wives. The increase, for example, in the crime rate and in drug addiction in Muslim societies are seen as a mirror-image of what exists in Western societies and which can be controlled only through an Islamic system of law and order. There is a recognition of the influence of the media, particularly on Muslim youth, which is partly why the Islamists constantly stress that the media are among the main areas that need to be 'islamized'. It is on the basis of social concerns and a rejection of what is considered to be a Western life-style that the Islamists find increasing support in Muslim societies.

The phenomenon that may prove among the most significant in relation to Islamism is the spread of Islam in Western Europe.[13] The number of conversions of non-Muslims to Islam is growing (at a rate greater than any other religion in Western Europe). A whole new generation of Muslims is attracted to Islam spiritually and culturally. This is occurring within the broader context of the growing number of ethnic and religious groups becoming integrated into their host societies, as well as confronting increasing racism. The attraction of Islam as a religion during the twentieth century has occurred in parallel with its success as a political movement that has grown in strength in the vast majority of Muslim states to form the main opposition to governments and in some cases to come to power.

However, the success of Islamism in power in achieving economic and technological progress is likely to be undermined by a number of factors, namely the quality of leadership, the reluctance for cooperation and integration between Muslim states on a level that could alter their potential power, and the isolation of new Muslim regimes by the West and their deprivation of aid and trade. Islamism, despite achieving power in Iran and Sudan, has failed to create a power base that has either strengthened its respective nation-states, or, more significantly for Islamism, transcended the nation-state in order to forge a new Islamic bloc.

What Islamists seem to be saying in the political, economic and social spheres in relation to the current world order is that the different regimes in Muslim states and the international system as it exists have left their states defenceless, divided and poor during much of the twentieth century. The Islamists wish to modernize their societies within a frame of reference they see as their own, devoid of those legal and social aspects that are considered to undermine the basis of Muslim identity. It is partly the old story of combining Western know-how with Islamic values but in its present stage it is also the story of domestic power struggles against unpopular regimes that are seen as promoting an unjust order.

Islamist attitudes to the current world order are not marginal. They represent much of what is being voiced in Muslim societies and more generally in the developing world. The main success of Islamism is that it has come to represent the concerns of vast numbers in Muslim societies in their search for regime accountability, development and independence. So long as these concerns are not addressed (and they are unlikely to be by present regimes) then Islamism will continue to appear an attractive alternative for many.

If Islamism is judged primarily as a political movement engaged in a domestic power struggle and as a movement that has contributed to religious revival then, on balance, its gains so far are substantial and its potential to come to power is likely to be realized. However, if Islamism is about the formation of an Islamic power that would change the balance of power between Muslim states and the West then it remains a long way from realizing its goal.

Notes

1. Some of these rejected rebellion against authority, such as the eleventh-century jurist al-Ghazali, while others, such as Ibn Taymiiyya, a thirteenth-century jurist much quoted by contemporary Islamists, legitimized opposition to governments if they were seen to err. See H. Ennayat, *Modern Islamic Political Thought* (London, 1982).
2. For a hypothesis on the dominant source of conflict being cultural on a new phase of world politics, see Samuel P. Huntington, 'The clash of civilisations?', *Foreign Affairs*, lxxliii/3 (1993), pp.22–49.
3. For a general survey, see J. Piscatori, *Islam in a World of Nation-States* (Cambridge, 1986).
4. The most notable of which is the Hizb al-Tahrir, originally established in Jerusalem, although now more widespread. However, other radical groups in Algeria and Egypt, for example, have similar beliefs.
5. K. Ohmae, 'Rise of the region state', *Foreign Affairs*, lxxii/2 (1993), pp.78–88.
6. For a translation and discussion of one of the most important texts promoting this idea, see J. Jansen, *The Neglected Duty: The Creed of Sadat's Assassins and Islamic Resurgence in the Middle East* (New York, 1986).
7. Note, for example, the way Sadat presented himself through the government-controlled media as a devout and practising Muslim.

8 See *A Model of an Islamic Constitution* (London, 1983), p.3 and *The Constitution of the Islamic Republic of Iran* (Tehran, 1980).
9 See N. Hijab, *Womanpower: The Arab Debate on Women at Work* (Cambridge, 1988), pp.63–92.
10 During the heyday of socialism in the 1960s several popular works attempting to read Marxist and Socialist principles in Islam were published.
11 For an interesting and informative set of ideas on Islam and economic development, see Khurshid Ahmed, 'Economic development in an Islamic framework', in Khurshid Ahmed and Zafar Ishaq Ansari (eds), *Islamic Perspectives: Studies in Honour of Mawlana Sayyid Abul A'la Mawdudi* (London, 1979).
12 For an alternative view on the fear of North African migration, see Y. Courbage, 'Demographic transition among the Maghrib peoples of North Africa and European communities abroad', in P. Ludlow (ed.), *Europe and the Mediterranean* (London, 1994).
13 See J. Nielsen, *Muslims in Western Europe* (Edinburgh, 1992).

10. COMMUNITY

Andrew Linklater

The twentieth century has been the century of the sovereign state. In this period the state surpassed the remarkable achievements of its predecessors not by expanding overseas empires, as they had done, but by augmenting other forms of state power. The surveillance of society, intervention in economic and social life and the capacity to wage destructive war have increased dramatically in recent decades. In the twentieth century, moreover, the territorial state became the dominant mode of political organization across the entire world.[1] Some new states are failed states,[2] sovereign only in name, and most require the supporting role of international institutions, yet the modern territorial state has long been without peer in the sphere of close political cooperation.

One reviewer of James Hutchinson Stirling's *The Secret of Hegel* castigated the author for keeping Hegel's secret to himself. No such mystery shrouds the labour of the sovereign state. 'In India', according to Hegel, 'five hundred men conquered twenty thousand who were not cowards, but who only lacked [the] disposition to work in close cooperation with others'.[3] Earlier forms of European political organization also lacked the level of close cooperation which gave the modern state its spectacular global reach.

Sovereignty can exist in the absence of community just as there are communities without sovereignty but political movements usually arise in such circumstances to eradicate the gulf between the two. The modern state has been successful because it has been able to create community out of the diverse groups brought within the same boundaries by chance or force. A great array of mechanisms have been used to create political community. Some states have simply absorbed minority groups within the dominant national culture; others have moved outsiders to other places where, allegedly, they really belong; some have exterminated or sidelined groups with whom close cooperation is thought to be impossible. Despite the atrocities and injustices committed by the state there has been no serious challenge to its desire to unite community and sovereignty and surprisingly little support for alternative models of political life during the twentieth century.

A myriad of factors are currently transforming political communities across the world and, as the century comes to an end, the time is indeed ripe for enunciating new principles of political life which break with the tyranny of the concept of the state.[4] Sub-national groups, various social movements and migrant populations are challenging the symbols of national unity which underpinned close cooperation in the past. Globalization is eroding much of what is distinctive about national cultures by disseminating one set of attitudes and beliefs (predominantly Western or American) across world society. Partly in response to one effect of globalization, namely mass migration, minorities continue to suffer from acts of violence and discrimination in many societies, yet the loosening of the ties between citizens and the state is a striking new trend within the same areas. This trend creates possibilities of different forms of community in which sub-national and transnational loyalties and identities acquire greater representation and voice. While an awareness of the fragile, even troubled, nature of modern political communities exists, and may even be growing as the century ends, a sense of the openness of the future is significantly stronger than in recent decades. At the end of the century, the fate of political community depends on the outcome of the struggle between divisive acts of cultural enclosure and efforts to open social arrangements simultaneously to sub-national and transnational claims.

This chapter is in five sections. The first considers Hegel's claim that the modern state triumphed over other forms of political association by reconciling several potentially competing political principles. The second addresses the modern state's failure, as E. H. Carr put it, to balance two competing principles (nationalism and internationalism) in the early part of the century. The third considers some of the implications of Carr's discussion for the still embryonic project of constructing a sociology of the shifting boundaries of moral and political communities. The fourth uses the principles developed in this section to analyse the forces which are undermining tightly bound and sharply separate communities and which require that political communities balance the national idea and internationalism in innovative ways. The fifth returns to Hegel's account of the modern state and argues that the state can best play a positive role in world affairs by balancing the different spheres of sub-national, national and transnational loyalties thereby combining a commitment to moral universalism with sensitivity to cultural difference.

Hegel's claim for the modern state

Hegel argued that the modern state succeeded by reconciling the competing imperatives of individualism and community, market and welfare, sovereignty and international responsibility. The modern state made it possible for its citizens to enjoy membership of a cohesive community (so recapturing the essence of life in the Ancient polis) while satisfying the modern subject's demand for personal freedom. Market forces were granted real autonomy, and self-regarding voluntary economic associations were allowed to develop, but poverty (an inevitable product of civil society) had to be alleviated by state provision for the poor. War was necessary for the community to cohere, sovereignty was unqualified by international legal obligations, but the state had to take account of international responsibilities to control the use of force. The state aimed to count on the loyalty of citizens in times of crisis and war without requiring their unconditional political obedience and without denying the rights of other sovereign communities. So it was in Europe at any rate. The perception that other peoples have no experience of political freedom has been a recurrent theme in Western constructions of community since the rise of Greek civilization. The modern state established its identity as a community through otherness, specifically by subjugating non-European peoples.

Not all twentieth-century states have been Hegelian communities balancing the principles mentioned above. Some have destroyed private property in the means of production in the name of socialist humanism; others have trimmed welfare to the bare bones in the name of individual self-reliance; and some have become family firms in names known only to the managers of Swiss bank accounts. Several have waged war without regard for the rights of individuals and peoples and they have placed the nation before the individual as well as before racial, ethnic and other minorities. Notwithstanding these differences, the similarities between modern states is one of the salient characteristics of the twentieth century. Good Hegelian states take part in the same kinds of political debate. They have disputed whether the balance has swung too far towards individual freedom or state control, whether market capitalism needs constraining or protecting against unwarranted state interference, and whether the nation is in danger of losing its identity in the face of global forces and emerging regional blocs or of tilting too far towards national egoism.

Not only have many states given surprisingly similar answers to these questions but the likenesses between them seem to be growing in the last decades of the century. Almost all states recognize the need for domestic market autonomy and virtually all now open their economies to global competition. Convergence is evident in economic policy as Patricia Clavin argues in chapter 7, and, some would argue, in type of regime. Pressures to create less authoritarian, if less than wholly democratic, regimes exist everywhere although, as Fukuyama observes, the logic of democratization may not reach far beyond the Western industrial world. Elsewhere, for example in East Asia, political systems may be evolving distinctive forms of paternalistic authoritarianism.[5] At this point in the century it is unclear whether convergence or divergence will prevail but clearly much hangs on the outcome if the argument that liberal-democratic states tend to be peaceful in their relations with each other is even only partly right.[6] For most of the twentieth century the main approaches to the state and world politics have assumed the immutability of the states-system and the probability of eventual war. The fact that it is now possible to contemplate the obsolescence of major war between the main industrial states is a new consideration which separates the last part of the century from the first.

Nationalism and internationalism
References to the obsolescence of major war existed early in the century yet they were soon abandoned when it became apparent that state behaviour would continue to be driven by calculations of war rather than by the principles of liberal internationalism. According to E. H. Carr, a crisis of community arose because states failed to strike the balance between sovereign rights and international responsibility which had characterized the society of states in the nineteenth century.[7] It is important to consider Carr's argument further since striking the right balance between the national idea and the international one remains the

pressing issue facing contemporary political communities in the modern world.

Carr distinguished between three phases in the development of modern state structures. In the first phase, which dominated much of the eighteenth century, economic and political power were harnessed to the central sovereign project of building powerful state structures. In the second phase, marked by the rise of bourgeois national movements in the nineteenth century, the mercantilist marriage of economic and political affairs was dissolved. Many state structures became broadly committed to the idea that free trade would lead to international harmony. New nations formed out of secession or unification became equal members of the society of states without seriously disrupting world peace while the free movement of goods and labour increased during an era of high migration. Nationalism and internationalism were balanced for the greater part of the century.

The third phase witnessed the end of the compromise between nationalism and internationalism. The balance between the two began to fail in the 1870s but the years between 1914 and 1939 revealed the true magnitude of the crisis. Nationalism began to operate within new economic and political circumstances as a result of three forces which brought the previously peaceful epoch to an end. With the extension of the male suffrage, ascending social movements used their new-found industrial strength to protect themselves against the vagaries of the market. New social strata embraced nationalism. Second, state structures began to pursue economic policies aimed at protecting national wages and employment. Economic and political power were reunited as the state abandoned *laissez-faire* to provide social services and resultant forms of economic nationalism undermined the open world economy. Third, between 1871 and 1924 the virtual doubling of the number of states first by reunification and then by secession created new international instabilities. The growing appeal of the principle of national self-determination linked with economic nationalism among the weaker states challenged the hegemonic internationalism of Britain, the main stabilizer of the world system.

What Carr called the socialization of the nation, the nationalization of economic policy and the geographical extension of nationalism led to the great wars and totalitarianism. Economic nationalism created new pressures to end large-scale immigration, and intense rivalry between nation-states became inevitable after the critical step of closing national frontiers was taken in 1919. Inflamed initially by the economic transition, nationalism from the First World War onwards encouraged total war: popular hatred blurred the important distinction between military and civilian targets. Coupled with the decline of international law in the 1930s, the deportation of peoples to tidy the frontiers signalled the end of the era in which the national principle and internationalism were in balance. The twenty-year crisis, as Carr described it, revealed the final bankruptcy of nationalism in the West.

In the first part of the twentieth century the reconciliations which Hegel thought unique to the modern state gave way to destructive contradictions. The state continued to secure the pacification of its domestic territory but the propensity to use violence in foreign affairs increased. Social welfare became a prominent concern but protectionism and greater international economic and political competition were its unwanted side-effects. National culture became more inclusive with the extension of citizenship rights from the legal and political to the economic domains, but national exclusiveness in the conduct of foreign policy and tighter national control over the admission of refugees intensified. International order was weakened as political communities became more tightly bound and more sharply divided from one another.

Moral and political communities

In the three phases discussed by Carr, mercantilist states were superseded by more open *laissez-faire* states which were replaced in turn by closed nation-states. Carr believed that new forms of political community might emerge in a fourth period beginning in the second part of the century. What he thought might eventuate remains significant for the present time. His basic insight was that the 'exclusive solution' to community which had limited membership to powerful groups within the state (to 'white men, landowners, propertied classes and so forth') could no longer command the loyalty of modern societies.[8] As with domestic politics, so with international relations: an international community limited to the great powers could not be legitimated. Carr referred to 'the impossible task of creating an international community out of units so fantastically disparate ... as China and Albania, Norway and Brazil', but he defended international planning to promote the equality of individual men and women across the world.[9] International planning had to proceed with regard for cultural differences. Like domestic society, the international community had to 'admit something of the same multiplicity of authorities and diversity of loyalties'.[10] Building the nation into a new world order committed to the welfare of all individuals would 'mark the beginning of the end of the destructive phase of nationalism'.[11]

Carr recognized that the boundaries of community are not fixed and that community can be defined in many ways, some more exclusionary than others. With rare exceptions the literature on political science and international relations has failed to develop Carr's schematic analysis of the diverse ways in which communities have been constructed.[12] Too little is known about the ways in which communities come to be bounded and distinct from one another and too little is known about how boundedness and separateness change over time. Some important clues to further research exist in the sociological literature, in Benjamin Nelson's writings on civilizational complexes, for example, which refer to Maine's emphasis on the expansion and contraction of the boundaries of moral and political communities, and to Durkheim's and Mauss's essay on how internationalization develops unevenly across frontiers – more quickly with respect to religious and political ideas than with respect to political structures and law.[13] Nelson was mainly concerned with the extent of boundary-crossing and boundary-closure at the level of great civilizations but the same themes arise in conjunction with the nation-state and the international states-system. To take this further it is useful to return to the theme that contradictions emerged in the exercise of state power in the early part of the century. These contradictions shed light on the forces which shape the development of communities.

Three monopoly powers define the modern state.[14] First, the state has claimed the right to exercise a monopoly of control over the instruments of violence. Its legitimacy has depended on its capacity to pacify society and defend the realm from physical threat and military attack. Second, the state has claimed the right to exercise monopoly control of the right of taxation. It first claimed this right so as to finance the creation of state bureaucracies and standing armies,[15] but more recently this power has become anchored in the idea that the state has a duty to levy and redistribute a share of the national income in order to secure its citizens' welfare, education and health. Undertaking this responsibility is a second reason for the state's relative success as a political community. Third, the state has claimed the right to determine priorities between political allegiances and loyalties. It has claimed this right in order to be sure that popular allegiances remain undivided in times of war although rarely have states endeavoured to destroy subnational identities and supranational loyalties entirely. Establishing priorities among political loyalties so as to leave some space for subnational and transnational loyalties is a third reason for the success of the modern state.

These monopoly powers point towards the different factors which shape the boundaries of community. The state's monopoly of control of the instruments of violence reveals the importance of state-building, pacification and war. The state's control of the right of taxation is a reminder of the impact of production and exchange (domestic and international) on the evolution of community. The state's role in shaping political identity illustrates the place of culture, specifically constructions of self and other, in the constitution of political community.

Stressing force, taxation and identity points to the fact that communities are shaped by the intersection of several phenomena: state-building and war, production and exchange, language, culture and belief. Developments in the social sciences since the mid-1980s have argued for synoptic explanations alert to the interplay between multiple phenomena and distinct therefore from earlier approaches which tended to focus on one logic (strategic competition and war in the case of realism, production and exchange in the case of Marxism).[16] Multi-logic approaches, surveying the forces mentioned above, have been used in the analysis of state-building and social power but no similar approach has appeared explaining how the boundaries of communities expand and contract, how societies become more or less particularistic and more or less sympathetic to balancing moral universalism and cultural difference.[17]

To return to Hegel and Carr with these themes in mind, the first point to note is that the state which Hegel described used its monopoly powers as follows. The state pacified its territory, reserved the right to use force to promote its interests against other states, recognized constraints as a member of an exclusionary society of states and assumed rights of conquest of non-European peoples. It combined market with welfare, recognized the rights of individuals to participate in a civil society which had outgrown the territorial state, and defended economic colonialism. It aimed to balance freedom and community within its territory, recognized the unifying force of civilization, but established its nature as a community in assumptions about its superiority over non-European peoples.

Carr's analysis of the rise of the nationalist state reveals how monopoly powers were used to create tightly bound communities more sharply separated from one another. The state continued to pacify domestic territory but was now more ready to use force in relations with other European states. It used its fiscal powers to improve the welfare of citizens but protectionism imposed great costs on outsiders and weakened the bonds of European international society. It used its capacity to shape political identity to create nationalistic communities which were at odds with other European states as well as non-European peoples. The first part of the twentieth century witnessed the development of more closed communities. The question which arises is whether current trends demonstrate that this process is being reversed.

The undermining of communities

Open communities are communities which respect the rights of minorities and demonstrate internationalism. The possibility of such communities has received either little or no analysis in modern social and political thought. Nineteenth-century precursors of modern writers on globalization (such as Marx) argued that the nation-state would be opened up by industrialization and internationalism. They attached too much importance to economic processes and too little to the countervailing power of nationalism. Other analyses of community such as realism have emphasized the tenacity of the modern nation-state, noting that states have homogenized their populations and constrained international loyalties and organizations not least given the probability of war. This approach to the shape of political community looks increasingly insecure in the light of current patterns of economic and cultural change. The Austro-Marxists writing at the beginning of the century were a striking exception to these trends. Recognizing the tenacity of the nation and the advance of globalization they argued that the central political question of the modern age was how the right balance between national groups (especially those lacking sovereignty) and internationalism might be struck.[18] This remains the key question to ask.

Regarding state-building and force, the main issue as the century ends is whether the pacification of the core marks a watershed in the evolution of international society. Pacification has three dimensions. After a long period in which war has been central, the civilianization of government is now a pronounced trend in modern states, the percentage of the population under arms having fallen steadily throughout the century.[19] Further, wars between the great powers are fewer in number and far less concerned with the conquest of territory, if significantly more deadly in their effects.[20] Even such deadly wars may now be obsolete within the Western security community. Finally, although the state retains its control of the means of violence it is increasingly reliant on international policing and surveillance to deal with transnational crime and violence.

Several explanations have been offered of what many regard as the great transformation of the modern age – the obsolescence of war between the major industrial powers since 1945. Some stress shifts in moral consciousness which have led war to be likened to slavery as unacceptable coercion.[21] Others stress the rise of the trading state geared to global trade and investment and secure in the knowledge that economic gain can occur (indeed can only occur) without the burdensome conquest of territory.[22] Still others emphasize the pacifying role of the nuclear revolution noting that modern populations prefer the lightning strike to the protracted struggle with the adversary, assuming that conflict occurs at a safe distance from national territory.[23] Whatever the reason, modern industrial states have become more responsible to the international community in the second half of the century for the use of the instruments of violence. The probable consequences of the obsolescence of major war are profound. Sacrifice in battle has been one of the main forces which has kept national communities together, as Hegel observed. States will find it more difficult to maintain cohesive communities where force is a less significant feature of national political life. The state retains control of the instruments of violence but one of the factors which has confined close cooperation to sovereign communities is weakening particularly in the Western world.

Such trends are not universal. Assumptions that the Western experience of state-building would be repeated across the world have turned out to be erroneous. Post-colonial states inherited overdeveloped administrative infrastructures, extensive military capabilities but low levels of competing urban-based economic power. The civilianization of government is not taking place in all non-European societies and many states which are relatively free from external threat maintain powerful armed forces which specialize in domestic repression and violence. Such is the legacy of the modern nation-state in non-Western regions of the world.

The future of international society regarding pacification depends in part on how peaceful states will act to influence state-formation in the more autocratic, unstable and dangerous areas. Many crucial questions about the relationship between the more and less pacific domains have yet to be answered: whether international action to prevent states from intimidating and oppressing their subjects will emerge, whether the society of states will prevent regimes which flout international standards of legitimacy from possessing the instruments of mass destruction and whether international action will be taken to prevent national boundaries being changed by force. Important issues concerning sovereignty, non-intervention and standards of legitimacy in international society are raised by these questions. Suffice it to add at this point that such issues concern the international role and responsibility of political communities in the post-imperial age.

As for production and exchange, the main question is how far these reinforce the logic of pacification. Evidently, material progress and the closed Fichtean state cannot go together. The phenomenon of globalization has undermined the separateness of nation-states. The tax haven for foreign capital is a striking example of how the state's monopoly of the right of taxation has waned in importance following the rise of the global economy, transnational production and the rapid mobility of huge reserves of international capital. Strong regional contenders for the state's fiscal power have arisen in many European countries and it seems reasonable to suppose that pressures will increase to allow international bodies to levy funds directly. In the main, states retain their monopoly of the right to tax and distribute significant portions of the national income but globalization means that insular communities are impossible to reproduce.

Globalization has important consequences for the culture of violence in the main industrial states. In the fifteenth and sixteenth centuries, war-prone states were unable to establish an empire within Europe which could control trading networks anchored in the geographically scattered towns.[24] Hegemonic powers created overseas empires administering peripheral regions but failed to subdue the core. Even that hegemony came to an end as capital migrated to regions with low labour costs, so eroding the economic foundations of military power.[25] In the twentieth century globalization has further diffused economic power, creating powerful centres of economic power within the former periphery and destroying ideas of imperial conquest. Using force to create overseas empire no longer features in the language used by great powers to define the purposes of political community. Previous states-systems were destroyed by empire but in the context of globalization it is feasible that the modern states-system will be the first one which evolves into a post-sovereign order by peace rather than war. The significance of the boundaries between nation-states may become less important than those between the pacified and the non-pacified world and, more significantly, between the global rich and the global poor.

As for identity, in the late twentieth century the state's ability to control human identity is weaker for at least three reasons. First, mass migration has replaced fairly homogeneous communities with diverse, multi-ethnic societies. The politics of indigenous peoples and national minorities demonstrate the rejection of national-assimilationist ideologies. Modern communities are under growing pressure to recognize cultural diversity and to abandon the assumption that the state is rightly the vehicle of one dominant nation. Second, these communities are now locked into global communication and information networks embodying new forms of socio-cultural power. Diverse consequences result. Elite and mass in many differed societies enjoy the 'cosmopolitan culture of modernity',[26] but many other elites and social movements are sharply opposed to the homogenizing tendencies of globalization. Groups espousing cultural closure and groups which favour greater openness to the outside world are evident in most parts of the world. The nature of the bond uniting 'members of the same society' and the extent of separateness from the world 'outside' have become keenly contested in most societies. Third, globalization faces states with painful choices about their future role in regional organizations. Political debate about the degree of regional integration further underscores the difficulty of acquiring a commanding consensus about the increasingly vexed question of national identity.

The bonds between the citizen and the state may be weakening but there is no reason to suppose that greater internationalism will eventuate. Globalization has often been welcomed as a liberating force which releases peoples from the grip of parochial cultures and ushers in a cosmopolitan culture with the vestiges of nationality allowed to linger, as Marx put it, on the guinea's stamp. Though not wholly incorrect, such writers overlooked Aristotle's observation that building a wall around the Peloponnese does not create the spirit of close cooperation integral to any community. The Stoic quest for a community which was wider than the polis failed because the vision of a universal society was advanced in the absence of a strong sense of 'a life of common involvements'.[27] With globalization the life of common involvements may be thought to reside in the old nation-state or in the older ethnic groups of which it is composed. Clearly, national differences survive globalization and may even be intensified by it. Uneven economic development recharges national differences as the disadvantaged look to the state for protection against the effects of globalization and the perceived threat of growing numbers of migrants and refugees. The sub-national revolt, currently the most potent form of nationalism, challenges the existing boundaries of many nation-states.

This is a fundamental shift in the latter part of the century which raises new questions about the state as the main form of political community. What is now much less compelling is the argument once frequently directed at Marxism which maintains that nationalism reveals the tenacity of the state, the immutability of the nation-state system and the impossibility of more inclusive communities.[28] Nationalism is not the ideology on which to build political community in the late twentieth century but demands for national rights must nevertheless be satisfied. The issue is how to reserve a place for the nation while ensuring that such solidarity does not become a form of power against others and while recognizing that political life can no longer 'be decided at the lesser level of small associations'.[29] Returning to Carr's phraseology, this requires a compromise between the national idea and internationalism.

The nature of the compromise will necessarily vary from place to place. What might be relevant in Europe, for example, will not be relevant across the world at large given disputes surrounding the meaning of internationalism. Concerning Europe, first of all, it is useful to return to the Austro-Marxist answer to the question of who should be included and excluded from the community. Recognizing how national minorities had often suffered at the hands of sovereign states, Austro-Marxists such as Otto Bauer and Karl Renner affirmed the principle of national-cultural autonomy. Autonomy was defended to ensure that national rights would be guaranteed but sovereign rights were withheld in the interests of internationalism. Austro-Marxists recognized that internationalism would not proceed far if national differences were disregarded but they clearly believed that more was required from national groups than the celebration of cultural difference. Indeed internationalism as defined by the Austro-Marxists rested upon basic respect for other nationalities.

Current illustrations of this approach to balancing nationalism and internationalism include the idea that societies should be accountable to the international community for the treatment of minorities who might reasonably take complaints against the state before international organizations. It includes arguments about the possibility of overcoming the democratic deficit by promoting regional representation within European political organizations, so institutionalizing the networks formed by representatives of different regions who often bypass their respective central governments. Here the regional organization might be the vehicle through which local identities acquire greater representation and a more powerful voice. Representing national minorities within regional organizations can extend social and cultural rights within the context of post-statist democracy. Current writings about cosmopolitan democracy which argue that globalization undercuts the value of democracy within the territorial state and which stress the need to secure democratic rights within new forms of political community invite discussions of how attachments to the nation might be represented within international organizations.[30] Clearly, the security provided by national citizenship has decreased with the rise of globalization and with the greater vulnerability of societies to forces which originate outside their borders and which escape democratic control – hence the need to re-create citizenship rights in post-sovereign arenas.

In the context of Europe it is possible to imagine new forms of community which balance nationalism and internationalism in such ways but it is difficult to envisage such models of community developing on a global scale. Intricate balances between the two principles are possible where groups share the same civilization but they are more difficult to imagine where different civilizations or cultures are involved. Arguably the Austro-Marxists gave little thought to the question of whether global arrangements could be created which would ensure justice between civilizations. Carr identified the problem of creating global structures which would do justice to fantastically different societies. In Hegel's era the question hardly arose. The question of justice between civilizations is, however, inescapable at the end of the twentieth century.[31]

Hegel's argument that the modern state succeeded by balancing individual and community, market and welfare, sovereignty and international responsibility assumed the modern state's clear cultural and political superiority over the rest of the world. The right to exercise power over non-European parts of the world has been central to the constitution of the identity of Western political community. Even those who disputed this right of conquest were relatively secure in their belief that the Western world had the right to judge the adequacy of other forms of life.[32] The supposition that the West represented the normative destination for other societies has been confidently displayed in many forms – in the claim that the West had to prepare other peoples for entry into the society of states and in the argument that nationalism is essentially the revolt of peoples who are converging towards similar patterns of economic and political development. It may be that the stage in which the nationalist revolt was undertaken by peoples who aspired to live according to the same principles and procedures has already come to an end.[33] Be that as it may, the notion that advanced political communities belong to an international society of states which is rightly limited to Europe no longer holds. The political exclusion of non-European peoples from that society has largely broken down and the trend towards a more culturally diverse international system is unmistakable. How are communities to balance nationalism and internationalism in a context in which the meaning of internationalism is exceedingly difficult to define?

The crucial point is the observation that what once passed for internationalism is simply the unsolicited projection of specifically Western values. Many of the states which have joined international society during the twentieth century have no wish to emulate Western ways of life. The West's alleged right to judge the adequacy of other forms of life, including their human rights record, is rejected in many parts of the world. Some argue that there is no modern requirement, no standard of civilization, which enables one society to judge another.[34] The rise of such arguments in the postmodernizing West is testimony to the loss of confidence in the idea that Western states are more advanced than other forms of political community or especially moved by internationalist concerns. The postmodern political community denies the existence of any Archimedean vantage point and questions the capacity of the modern state to balance nationalism and internationalism in ways which ensure justice between civilizations.

Shaped by such beliefs, the modern political community doubts its capacity for international action. The state which Hegel so obviously admired had no such doubts and demonstrated the power of close cooperation by the alleged ease of its conquest of India. Modern political community lacks confidence in its own way of life or the necessary internationalist commitment to project its military power. Returning to pacification of international society: sceptical writings on humanitarian intervention point out that modern populations are fickle enough to press their national governments into military action but easily disenchanted when drawn into protracted conflicts with local warlords in areas where no obvious political settlement is in store.[35] The sceptics point out that pacification may require a significant shift away from the idea of sovereignty and the corollary principle of non-intervention, adding that dangerous precedents are set when great powers are allowed to intervene in the internal affairs of other societies. They suggest that in the end provincial considerations rather than international ideas will weigh heavily on the minds of intervening governments. They argue that great powers will set the international standards of legitimacy which define the pariah state and lead to action (possibly military action) to prevent it from acquiring the instruments of mass destruction. What they doubt is that states will project national power in accordance with a sense of obligation to the society of states and the community of humankind. With equal veracity they might doubt the absence of any strong commitment to reduce global economic inequalities. In short, at the end of the century national communities have lost their former assurance in their right to project their power and have yet to find in internationalism an alternative rationale.

To some observers the demise of internationalist states may seem no great loss, but the reaction against universalism has now gone too far and the current absence of internationalist ideals from the purposes of political communities is a matter of regret. Cosmopolitanism is often accused of failing to take sufficient account of cultural differences; however, the defence of cultural difference is a cosmopolitanism of sorts. No defence of cultural difference can easily stand up for the principle of sovereignty, given past relations between states and national minorities or indigenous peoples. International support for groups which are the victims of violence and national-assimilationist ideologies is one element of the modern requirement. Other principles, including support for the starving and the victims of genocide and racism, have been defended but they still have too small a role in debates about the purposes of political community.[36]

Community and citizenship

In summary, the transformation of state structures in the early part of the century revealed how multiple processes can interact to create more closely bound communities intent on aggressively promoting their interests and rights. Since the Second World War political communities in the West have enjoyed relative stability in the context of the nuclear peace and a stable global economy. The Western pattern of nation-building looked as if it might be repeated in post-colonial societies. But as the century ends, the tenacity of sub-national cultures, the obsolescence of major war between great powers and the imprint of globalization upon whole societies are weakening the nationalist identities which converge with the boundaries of sovereign states. Post-colonial states are not alone in wrestling with the implications of their fracturing ethnic mosaics. Support for ethnic-based community proceeds in conjunction with a timid response to universalistic claims. The supposed superiority of Western culture is losing ground within the West, and Western ideas are increasingly criticized and condemned in the non-Western parts of the world. As Hegel observed, the modern state has enjoyed unprecedented mobilizing power and global reach. Loss of national purpose in modern states, the absence of alternative political structures with equivalent administrative range (transnational corporations aside) and hesitant support for internationalism result in feeble responses to global problems. Patterns of global change at the end of the century are eroding traditional political structures but new models of community are not emerging in their place.

In this fluid context the main theoretical challenge is to envisage new configurations of community which ally cosmopolitan principle and national sentiment. As many observers have noted, political theory fixed its sights on the relationship between citizens and the state. The study of international relations provided sonorous accompaniment by depicting the world of states as a realm of recurrence and repetition. The consequent failure to theorize the world outside the state has left the modern political imagination profoundly impoverished. Yet the transformation of modern society and politics demonstrates the mutability of international relations and invites reflection on the prospects for meliorist strategies. Specifically, it invites consideration of new forms of community and new modalities of citizenship.

To the possible horror of the classicists it might be argued that the modern states-system has reached a crossroads which is reminiscent of the late Hellenistic world, at least as it appears in some accounts.[37] After celebrating the city-state for several centuries, Greek political thought began to grapple with notions of federal communities and conceptions of dual citizenship. The current challenge is very similar: to envisage forms of community which grant citizenship a meaning and significance which extend the achievements of the modern sovereign state. The emphasis is on citizenship because it has underpinned the close cooperation peculiar to the modern state. By defining what members of the state have in common and what sets them apart citizenship has provided the key to modern political community. Citizenship has been set within national bounds because alternative settings proved to be unattainable. With the extension of state power in the eighteenth and nineteenth centuries, sub-national groups had to decide whether to aim to locate power in the regions or to assume the centralized state was given and concentrate on the struggle to democratize power. Geopolitical struggle eliminated the first of these options by favouring the development of centralist rather than confederal states. In the nineteenth century citizenship came to signify a bilateral relationship between the individual and the state.[38] Citizenship was indivisible. Notions that minorities might have special citizenship rights conferred upon them were unwelcome and conceptions of transnational citizenship were uncommon.

Citizenship is a prized possession in modern states because it encompasses a range of undeniably important legal, political and economic rights.[39] However, citizenship has been simultaneously too universalistic and too particularistic: too universalistic because the needs of national minorities or indigenous peoples have been neglected and too particularistic as the interests of outsiders have largely been ignored.[40] The claim that citizenship is too universalistic notes that modern societies need to rework the principles of community so that the particular needs of weaker cultures are properly recognized. This argument has been forcefully advanced in conjunction with the special plight of indigenous peoples, in circumstances where the gulf between the boundaries of community and the boundaries of the political system is abundantly clear.[41]

Breaking with the dominant categories of national citizenship to recognize the dissimilarity of groups within the modern state is one dimension of the restructuring of modern societies. Just as important is the theme of creating universal citizenship which introduces international guarantees for individual and collective rights. The notion of cosmopolitan democracy maintains that the democratic rights of citizens should now be embodied in regional political bodies. Similarly, the argument that sub-national groups should be able to take their grievances against the state before international institutions envisages another instance of transnational citizenship. In this context, it should be stressed, the universalization of citizenship rights within international organizations and the particularization of citizenship rights within the state to recognize the specific identities of minority cultures can develop hand-in-hand.

Late in the twentieth century the problem of organizing human beings still requires states, but states which are less guarded about old sovereign rights. Other political associations may have close cooperation but they mainly lack the state's organizational scope and capacity.

Solving the problem of organizing human beings requires states which are less insistent on sovereignty and more tolerant of the sub-national and transnational loyalties on which future sites of organizational power may come to rest. In this context, the political theory of the modern state might focus on its future role in balancing membership of different communities – sub-national, national and transnational. Deprived of the worst side of nationalism and sovereignty, the state can continue to play a positive role in world affairs. To return to the themes introduced at the start of this chapter, the state will remain charged with balancing the claims of the individual and the requirements of community, the welfare principle and market economics, but it will need to rethink the relationship between sovereignty and international responsibility. This last dimension entails a fundamental re-examination of the purposes of political community and the uses to which the state should put its monopoly powers.

On this last subject, in the early twentieth century the state misused its monopoly powers. Internal pacification was accompanied by increasing tolerance of the use of force in foreign affairs. The promotion of welfare was pursued by shifting costs on to other societies. The intensification of national identity clashed with the need for international order. Late in the century states in the Western industrialized world enjoy domestic pacification and membership of a security community. National economic policies observe some multilateralist canons in the Western world, enough to hold economic nationalism at bay. But national purposes have yet to be enlarged to include the pacification of conflict-ridden areas and the obligation to promote the material well-being of men and women everywhere.

Weakened as it is by the constraints of globalization, the state still plays a crucial role in shaping political identity. Whether or not new forms of political community emerge which admit a greater range of loyalties and identities depends very much on the role played by the state. It is clear that the state is much less tightly bound and less sharply separated than its predecessors earlier in the century and that the importance of imagining alternative forms of political community has greatly increased. It is also abundantly clear that many seek refuge in dangerous versions of closed nationalism. Hegel's observations about the decline of the Greek polis have some relevance for the modern period. Close cooperation at the level of the polis was destroyed by individualism and universalism just as cooperation at the level of the nation-state is now being challenged by the sub-national revolt and globalization.

Hegel believed that the decline of the polis was necessary so that a higher form of political community could emerge – the modern state some two millennia later. At the end of the century it is unclear whether the close cooperation which was provided by the modern state is finally coming to an end and an unavoidable period of estrangement between different cultures awaits, or whether new communities which extend universality and difference can be designed. Herein lies the problem of community at the end of the century.

Notes

1. Hedley Bull and Adam Watson (eds), *The Expansion of International Society* (Oxford, 1984).
2. Gerald B. Helman and Steven R. Ratner, 'Saving failed states', *Foreign Policy*, 89 (1992–3), pp.3–20.
3. Georg Wilhelm Friedrich Hegel, *Philosophie des Rechts* (1821); trans. T. M. Knox as *The Philosophy of Right* (Oxford, 1952), paragraph 327, addition.
4. Hedley Bull, *The Anarchical Society: A Study of Order in World Politics* (London, 1977), p.267.
5. Francis Fukuyama, *The End of History and the Last Man* (London, 1992), pp.242–3.
6. Michael Doyle, 'Liberalism and world politics', *American Political Science Review*, lxxx/4 (1986), pp.1151–69.
7. Edward Hallett Carr, *Nationalism and After* (London, 1945), Part I.
8. Ibid., p.42.
9. Ibid., p.43.
10. Ibid., p.49.
11. Ibid., p.67.
12. Functionalism and neo-functionalism and especially the work of Karl Deutsch are important exceptions to the general neglect of this area.
13. Benjamin Nelson, 'Civilisational complexes and intercivilisational relations', *Sociological Analysis*, vol. 68 (1973), pp.79–105 and 'Note on the notion of civilisation by Emile Durkheim and Marcel Mauss', *Social Research*, xxxviii/4 (1971), pp.808–13.
14. Norbert Elias, *State Formation and Civilisation* (Oxford, 1982) and Andrew Linklater, 'Community, citizenship and global community', *Oxford International Review*, v/1 (1993), pp.4–7.
15. Charles Tilly, *Coercion, Capital, and European States, AD 990–1992* (Oxford, 1992), p.70, points out that the Prussian monarchy's main tax-collection agency began life as the Prussian War Commissariat.
16. Anthony Giddens, *The Nation-State and Violence* (Cambridge, 1985); Michael Mann, *The Sources of Social Power*, i: *A History of Power from the Beginning to AD 1760* (Cambridge, 1986); and Tilly, *Coercion*.
17. Andrew Linklater, *Men and Citizens in the Theory of International Relations* (London, 1990), pp.207–26.
18. Tom Bottomore and Patrick Goode (eds), *Austro-Marxism* (Oxford,

19 Tilly, *Coercion*, pp.123 ff.
20 Ibid., p.67.
21 John Mueller, *Retreat from Doomsday: The Obsolescence of Major War* (New York, 1989).
22 Richard Rosecrance, *The Rise of the Trading State: Commerce and Conquest in the Modern World* (New York, 1986).
23 John Mearsheimer, 'Back to the future: instability in Europe after the cold war', *International Security*, xv/3 (1990), pp.5–56.
24 Tilly, *Coercion*, p.52.
25 Christopher Chase-Dunn, 'Interstate system and capitalist world-economy: one logic or two?', *International Studies Quarterly*, xxv/1 (1981), pp.19–42.
26 Bull and Watson, *Expansion*, p.435.
27 Sheldon Wolin, *Politics and Vision: Continuity and Innovation in Western Political Thought* (London, 1961), p.434.
28 I refer to arguments that Marxism failed to predict the end of the internationalism of the working class in 1914, to recognize that building socialism in one country would mean accepting the constraints inherent in the nation-state system, to predict the rise of nationalism within the socialist bloc and to foresee war between socialist states, for example in South-east Asia. For further discussion, see Linklater, *Beyond Realism and Marxism: Critical Theory and International Relations* (London, 1990).
29 Wolin: *Politics and Vision*, p.427.
30 David Held, 'Democracy, the nation-state and the global system', in D. Held (ed.), *Political Theory Today* (Oxford, 1991), and 'Democracy: from city-states to a cosmopolitan order?', in D. Held (ed.), *Prospects for Democracy: North, South, East, West* (Cambridge, 1993).
31 Chris Brown, 'The modern requirement? Reflections on normative theory in a post-European world', *Millennium*, xvii/2 (1988), pp.339–48.
32 Tzvetan Todorov, *The Conquest of America* (London, 1984).
33 Bull and Watson, *Expansion*.
34 Brown, 'Modern requirement?'.
35 Adam Roberts, 'Humanitarian war: military intervention and human rights', *International Affairs*, lxix/3 (1993), pp.429–49.
36 Mark Hoffman, 'Agency, identity and intervention', in I. Forbes and M. Hoffman (eds), *Political Theory, International Relations and the Ethics of Intervention* (London, 1992).
37 F. Wallbank, *The Hellenistic World* (Glasgow, 1981).
38 Michael Mann, *The Sources of Social Power*, ii: *The Rise of Classes and Nation-States, 1760–1914* (Cambridge, 1993), pp.250–1, 354.
39 Thomas Humphrey Marshall, *Citizenship and Social Class* (Cambridge, 1950).
40 Linklater, 'Community, citizenship and global politics'.
41 Will Kymlicka, *Liberalism, Community and Culture* (Oxford, 1989).

11. THE FIN DE SIÈCLE

Charles Townshend

'The *Nineteenth Century!* It seems an inexhaustible theme, and so it really is', as Houston Stewart Chamberlain gushed at the start of his bore into *The Foundations of the Nineteenth Century*, first published in German in 1899.[1] But he added, 'and yet it is only by including more that it becomes comprehensible and possible of achievement'. Chamberlain's subject was not really the nineteenth century, but the future of civilization, or rather of *Kultur* in the German *volkisch* sense. The substance of his two hefty volumes was the whole of Western history from ancient Greece to the year 1800: 'the bases upon which the nineteenth century rests', the aim being to locate 'the turning-point of the history of Europe: The awakening of the Teutonic peoples to the consciousness of their all-important vocation as the founders of a completely new civilization and culture.'

We might well think that one of the ways in which centuries end is with the publications of such large ruminations on human destiny: Fukuyama's *End of History* and Paul Kennedy's *Preparing for the Twenty-first Century* are surely but the vanguard of the great cohort we may expect in the next quinquennium. (Of course, size does not matter as far as 'largeness' is concerned: the fact that Kennedy's is smaller than Chamberlain's reflects a shift in publishing assumptions which marks this century.) Timing is more important. It was definitely odd of Kenneth Boulding to write a book called *The Meaning of the Twentieth*

Century in 1964. But his title, if not his argument, reinforced a basic aspect of modern perception. We think in centuries; we expect them to bear a meaning. Because we fashion them into entities, we now approach the end of a century equipped with a special label which can be pinned to a bewildering variety of cultural and political manifestations. The signs have gone up: we are entering the *fin de siècle*. (Indeed, Britain has even set up Millennium Commission to find out how people think it should be marked.)[2] It was not always thus.

'**Fin de siècle.** 1890 [Fr.] ... : characteristic of the end of the (nineteenth) century; advanced, modern; also, decadent.' As always, the *OED* tells us much – first and foremost, that there has been only one *fin de siècle* so far. (Though it seems to be a few years adrift on its start: the play of this title by Jouvenot and Micard was first performed in Paris on 17 April 1888; and the *Trésor de la langue française* has Zola using the phrase a couple of years before that.) And it does not concern itself with the tricky debate about *when* centuries actually end, which which would provide an instructive contrast between accuracy (31 December 1900) and instinct (31 December 1899), the latter surely dominant. Many, indeed all, centuries had come to an end before then, but – with the exception perhaps of the tenth – the event had not been seen as bearing any unique significance. Millennia possess a certain universal charm, but the nineteenth hundred of the Christian era did not on the face of it contain a special magic. Its selfconsciousness was, one might say, revolutionary. The century as a secular unit is a distinctly modern vessel of awareness; it is the fourth meaning assigned to the word by the *OED*. Until 1598 century had only two meanings in English: the half-maniple of the Roman army, and the 193 voting divisions of the Roman *Comita centuriata*. It then began to be used as a collective noun with no specific content, finally acquiring its special relationship with time in 1626. At the end of the eighteenth century the secular ladder was almost kicked away; 22 September 1792 became (retrospectively, in the French revolutionary calendar introduced in October 1793) the first day of Year I. The new calendar barely outlasted the old eighteenth *centur*, but even if it had not fallen victim to Napoleon's reconciliation with the Pope, the next century would most likely have basked in the new light of metrication. Only it would have been a slightly different set of years, which may remind us that the tension between scholarship and instinct has given the century a fair amount of elasticity. The attempt to supply some real content for the aesthetic container has produced long and short centuries, as well as skidding centuries, of which the nineteenth (1815–1914) is indeed a prime example.

Despite the sober return to the Gregorian numeration, the nineteenth century retained a whiff of the secular-millennarian energy of the revolutionary calendar. One of the most remarkable discoveries of the revolutionary generation was the *Zeitgeist*, a potent formulation of the way in which great historical processes manifest themselves in the apparent insignificance of everyday life. Romantic sensitivity to the inner values of societies, the historical and cultural relativism propounded by Herder[3] which revolutionized the academic discipline of historical research, fuelled this alertness to the grammar of change. The unprecedented scale and pace of change was what impressed the nineteenth century with its uniqueness, and lapses of decades rather than centuries or millennia began to be felt as substantial. The decade (born in 1594, according to the *OED*) was a principal beneficiary of the French Revolution, whose calendar had set the ten-day *decadi* in place of the seven-day week. From the starving forties to the naughty nineties, the decade was set on a career which has given it for us not merely descriptive but even prescriptive power. Indeed the 1890s, when even the English (according to Holbrook Jackson) awoke to the idea of the *Zeitgeist*, was the most self-conscious decade so far.[4]

Insofar as we are all poststructural wordplayers now, we will not miss the connection between decades and decadence. The dictionary tells us that the *fin de siècle* was advanced, modern, decadent. On top of all this, of course, it was French. The concurrent sense of progress and decadence was central to it, as it is to the angst of modernity in general. The dizzying range of attitudes to the approaching end of the century is hardly narrowed by confining our attention to a single country, or even a single city, as Eugen Weber's study of France and Carl Schorske's of Vienna demonstrate. 'The words were everywhere; they could be applied to anything and everything: "Fin de siècle! partout, partout/ ... il sert a designer tout".'[5] It did not imply a sense of crisis, though such a sense was widespread – there was even, indeed, a 'crisis in the Church' in England. All that seems clear is that the negative implications of the phrase soon overwhelmed the positive. Through the decade the popular philosopher Max Nordau persistently invoked the 'traditional belief in the evil destiny of the closure of centuries'. To him;

> *fin de siècle* is at once a confession and a complaint ... In

our days there have arisen in more highly developed minds vague qualms of the Dusk of Nations, in which all suns and all stars are gradually waning, and mankind with all its institutions and creations is perishing in the midst of a dying world.[6]

For France, the emblematic figure of the *fin de siècle* was preeminently the Duc des Esseintes, antihero of Joris-Karl Huysmans's masterpiece *A rebours* (1884), trying 'desperately to escape from the penitentiary of this century'.

In large measure, Huysmans's taste still governs our sense of what was going on: the *fin-de-siècle* painters *par excellence* are Gustave Moreau and Odilon Redon, not that baffled anarchist Camille Pissaro or Paul Gauguin (nor, though he might fit better, Gustav Klimt).[7] Pissaro and the Impressionists are nineteenth-century artists, notwithstanding that Monet was in the midst of his series paintings at the turn of the century, and did not complete the water lilies until 1923.[8] Gauguin and the Post-Impressionists belong to the twentieth century, though Gauguin died in 1903 and his *Whence come we? Where are we? Whither go we?* of 1897 could, one might think, scarcely be bettered as a symbol of the *fin de siècle*. The aesthetic mood of the international 'decadence', set by Huysmans, was deepened by the works of Walter Pater in England, Oscar Wilde's Huysmanesque *The Picture of Dorian Gray* (1891) and the brilliant though short-lived journal *The Yellow Book*.

And the *fin de siècle* seems overwhelmingly literary and visual, because music played little part in the private world created by des Esseintes: there is nothing in it like Proust's fascination with 'Vinteuil'.[9] Des Esseintes would no doubt not have liked (as Proust later did) the intrusion of a live string quartet into his hermitage, preferring to sidestep reality with his 'mouth organ' through which he could taste musical instruments in the form of alcoholic liquors. Would it have been different if the phonograph had been available? The privacy and power of a quadrophonic hi-fi would surely have suited him exactly, and he would have luxuriated in *Parsifal* at full volume. But can we imagine des Esseintes with a television? Would the attraction of its artificiality have been swamped by the horror of its popularity? Much of the inner contradiction of the *fin-de-siècle* mood (*Zeitstimmung*) is almost tangibly contained in Huysmans's untranslatable title: against the nap, against nature, a deliberate assault on normality. Symbolist pictures convey this unease in ways that are hard to pin down. How do we know, for example, that Lucien Levy-Dhurmer's breathtaking pastel *The Creek* (c.1898), coruscating with light-on-water effects as it is, is a Symbolist and not an Impressionist work? Because the light is in the wrong place, just outside the picture?

All this is merely to say that *fin de siècle* is an attitude of mind, not a chronological moment. We cannot read it off – elegant though this would be – from even so selfconscious an event as the Paris Exhibition of 1900. If we accept that we cannot fix the *fin-de-siècle* mood in any straightforward way, we can see that it involved two distinct processes – taking stock of the past, and facing (or flying from) the future. They are connected, certainly: attempts to project the shape of the future must arise out of a grasp of the past. Some versions of the past determine the future, as nineteenth-century racial studies pessimistically did. But retrospection can be done without projection, and feels safer that way. Balance-sheets for the century were popular, and none was more impressive than that compiled by the great evolutionist Alfred Russel Wallace under the upbeat title *The Wonderful Century* (1898). With the assurance of the mid-century generation Wallace drew up a list of first-rank inventions or scientific applications: those 'which are perfectly new departures, and which have also so rapidly developed as to have profoundly affected many of our habits, and even our thoughts and our language'. He found thirteen in his own century, as against no more than five in all of preceding time. An almost equally drastic acceleration was evident in the realm of theory: twelve great discoveries in the nineteenth century, eight in all previous history. Though Wallace recognized that 'numbers are not absolute', the contrast was plainly awe-inspiring. The century had produced wonders, and opened up limitless possibilities; but it also had its failings. Wallace's estimate of these may surprise us. His fierce denunciation of the 'reckless destruction of the stored-up products of nature' caused by the pursuit of profit will strike a greenish contemporary chord, but this nine-page ecological diatribe was dwarfed by his laments over the opposition to hypnotism and the neglect of phrenology, and his tirade against vaccination, this last running to no fewer than a hundred blistering pages.[10]

Prediction was more chancy.[11] W. E. Gladstone confessed with humility (or maybe complacency, but surely without anxiety): 'The future is to me a blank.' Systematic analysis of trends in either politics or business (through opinion polling or market research) was in its infancy, and futurology was still a species of prophecy belonging to imaginative literature. Its most prolific exemplar, Jules Verne, was on his 37th book at the end of the century. Edward Bellamy's millennial bestseller *Looking Backward 2000–1887* had come out in 1888; its vision of a universally socialized state was still resonating.[12] The most impressive seer of the *fin de siècle*, however, was H. G. Wells, whose astonishing sequence of novels in the late 1890s – *The Time Machine*, *The War of the Worlds* and *When the Sleeper Wakes* – was capped by a shot at full-scale real-world prediction in *Anticipations of the Reaction of Mechanical and Scientific Progress upon Human Life and Thought* (1902). Systematizing much of the vision imaginatively presented in *When the Sleeper Wakes*, this is a humbling book, demonstrating both the power of insight and the timebound limits of foresight. Try this for size:

> I imagine that the German Empire – that is, the organized expression of German aggression today – will be either shattered or weakened to the pitch of great compromise by a series of wars; it will be forced to develop the autonomy of its rational middle class in the struggles that will render these compromises possible, and it will finally not be Imperial German ideas but central European ideas possibly more akin to Swiss conceptions, a civilised republicanism finding its clearest expression in the French language, that will be established upon a bilingual basis throughout Western Europe, and increasingly predominant over the whole European mainland and the Mediterranean basin, as the twentieth century closes.[13]

Not bad – up to a point. Wells's approach derives its persuasiveness from its ostensibly technical logic, but it shows that technological prediction is hardly more secure than the projection of attitudes. Wells got the process of economic unification around a Rhenish core right, and he spotted the long-term significance of the Spanish language, and Japanese power. He was at his most inspired on the subject of transportation, which the nineteenth century had revealed more clearly than ever before to be the keystone of the social fabric. Dismissing railways as a messy compromise, he conjured up visions of dual-carriageway *Autobahnen* to warm the heart of our own Department of Transport: 'Through the varied country the new wide roads will run, here cutting through a crest and there running like some colossal aqueduct across a valley, swarming always with a multitudinous traffic of bright, swift (and not necessarily ugly) mechanisms.'[14] Alongside this, however, he rashly projected a starring role for that most brilliant of all *fin-de-siècle* vehicles, the bicycle. To him (as to all sane people no doubt) it was plain that the velocipede, which had taken the bourgeoisie by storm in the early 1890s and was just becoming available to the workers, offered a miraculous prospect of pollution-free, zero-energy speed and liberation. In France, above all, the mania for *cyclisme* accelerated exhilaratingly in the decade before the first Tour de France in 1903.[15] It offered not only independence and excitement, but also an antidote to the neurotic enervation of decadence: as Zola strenuously put it in *Paris* (1898),[16] cycling – in cities especially – was 'a continuous apprenticeship of the will, an admirable lesson in steering and defence'. Unfortunately this last quality was to remain all too evident: even in France, no coherent provision for mass riding was made. The merest sight of the first real automobiles was to transform humanity, like Toad, into devotees of power and speed.[17] Only the serendipitous creation of the mountain bike by Marin County hippies in the 1970s was to rescue the bicycle from dull relegation to the margins of transport history and revive something of the original *fin-de-siècle* vision.

The nineteenth century was perhaps too businesslike to grasp the pivotal role of serendipity (here, however, we really need a new word to express the distance we have come from Horace Walpole's enlightenment optimism) in the process of technical development. When Wells contemplated the future of war, he extrapolated from the notions that were already dominant in German military science. He foresaw 'total war': non-combatants would no longer exist; 'the State will be organized as a whole to fight as a whole'. He grasped instinctually the possibility of air power, and envisioned the armies of a 1950 war burrowing into two-man foxholes for shelter – as if in Korea, but they are attacked by dirigible balloons, not jet fighters. He thought that twentieth-century sea wars would be won and lost in a week, and saw no role for 'the slow fumbling treacheries of the submarine'.[18]

Wells predicted great wars but he also believed in the inevitability of internationalism: only a world government could ultimately save the world. With a confidence which is now disconcerting, Wells cast his social vision around the inevitable divergence between the elite – the New Republic which would sweep away national sovereignty and sexual repression alike – and 'the People of the Abyss'. What could be more chilling than the question he put in the mouth of the latter: 'What will you do with us, we hundreds of millions, who cannot keep pace with you?' He saw that everything would depend on the answer, but he did not provide it. He was merely sure that it would not lie in liberalism or democracy. 'Liberalism is a thing of the past, it is no longer a doctrine, but a faction'; 'some newborn thing' must appear – but what? The New Republic provides oddly few clues, beyond a moral code which embraces a kind of critical pantheism and eugenic determination. Only full, beautiful and efficient life will count as life.

> For a multitude of contemptible and silly creatures, fear-driven and helpless and useless, unhappy or hatefully happy in the midst of squalid dishonour, feeble, ugly, inefficient, born of unrestrained lusts and multiplying through sheer incontinence and stupidity, the men of the new Republic will have little pity and less benevolence. ...
> They will hold that a certain portion of the population – the small minority, for example, afflicted with indisputably transmissible diseases, with such hideous incurable habits of mind as the craving for intoxication – exists only on sufferance, out of pity and patience, and on the understanding that they do not propagate; and I do not foresee any reason to suppose that they will hesitate to kill when that sufferance is abused.[19]

The gender of these grim philosopher-republicans will strike the present-day reader as significant, and we must note in passing that as regards the social role of women the vision of the seer – though free of the pervasive misogyny of so many of his contemporaries – was restricted in a way surprising in the age of the Woman Question, and especially for the future author of *Anne Veronica*.[20] Wells did not reach a satisfactory synthesis of the clash between the eugenic and liberal versions of women's destiny which was to mark the next generation.[21]

Wells's ultimate vision was positive, piercing through to 'that still ampler future of which the coming hundred years is but the opening phase'. But his fellow intellectuals were more often of a different outlook. Huysmans wrote, 'Society disgusts me ... The ruling classes are repulsive, the ruled infuriate me.' At the end of *A rebours*, Des Esseintes exclaims, 'Crumble, society! Die, old world!' ('croule donc, société! meurs donc, vieux monde!'). The sense of decay was pervasive, if not always as violently expressed as it was by Derain to Vlaminck: 'the degeneration of the race oozes out of our every pore ... We are the mushrooms of ancient dunghills.' It has been suggested that the verb-noun shift of 'degenerate' was a signpost of the *fin de siècle*, and it would be convenient if such mechanical markers could be routinely found: we should know what to look out for.[22] But in any case there is no mistaking the apprehensions of those who, unlike Wells, could not even believe in the survival of the best. This was not only the wilder fringes of racial pessimists in the Gobineau mould. The notion of nervous disease – from which des Esseintes was a spectacular sufferer – was widely regarded as the *maladie du siècle*, definitively diagnosed in Dr Maurice de Fleury's *The Major Symptoms of Neurasthenia* (1901) and frequently invoked in the criminal courts.[23] Freud's therapy was not yet available: *The Interpretation of Dreams* was published at the end of 1899, though his publisher dated it 1900, and the first 600 copies took eight years to sell. But much of the movement towards organized sport (of which the first Olympic Games was a vital symbol) was conceived as therapeutic.[24]

One of the indicative essays with which that estimable journal *Nineteenth Century* approached its end (in August 1899) posed the arresting question 'Why are our brains deteriorating?' The answer offered was (like all good answers) in three parts. First, the stupendous – and stupefying – increase in the volume of knowledge since the age of Euclid, when 'an intelligent lad could master all that was known of mathematics by the age of eighteen or nineteen'.[25] Prolonged apprenticeships would reduce the capacity for original thought, and 'produce a feminine rather than a masculine kind of intellect'; true originality would be confined to 'a very few exceptional men' whose 'number must tend steadily to decrease'. The second problem was 'the mental impatience of the age', the result of 'nerve strain, ... worry and overpressure in modern life', reducing the capacity for sustained attention. The new mass circulation press, a crucial growth industry of the *fin de siècle* (and, as Holbrook Jackson noted, the decisive victor in an ominous kind of cultural showdown between 'Yellow Book and Yellow Press'),[26] fostered this 'degeneracy' – 'The root idea of all these journals appears to be that the mind of the reader must not be occupied and his attention strained over any subject for more than a minute, or at the outside a minute and a quarter.' Finally, the 'levelling and democratic spirit of the age' was tending to eradicate individuality, and with it independence of thought. 'The stream of human knowledge is growing broader and broader no doubt, but at the same time it tends to run shallower.' In the light (or gloom) of such a systematic indictment of the inescapable process of decline, only one escape route remained: 'Great wars may come upon us like a refiner's fire, and set up worthier national ideals ... in place of the mammon-worship, the luxury, sloth and selfish ease which now prevail among us.'[27]

Peace had become a problem. Pacification was crucial to the ordered calm of bourgeois society. In Britain the 'conquest of violence' had happened suddenly around the mid-century, for reasons which were slightly obscure, but evidently part of the general progress of civilization. Once it had come about, it was vital that this pacification should be complete, and permanent. Any rupture would now seem far more dangerous than a century earlier, since it imperilled the whole logic of progress. Hence the century ended with a good deal of earnest heart-searching about the finality or inevitability of peace. On the domestic front, there was real alarm here about the incidence of crime, above all 'hooliganism' – a label which appeared in 1898[28] – a product of urban blight and insubordination. ('The tendencies of modern life incline more and more to ignore, or disparage social distinctions, which formerly did much to encourage respect for others and habits of obedience and discipline', as a Brighton magistrate put it in 1898.) That great *fin-de-siècle* creation, the Football League, founded in 1888, quickly generated the fears of violent disorder expressed in Ernest Ensor's article entitled 'The Football Madness' (1898).[29] How serious a problem was youth crime? Insofar as it was, like degeneration, a product of long-term structural processes, it was very serious. At the same time, it was by the same token ultimately amenable to social engineering. The state had the capacity to perform such engineering; all that was required was correct diagnosis and the will to act. External war was, however, by its nature outside the state's power. If it was to be eliminated, it could only be either by the agency of a world state, or by the force of general progress.

Since the former remained a vanishingly distant prospect, much depended on the latter. The kind of optimism required was well displayed in Alexander Sutherland's short article on 'The natural decline of warfare' (1899). He argued that history 'beyond a doubt' supported the 'happier conclusion' (as against 'those who drearily believe that war is an incurable evil'), by evidencing the gradual development of 'human sympathy' and sapping of the military spirit. He achieved this result by identifying the core of this military spirit in the centrality of fighting to life in the seventh century, and the absence at that period of any controls on slaughter and brutality. Starting from this low point (which, one must note, rather ignored the ups or downs of civilization over the preceding millennium) he was able to demonstrate measurable improvements, for instance in the treatment of women and children: whereas in the seventh century it was a favourite and common sport to throw infants up in the air and catch them on the point of a spear as they fell, by the eleventh century it had 'ceased to be consistent with the spirit of the times that women and children should be slain'. Men had definitely 'moved on from the stage in which they quaff wine from enemies' skulls'. (One must wonder whether Sutherland would have seen as an equivalent sign of progress – if he knew of it – the fact that Lord Kitchener had, after the battle of Omdurman the previous September, had the skull of the Mahdi dug up for his use as an inkstand.) The most dramatic shift had occurred by the sixteenth century: the old lust of killing had gone, non-combatants were molested as little as possible, even prisoners taken in arms were now spared, and 'men make war with grave and sad regret; it is not the aim and object of life, but a sad necessity reluctantly complied with.' By the end of the nineteenth century there was (in the developed world) 'absolute peace' internally, while externally 'the total amount of warfare is immensely diminished': while the scale of warfare had become vast, its incidence and duration had both reduced.[30]

Plainly there are unsatisfactory aspects to this argument and the many others like it. The linkage of the military spirit to war, physical violence and brutality was too simple, and militarism was coming to be seen by many of its critics as a distinctly political phenomenon (indeed Alfred Vagts, in his famous study, argued that in the later nineteenth century militarism became fatefully decoupled from war). Among his assessments of the failures of *The Wonderful Century*, Wallace linked war together with penal policy under the title 'Militarism – the Curse of Civilization'. His principal target was the waste of resources poured into military establishments, and his evidence for an increase in the war spirit in the latter part of the century was the 'inordinate increase in armaments' and their greater deadliness. His unease was in part aesthetic: in a judgement which would have been despised by des Esseintes (who thought steam locomotives more dazzlingly beautiful than any product of nature), he lamented the fact that armoured steam warships bore no resemblance at all to 'the majestic three-deckers and beautiful frigates with which all our great naval victories were gained'.

On the other hand, the fact that modern guns, by contrast, were 'elaborate pieces of machinery finished with the greatest perfection and beauty', brought no comfort: 'it makes any thoughtful person sad to see such skill and so much of the results of modern science, devoted to purposes of pure destruction.'

The one bright spot detected by Wallace in all this, earlier in the century, had been the abolition of duelling. (The *Saturday Review* had observed in 1858 that 'Duelling belongs to a coarse and barbarous state of society', or is symptomatic of 'a deep social disorder'.) But the survival of the *Mensur* in Germany alerted some observers to the fragility of pacification. In 1900 Jerome K. Jerome took a bicycle tour through Germany to write his follow-up to *Three Men in a Boat*. *Three Men on the Bummel* never achieved the same celebrity, but it produced a set-piece which might project a tremor into the new century. Jerome stressed the contrast between the German belief that the duel was a school of coolness and courage, and the reality of the event: 'no movement, no skill, no grace', 'the whole interest is centred in watching the wounds'. He spared his readers no ghastly detail of the bloodbath, but his primary purpose was to chart his own reactions. He believed himself to be 'not of an unusually bloodthirsty disposition', and had been anxious about whether he would be able to go through with the experience; 'as the blood began to flow, and nerves and muscles to be laid bare, I experienced a mingling of disgust and pity', but 'by the time the third duel was well upon its way, and the room heavy with the curious hot odour of blood ... I wanted more'.[31] His conclusion, that 'beneath our starched shirts there lurks the savage, with all his savage instincts untouched', banal enough perhaps, makes a suitable epitaph to the nineteenth century and leitmotif for the twentieth, whose central lesson has been the banality of evil. Terrorism, total war, genocide: the lineaments of a century's agenda were indeed in place.

It is worth recalling that Huysmans (usually described as 'a minor civil servant') was deputy head of the branch of the Sureté which was responsible for surveillance of anarchist and subversive activities. The destructive ferocity of des Esseintes, for instance where he concocts a plan to turn a downtrodden apprentice into a violent criminal, taps straight into a deadly stratum of *fin-de-siècle* fashion. The nineteenth century ended with a spate of terrorism, indeed one might say with the invention of modern terrorism. No political philosophy could have been more *a rebours* to this improving century than nihilism, and no action more subversive of liberal political culture than indiscriminate violence. Among the most poignant moments of the *fin de siècle* may be the coverage of the trial of the French terrorist Ravachol by Theodor Herzl, Viennese journalist and founder of Zionism (who would publish *The Jewish State* three years later, in 1896). Herzl perceived that the terrorist had 'discovered a new voluptuousness: the voluptuousness of the great idea and martyrdom'; at the same time, he saw the jury's failure to recommend the death penalty as signalling the crisis of liberal democracy. Popular sovereignty had lost its courage, and society was 'ripe for a saviour once more'.[32]

A few months after Sutherland's essay, Britain went into the second Boer war, and the century went out (on the popular measurement) in the gloom of 'Black Week'. The gloom enveloped not only gung-ho patriots but also the opponents of the war (viciously branded 'pro-Boers'). Beatrice Webb mused on 31 January 1900:

> The last six months have been darkened by the nightmare of war. The horrible consciousness that we have, as a nation, shown ourselves to be unscrupulous in methods, vulgar in manners as well as inefficient, is an unpleasant background to one's personal life ... I sometimes wonder whether we could take a beating and be better for it? This would be the real test of the heart and intellect of the British race: much more so than if we succeed after a long and costly conflict. If we win, we shall soon forget the lessons of the war. Once again we shall have "muddled through" ... Once again the English gentleman, with his so-called habit of command, will have proved to be the equal of the foreign expert with his scientific knowledge.[33]

Certainly the English gent shortly proved capable of devising the concentration camp, thereby laying a foundation on which foreign experts could later build.

The gloom of the unlooked-for stumble of the 'weary titan' fed the larger fear of race degeneration.[34] The very signs which Sutherland and his like would read as indications of progress – above all 'the growth of human sympathy' – would be read by others as symptoms of a fatal decay of race energy. The onset of the mass age triggered pessimistic visions ranging from Gustave Le Bon's semi-scholarly study of crowd psychology (1895) or James Ensor's nightmarish 'Entry of Christ into

Brussels' (*L'Entrée du Christ à Bruxelles*, 1888), to the sweeping declinism of Brooks Adams (*The Law of Civilization and Decay*, 1896) and Oswald Spengler.[35] But while we can find in the *fin de siècle* the philosophy of anti-Semitism (if that is what Chamberlain's work is), a missing feature is the possibility of the Holocaust, the defining event of the twentieth century. Jerome hardly glimpsed this abyss in his revulsion from the bloodlust of the *Mensur* (other observers saw it as a means of containing rather than creating violence). Wallace, once again, was unusual in singling out as 'the crowning proof of the utter rottenness of the boasted civilization of the Nineteenth Century' the Armenian massacres of the mid-1890s. And for all the bleakness of his judgment, the source of barbarity still lay outside Europe (just); the European crime was one of omission, not commission: 'a hundred thousand Armenians murdered or starved to death while the representatives of the great powers coldly looked on – and prided themselves on their unanimity in all making the same useless protests'.[36] The English at any rate did not even have a word for it until 1944, and would have to wait until the next *fin de siècle* for 'ethnic cleansing'.

Chronologically, at least, we are in a position to survey, Wallace-like, the achievements and failures of 'our' century. Psychologically, can we face them? The simple project of a balance sheet now seems intolerably positivistic; but it is surely not just our sense of its naivety which inhibits us from plugging away with a list of great discoveries: insulin, penicillin, DNA, nuclear fission ... (or even of life-easing little ones like Velcro or the Post-it note).[37] It is the realization that the successes and failures of our epoch are no longer cause for a pat on the back or a rap over the knuckles – not even the sharpish sort of rap delivered by Wallace. (One of our easier admissions would be that we have persisted in neglecting both mesmerism and phrenology, while indulging ever more freely in vaccination.) As a recent newspaper editorial put it, 'the most benign innovations of one decade – pesticides, for instance, or the chlorofluorocarbons used in refrigeration and air-conditioning – become the nightmares of the next.'[38] The nature of our enterprises has engineered an incipiently catastrophic future: the only chance of avoiding it lies in accurate prediction. If retrospection is no longer comfortable, prophecy is no longer a luxury to be left to imaginative literature.

Does this mean we are better at it than Wells was? Clearly we need to be. He was most wrong about the life-prospects of liberalism. The 'collapse of communism', a process which has transformed both the mental and the economic framework of the *fin de siècle*, may have been hard to predict, as are its implications. But even those who are unimpressed by Fukuyama's Hegelian design must admit that the resilience of liberalism has been remarkable. It was never more impressive, perhaps, than under the pressure of two total wars, and such heroic passages seemed to vindicate the liberal dogma that pluralism and openness were strengths, not weaknesses.[39] But tolerance has proved less happy in adjusting to – say – the resilience of terrorism, and if we add to this renewed ethnic and religious intolerances, we are bound to wonder whether the old belief was ever right.[40] A great deal hinges on this. When Kenneth Boulding told us *The Meaning of the Twentieth Century* in the mid-1960s, he was still able to deploy a strong version of liberal modernization theory, holding that 'the rise of modern science is quite closely associated with the development of democratic and pluralistic institutions'. This was important because the programme for the century, in his view, was to carry through the 'great transition' from civilization to post-civilization, a situation characterized by 'a continuous process of scientific and technological development'. The signals of this transition were such things as the closeness of the date dividing history into two equal parts (in the field of publications in chemistry, for example, he noted that the watershed was then about 1950), or the fact that 'something like 90 per cent of all the scientists who have ever lived are now alive'. The importance of scientific development lay, of course, not in this dizzying acceleration itself, nor even in specific technical achievements however useful, but in the unique capacity of science to generate better – i.e. more realistic – images of the world. In a crucial sense, therefore, the primary function of science was political. Only if people accept realistic images of the world is there a chance of escaping from the influence of rhetoric, enthusiasm and sectarianism (as Boulding noted, the skills of the debater are totally irrelevant to the solution of real problems, yet they remain at the heart of politics).

This 'great transition' was threatened by great 'traps', pre-eminently the war trap, the entropy trap and the population trap. Contemplating these, especially the last, Boulding's guarded optimism took on a tightrope-walking quality. Only if the momentum of science was maintained could the steady 'learning of realistic images for the future of mankind' provide a possibility of overcoming lethal traditions. Thus a greater weight rests on education than used to be the case: it is not just a question of bringing mass democracy up to the aesthetic standards of the old elites, but a matter of making a future possible. The undoubted failure of the education project even in the most developed societies baffles us into silence. (How do we deal with the fact that 40 per cent of British people still think the sun goes round the earth? Answer: we ignore it.) Nor do we know if there is any way of dealing with the fact that the transition project, conceived as a whole, has stalled if not failed. Even optimists must feel that emancipation (whether sexual or racial) has not gone as far as it should. The end of imperialism, or at any rate colonialism – one of the most cheering and apparently decisive steps of the 1960s – has been virtually negated by the persistence of backwardness. Wells's 'People of the Abyss' are much in evidence but there is little sign of any of his remedies. The ruthless exploitation of natural resources condemned by Wallace has engendered a catastrophic trend which outstrips moral outrage; yet we have no other means of responding to the fate of the Amazon rainforest. One blow too many in the fight against nature has revealed the shocking vulnerability of the old enemy: a hole in the ozone layer makes a new enemy of the giver of life itself, the sun. Where turn-of-the-century explorers pitted their frail bodies and boats against the terrifying might of the Antarctic, children of the 1990s have worrisome wall displays of the 'fragile wilderness' loaded with ever-lengthening lists of endangered species.

We go into our *fin de siècle* with plenty of the *fin-de-siècle* anxieties still in place; but the exciting side of angst seems to have been lost on the way. Racism abounds, but it does not carry the thrilling apocalyptic fears of degeneration and race suicide that raised the temperature of nineteenth-century *fin de siècle* alarms. We are still in the thrall of rhetoric – indeed no epoch was ever more so than the age of mass communication – and feel good by relying on euphemism or metaphor: international community, green shoots, fledgling democracy.[41] Paul Kennedy's *Preparing for the Twenty-first Century* is characteristic, in both tone and approach, of what we are up against. Through an account of trends in demography, communications, biotechnology, robotics and ecology, he piles up a crushing statement of the inadequacy or irrelevance of existing political arrangements – i.e. the system of sovereign states – to the handling of global problems. All this may not be novel in itself, though it is striking when it comes from so traditional a student of states. The basic 'falling out of gear' had, as he points out, been recognized by *The Economist* as long ago as 1930: on 'the economic plane', the world had become a 'single, all-embracing unit', but on the political 'it has not only remained partitioned into 60 or 70 sovereign national [sic] States, but the national units have been growing smaller and more numerous and national consciousness more acute'. It was the tension between these antithetical tendencies which produced 'a series of jolts and jars and smashes in the life of humanity'.

The resilience of sovereignty would have mystified Wells. At the moment all the signs are that the partitionist tendency identified by *The Economist* is enjoying a new surge of life, jars and smashes and all. The millennarians now are not like the amiable theosophists of the 1890s, but the kind who invoke a new flood which will destroy all peoples but the Serbs. Douglas Hurd was not whistling in the dark when he labelled the European integrationist idea 'old-fashioned'. It appears that the partitionists' most powerful weapon is public opinion, so that liberal democracy itself could be the staunchest enemy of internationalism, and the biggest obstacle to 'learning realistic images for the future'. The only apparent alternative to nationalism is not internationalism, but religion. Andrew Linklater puts it mildly when he writes that 'the modern political community doubts its capacity for international action'. It has not come far from that community which fretfully watched the Armenian massacres of 1896, its purely verbal responses succeeding only in provoking an Islamic reaction.[42] Doubt, of course, is a good liberal quality. Only fundamentalists are free of such doubts. Only they have what Wells said the New Republic would need: the faith to kill. Is the future still in doubt?

Notes

1. H. S. Chamberlain, *Die Grundlagen des XIX. Jahrhunderts* (1899), trans. as *The Foundations of the Nineteenth Century* (London, 1909), i, p.lxi.
2. Appropriately, perhaps, *The Independent* reported on 17 September 1994 that several of the commissioners were 'confused' about the nature of their task.
3. See Sqiah Berwin, 'The Counter Enlightenment', in *Against the Current* (London, 1979), pp.1–24.
4. H. Jackson, *The Eighteen Nineties: A Review of Art and Ideas at the Close of the Nineteenth Century* (London, 1913, repr. Harmondsworth, 1939), p.36.
5. E. Weber, *France: Fin de Siècle* (Cambridge, MA, 1986), p.9, quoting Paul Desachy and René Dubrenil, *Fin de siècle, monologue en vers dit par F. Galipaux du Palais Royal* (Paris, 1891); for Schorske, see note 32 below.
6. Max Nordau, *Degeneration* (London, 1895), p.2. Nordau's influence has proved perishable, though *The Times* in reviewing his *Conventional Lies of our Civilization* compared him (albeit ambivalently) with Rousseau.
7. Jennifer Birkett, *The Sins of the Fathers: Decadence in France 1870–1914* (London, 1986), pp.61–98.

THE FIN DE SIÈCLE   215

8   John Rewald's celebrated *History of Impressionism* (New York, 1946) ends in 1886, with a cursory survey of the rest of his central subjects' lives.
9   Holbrook Jackson's 'review of art and ideas' found even less of a place for music, disregarding the significance of, say, the completion of Mahler's Third Symphony in 1896.
10 A. R. Wallace, *The Wonderful Century: Its Successes and Failures* (London, 1898), pp.213–314.
11 See Charles H. Pearson, *National Life and Character: A Forecast* (London, 1893), pp.1–10.
12 On its multifarious impact see W. H. G. Armytage, *Yesterday's Tomorrows: A Historical Survey of Future Societies* (London, 1986), pp.76–8.
13 H. G. Wells, *Anticipation of the Reaction of Mechanical and Scientific Progress upon Human Life and Thought* (London, 1902), pp.258–9.
14 Ibid., p.62.
15 Weber, chap. 10, *passim*.
16 Quoted in Weber, *France*, p.195.
17 Richard Overy, 'Heralds of modernity: cars and planes from invention to necessity', in M. Teich and R. Porter (eds), *Fin de Siècle and its Legacy* (Cambridge, 1990), pp.54–79.
18 Wells, *Anticipations* pp.192–3, 199.
19 Ibid., pp.229–300.
20 On other attitudes to women, see B. Dijkstra, *Idols of Perversity: Fantasies of Feminine Evil in Fin-de-Siècle Culture* (New York, 1986).
21 Karen Offen, 'Depopulation, nationalism, and feminism in *fin-de-siècle* France', *American Historical Review*, lxxxix (1984), pp.648–75.
22 Alison Hennegan, 'Personalities and principles: aspects of literature and life in *fin-de-siècle* England', in Teich and Porter (eds), *Fin de Siècle* p.189.
23 Ruth Harris, *Murders and Madness: Medicine, Law and Society in the Fin de Siècle* (Oxford, 1989), p.143.
24 Robert A. Nye, 'Degeneration, neurasthenia and the culture of sport in *belle époque* France', *Journal of Contemporary History*, xvii (1982), pp.51–68.
25 H. Elsdale, 'Why are our brains deteriorating?', *Nineteenth Century*, xlvi (1899), p.263.
26 Jackson, *The Eighteen Nineties*, p.47.
27 Ibid., p.272.
28 J. Trevarthan, 'Hooliganism', *Nineteenth Century*. vol. xlviii (1901), p.84.
29 E. Ensor, 'The football madness', *Contemporary Review*, (1898); see also G. Pearson, *Hooligan: A History of Respectable Fears* (New York, 1984), p.65.
30 'In spite of all the ingenuity of our great weapons of destruction, the loss of life in Europe by war during the present century has not exceeded one per annum out of every ten thousand of the population.' Pearson, *Hooligan*, p.576.
31 Quoted in Peter Gay, *The Cultivation of Hatred* (New York, 1993),

pp.9–12.
32 Carl Schorske, *Fin-de-Siècle Vienna: Politics and Culture* (Cambridge, 1981), p.154.
33 Beatrice Webb's diary, quoted in Stephen Koss (ed.), *The Pro-Boers: The Anatomy of an Anti-war Movement* (Chicago, 1973), p.58. Cf. Wells's caustic remark that 'If the cycle is to be adapted to military requirements, the thing is entrusted to Lt. Col. Balfour. If horses are to be bought for the British Army in India, no specialist goes, but Lord Edward Cecil.' *Anticipations*, p.154.
34 R. Soloway, 'Counting the degenerates: the statistics of race degeneration in Edwardian England', *Journal of Contemporary History*, xvii (1982), pp.137–64.
35 K.-D. Bracher, *The Age of Ideologies* (London, 1985), p.1. For acute studies of Spengler, and valiant efforts to reverse the judgment of history on him, see Erich Heller, *The Disinherited Mind* (London, 1952, repr. Harmondsworth, 1961), pp.159–74; and H. Stuart Hughes, *Oswald Spengler: A Critical Estimate* (New York, 1952).
36 Wallace, *Wonderful Century*, pp.377–8.
37 Henry Petroski, *The Evolution of Useful Things* (New York, 1993).
38 'Be a devil and take a walk in the sun', *The Independent*, 13 July 1994, p.13.
39 The classic paean is Clinton L. Rossiter, *Constitutional Dictatorship: Crisis Government in Modern Democracies* (Princeton, NJ, 1948).
40 There is an original discussion in Susan Mendus, *Toleration and the Limits of Liberalism* (London, 1989).
41 Cf. Heinrich Vogel, 'Mantras in Western transformation-rhetoric', Woodrow Wilson Center Occasional Paper 21, 1992.
42 'The Armenian question ... started in England as a humanitarian protest against the massacre ... at Sassoon [Sasun]. As such it has the sympathies of the educated Moslems of India, and even of Turkey. By degrees, however, it assumed, in the hands of designing Christian ministers imbued with a secret hatred of Islam, and Forward Liberals inebriated with party fanaticism, an anti-Islamic character.' Rafiuddin Ahmad, 'A Moslem's View of the Pan-Islamic Revival', *Nineteenth Century*, xlii (1897), p.517.

Index

Acton, Lord, 23
Adams, Brook, 211
Adorno, Theodor, 95, 96
African National Congress (ANC), 143
agriculture: collectivization of, 43, 49;
  state support for, 118
Akashi, Yasushi, 66
Algeria, 143, 144, 163, 164, 166, 168
Alsace, 77, 141
Angell, Norman, 12
Anglo-Japanese Treaty (1911), 58, 59, 60
Angola, 144, 151, 152
anti-Semitism, 211
appeasement policy, 79
A rebours, 201, 205
Arab-Israeli conflict, 163, 169
Armageddon, 90, 91
Armenian massacres, 211, 214
Armstrong, Louis, 114
Aron, Raymond, 92
Ataturk, Mustafa Kemal, 168
atomic bomb, dropped on Japan, 63
Auschwitz, 95, 97
Austria, 76, 114, 141;
  textile industry, 77
Austro-Hungarian empire, 74, 75, 76, 77
automobiles, coming of, 204
aviation, development of, 28
Axis powers, 32, 33, 38, 61

Baltic Republics, 155
Bangladesh, 154, 172
Bank of England, 123, 128
Barnaby, Frank, 103
Barry, Brian, 5, 6
Bauer, Otto, 189
Beard, Charles, 21
Bellamy, Edward, 203
Berlin, Isaiah, 142

Berlin Wall, 87;
  building of, 83
Biafra, 154
bicycle, development of, 204, 209
Black Wednesday, 130, 131
Blair, Bruce, 104, 105, 106
Bloom, Allan, 9
Boer War, 210
Bolshevik party, 46, 145
Bosnia, 86, 155, 156, 171;
  Muslims in, 169
Boulding, Kenneth, 198, 212
Boxer Uprising, 58, 75
Bretton Woods system, 120;
  US withdrawal from, 85
Brezhnev, Leonid, 44, 49
Briand, Aristide, 78
Bulgaria, 76
bullet, conoidal, invention of, 98
Bundesbank, 127, 131
Bundy, McGeorge, 102, 104
Burma, 63
Buzan, Barry, 93

caliphate, 163;
  abolition of, 160;
  obligation to restore, 162
Callaghan, James, 114
Camp David Accords, 165, 170
Canada, 25, 26
Carr, E.H., 178, 180, 181, 183, 184, 189, 190
Carter, Jimmy, 85
centuries:
  skidding, 200;
  varying length of, 1, 199
Chaloupka, William, 92
Chamberlain, H.S., 198
Chiang Kai-shek, 146

China, 58, 60, 61, 62, 65, 66, 67, 72, 75, 76, 146;
  five races of, 147
Churchill, Winston, 24, 90, 123, 124
citizenship, 73, 192-6;
  dual, concept of, 193;
  national, 194;
  seen as indivisible, 194;
  transnational, 194;
  universalism of, 194
City of London, 128;
  as money market, 123
city-state, Greek, 193;
  decline of, 195, 196
civilianization of government, 186
Cobban, Alfred, 141
Cold War, 7, 21, 43, 51, 87, 92, 104, 106, 145, 148, 149, 155;
  end of, 2, 129, 153, 154, 171
collectivization, 43, 46, 49, 54
colonialism, 213;
  and nation-state, 160-4
command and control systems, centralization of, 105
Common Agricultural Policy (CAP), 118
communication networks, 188
communism, 6, 13, 21, 25, 43, 81, 119, 146, 147;
  crusade against, 37;
  demise of, 3, 54, 146, 152, 153, 154, 211
Communist Party of USSR, 47 (banned in Russia, 43)
community, 177-97;
  closed, 185;
  creation of, 178, 179;
  crisis of, 180;
  international, 182;
  moral, 182-5;
  non-fixed boundaries of, 183;
  political, 182-5;
  undermining of, 185-92
Congress of Berlin, 141
Conservative Party (UK), 116, 122, 127, 130
Coolidge, John Calvin, 123
cooperation, 177, 195, 196
corruption, 173
Council for Mutual Economic Assistance (CMEA), 83, 152
credit transactions, deregulation of, 131
crime, 174, 207;
  among youth, 207

critical theory, 94, 95, 96, 97, 99, 100, 104, 106;
  of technology, 97
Croatia, 156;
  recognition of, 155
cultural differences, 192
cultural theory, 93
currency, speculation in, 131
Czechoslovakia, 77, 80, 145

Darwinism, social, 73
decolonization, 142, 154
Delors, Jacques, 129
democracy, 5, 10, 15, 33, 34, 56, 106, 111, 141, 143, 180, 189, 205, 212, 214;
  and globalization, 190;
  and Islam, 164-8;
  and planning, 51-4 (incompatible with, 45);
  and role of state, 55;
  cosmopolitan, 190, 194;
  representative, 6;
  Soviet, 51
Denmark, 84, 130
deportation of peoples, 182
Deutschmark, 127, 129, 131
disarmament, 97, 118
distribution of wealth, 113, 116, 172
Divine, Robert, 33
dollar: devaluation of, 113, 126;
  floating, 126
dress codes for women, 163, 165
drug addiction, 174
duelling, abolition of, 209
Durkheim, Emile, 183
dynastic principle, 141

Eastern Europe, 2, 80, 83, 85, 86-7, 152
eclecticism, postmodern, 17
economic aspect, relation with political, 110, 181
economic growth, 113, 115, 151
economic interests, influence of, 30
economic policy, 180;
  nationalization of, 181
economic power, diffused, 187
economism, 110-36
education, 212, 213
Egypt, 163, 164, 165, 166, 167, 168, 170, 172
Einsteinian model, 94
Enlightenment, 17, 73, 95, 139, 142

INDEX

Ensor, Ernest, 207
Ensor, James, 210
environmental issues, 118
Eritrea, 145, 155, 156
ethnic cleansing, 211
ethnic conflict, 118, 142
ethnic ghettoes, 155
ethnic identity, 141, 145, 152, 154, 188, 193
ethnic minorities, 146, 164
Eurocentrism, 16
Europe, 66, 71–89, 113;
 exclusion of non-Europeans, 191;
 reconstruction of, 31;
 rivalry with US, 85;
 widening of, 83–5
European Coal and Steel Community (ECSC), 81, 82
European Community (EC), 84, 120;
 full monetary union of, 129
European Free Trade Association (EFTA), 84, 86
European Monetary Institute, 128
European Monetary System (EMS), 84, 85
European Union (EU), 11, 120, 121;
 questioned, 87
Exchange Rate Mechanism, 111, 117, 122, 127;
 and Britain, 126–30
exterminism, 103, 104

fascism, 118, 138, 142, 147, 167, 168
Feenberg, Andrew, 97, 99, 100
feminism, 93, 118
Fichte, J.G., 138
fin de siècle, concept of, 198–216
finance capital, 12
de Fleury, Maurice, 206
Formosa, 59
franc fort, 129, 130
France, 24, 33, 74, 75, 76, 77, 78, 79, 80, 81, 83, 114, 122, 123, 125, 126, 130, 139, 141, 142, 143, 147, 149, 200, 201, 203
Franco-German Treaty, 83
Frankfurt School, 94
French Revolution, 8, 73, 139, 200
Freud, Sigmund, 206
Front de Libération Nationale (FLN) (Algeria), 144
Front Islamique du Salut (FIS) (Algeria), 166

Fukuyama, Francis, 2, 6, 7, 8, 9, 10, 44, 54, 180, 198, 212
full employment, 113, 115
fundamentalism, Islamic, 158
futurology, 202

Galbraith, J.K., 119
Gandhi, Mahatma, 149
Gauguin, Paul, 201
de Gaulle, Charles, 79, 82, 83
General Agreement on Tariffs and Trade (GATT), 21, 29, 85, 120
Germany, 10, 24, 33, 72, 74, 75, 76, 77, 78, 79, 80, 81, 82, 83, 84, 112, 113, 115, 116, 117, 119, 122, 123, 124, 125, 126, 130, 131, 141, 142, 145, 150, 203, 209;
 Nazi, 25;
 pact with Japan, 61;
 reunification of, 129, 154, 155;
 Weimar, 114
Ghana, 149
Gilpin, Robert, 22, 23
Gladstone, W.E., 202
globalization, 117, 178, 185, 187, 188, 192, 195;
 of credit markets, 131
gold standard, 127;
 Britain's membership of, 111, 117, 121-6;
 British abandonment of, 125
Gorbachev, Mikhail, 6, 43, 44, 54, 66, 85
Gramsci, Antonio, 5, 104
Gray, Colin, 100, 101, 102
Great Depression, 112, 125, 152
Great East Asia Co-Prosperity Sphere, 62, 63, 68
Great Terror (USSR), 49
Greece, 75, 76, 84
guerrilla movements, 144
Guinea Bissau, 151
Gulf war, 128, 169, 171

Habermas, Jurgen, 4
Habsburg empire, 140
Halliday, Fred, 7
Harding, W. G., 123
Havel, Václav, 4, 10
Hawtrey, Ralph, 130
Hayek, Friedrich, 46, 51, 53
Heath, Edward, 114
Hegel, G.W.F., 2, 3, 7, 9, 15, 16, 177, 178, 179–80, 182, 184, 186, 190,

191, 193, 195, 196
hegemonic stability, theory of, 23
hegemony, 5, 25
Heisenberg, Werner, 94
Herder, J.G. von, 16, 138, 200
Herzl, Theodor, 210
Hinduism, 149
Hiroshima, 63, 64, 90, 91, 92, 96, 97
history: developmental model of, 16;
  end of, 1–19, 44
  (particular, 16);
  materialist conception of, 2;
  meaning of, 2;
  varieties of, 16;
  world-, 137
Hitler, Adolf, 32, 33, 36, 37, 51, 61, 78, 118
hooliganism, 207
Horkheimer, Max, 95, 96
Howe, Geoffrey, 115, 128
human rights, 191
Hume, David, 13, 15
Hungary, 75, 80
Hurd, Douglas, 128, 214
Hussain, Saddam, 155, 156, 170
Huysmans, Joris-Karl, 201, 205, 209
hyperinflation, 124

imperialism, 12, 25, 27, 72, 102, 139–45, 213
independence, right to, 144
India, 14, 15, 16, 76, 148, 149, 154, 177, 191
Indian National Congress, 148
industrialization, 51, 52, 74, 111, 185
inflation, 113, 115, 122, 125, 127, 128, 132;
  'creeping', 114, 115;
  'Latin', 114;
  hyper-, 115;
  impact of, 114
information technology, 131
instrumental theory, 100
intelligentsia, 52
interest-based theory, 25–8
Intergovernmental Conference (Hague, 1986), 127
international economy, 120–1
International Monetary Fund (IMF), 14, 21, 29, 65, 151, 152
international relations, 10–14, 78, 91, 93, 193
internationalism, 31, 178, 180–2, 185,

189, 190, 191, 192, 204, 214
intervention, 112, 116, 117, 119, 127, 177, 191
investment abroad, 120;
  of UK, 27;
  of US, 26, 31
investment market, power of, 131
Iran, 15, 17, 161, 163, 168, 171, 174;
  revolution in, 168
Iraq, 13, 170
Ireland, 84, 141
Isaacson, Walter, 31
Islam, 16, 86, 158–76, 214;
  and democracy, 164–8;
  and politics, 159–60;
  expansion of, 71;
  golden age of, 160;
  radical, 15;
  spread of, in Western Europe, 174;
  varieties of, 159
Islamic corporate structures, 167
Islamic law, 160
Islamist groups, suppression of, 164
Islamization, 163
isolationism, 27, 31, 34
Israel, 21, 170;
  right to exist, questioned, 169
Italy, 78, 81, 82, 126, 130;
  unification of, 74

J.P. Morgan & Co., 31
Jackson, Holbrook, 200, 206
Japan, 7, 13, 16, 17, 21, 26, 33, 37, 58–70, 73, 75, 85, 119, 150, 203;
  collapse of industry, 64;
  declares war on Russia, 59;
  earthquake in, 60;
  foreign policy of, 65;
  growth of, 65;
  pact with Germany, 61;
  peace treaty with US, 65;
  power of military, 64;
  Self Defence Force (Jieitai), 66, 67;
  surrender of, 63;
  trade surpluses of, 65;
  treaty with US, 66
Japan-Britain exhibition, 59
Jena, Battle of, 8
Jerome, Jerome K., 211
Jordan, 166

Kampuchea, UN operations in, 66
Kant, Immanuel, 2, 11, 12, 15, 16

INDEX

Katanga, 154
Kato, Masahide, 92
Kautsky, Karl, 12
Kedourie, Elie, 137
Keegan, John, 28
Kennan, George F., 32
Kennedy, John F., 82, 83
Kennedy, Paul, 198, 213
Kenya, 14, 143, 144
Keynes, J.M., 77, 122, 147
Keynesianism, 55, 112
Khrushchev, Nikita, 44, 49, 50
Kindleberger, Charles P., 24
King, B.B., 114
Kitchener, Lord, 208
Klimt, Gustav, 201
Knorr, Klaus, 23
Kojève, Alexandre, 3, 8, 9, 10
Konoe, Prince, 62
Korea, 59
Korean War, 113
Krasner, Stephen D., 27
Kurds, 156, 164;
   Iraqi, safe havens for, 156
Kuwait, 156;
   invasion of, 155, 170

Labour Party (UK), 113, 122
labour shortages, 50
laissez-faire, 112, 115, 116, 117, 132, 182;
   abandonment of, 181
Last Men, 3, 8
Lawson, Nigel, 126, 127, 128
Le Bon, Gustave, 210
League of Nations, 21, 30, 59, 60, 78, 97, 153;
   credibility of, 24
legitimacy, 6, 164, 183, 187, 192;
   crisis of, 4;
   of state, 112;
   of USSR, 44
Leigh-Pemberton, Robin, 128
Lelth-Ross, Frederick, 123
Lend-Lease programme, 31, 32, 33
Lenin, V.I., 44, 110, 145, 146
Levy-Dhurmer, Lucien, 202
Liberal Democratic Party (Japan), 67
liberalism, 3, 4, 11, 15, 36, 138, 140, 143, 145, 147, 150, 152, 205, 211;
   really-existing, 12;
   resilience of, 212;
   Western, 6, 9 (triumph of, 7)

liberalization, economic, 15, 164–8
Linklater, Andrew, 214
Lippmann, Walter, 32
Liska, George, 36
Locarno, Treaty of, 78
Lome Convention, 152
Lorraine, 77
Luce, Henry R., 20, 34

Maastricht, Treaty of, 130
MacArthur, Douglas, 64
Maginot Line, 79
Maier, Charles, 131
Major, John, 128
Malaya, 62, 63
Malaysia, 161, 172
man, reversion to animality, 8, 10
Manchukuo, 60, 61, 63
Mandelbaum, Michael, 22
Manhattan project, 96
manufacturing industry, shift from, 118
Mao Zedong, 100, 101, 102, 146
Marcuse, Herbert, 96, 97
market economy, 5, 6, 7, 9, 12, 44, 51, 55, 115, 116, 173, 179, 184, 190
Marshall Plan, 21, 30, 31, 37, 80
Marx, Karl, 2, 7, 9, 16, 21, 44, 98, 119, 120, 185, 188
Marxism, 12, 15, 110, 138, 152, 184
Mau Mau movement, 144
Mauss, Marcel, 183
Mazzini, Giuseppe, 138
media, Islamization of, 174
Mediterranean, 71, 74, 75, 84
Mexican Revolution, 27
Mexico, 25
migration, 168, 178, 181, 182, 189;
   falling levels of, 120;
   from Europe, 72;
   policies, 148;
   Russian, 146
military spirit, 208;
   sapping of, 207
Mill, J.S., 138, 141
minorities: rights of, 185;
   treatment of, 189, 190, 194
Mitteleuropa, 84
modernity, 188
modernization, 160, 162, 174;
   without Westernization, 173
Monet, Claude, 201
money, magic of, 121
money markets, 121

money supply, control of, 115, 132
Moreau, Gustave, 201
Morgenthau, Hans J., 23
motorways, building of, 203
Mozambique, 151, 152
Mueller, John, 100, 101
Museum of Natural History (New York), 91
Muslim Brotherhood, 163, 167
Muslim states, poverty of, 172
Mussolini, Benito, 32, 78
mutually assured destruction (MAD), 104

Naga rebellion, 149
Nagasaki, 63, 64
Napoleon Bonaparte, 73, 199
nation: concept of, 138;
   socialization of, 181
nation-state, 77, 111, 121, 131, 139, 185, 186, 187;
   and colonialism, 160-4;
   boundaries challenged, 189;
   confidence restored in, 82;
   creation of, 161, 192;
   enhanced power of, 119;
   established by colonial powers, 143;
   interdependence of, 120;
   role of, 112;
   viability questioned, 79
national economy, 120-1
National Party (S. Africa), 143
National Rifle Association (NRA) (USA), 97, 100
national-cultural autonomy, 189
national security state, 104, 106
nationalism, 13, 78, 119, 129, 137-57, 161, 167, 178, 181, 182, 183, 189, 190, 191, 195;
   African, 149;
   and ideological conflict, 145-50;
   and internationalism, 180-2;
   as European invention, 137 138;
   as intellectually parasitic, 140;
   geographic extension of, 181;
   lack of substantive content, 138;
   socialized, 148;
   US, 38
nationalities policy of USSR, 146
Nazism, 95, 112, 113, 142
Nelson, Benjamin, 183
nervous disease, 206
New Deal (USA), 112, 113
New International Economic Order (NIEO), 172
New York, interests of, 30
Newtonian paradigm, 94
Niemeyer, Otto, 122
Nietzsche, Friedrich, 3, 8, 17
nihilism, 209
Nixon, Richard, 85, 113
Nkrumah, Kwame, 149
Nobutoshi, Hagihara, 69
Non-Aligned Movement, 143, 149, 172
Nordau, Max, 200
North Atlantic Cooperation Council, 86
North Atlantic Treaty Organization (NATO), 21, 81, 83, 86, 113
North-South conflict, 150
nuclear fission, 91, 211;
   as source of energy, 93
nuclear fusion, 91
nuclear revolution, 186
nuclear weapons, 28, 64, 82, 83, 90-109;
   arms race, 96;
   as paper tiger, 101;
   as technology, 100–6;
   environmental impact of, 92;
   mobilization against, 91;
   moderating behaviour of states, 103;
   peace obtained through, 192

Ohira, Prime Minister, 68
oil: crisis, 65;
   Japan's supplies of, 62;
   price, rise of, 113, 151
Open Door empire of US, 25
Organization for Economic Cooperation and Development (OECD), 11, 65
Organization for European Economic Cooperation (OEEC), 80
Organization of African Unity (OAU), 150
Organization of Petroleum Exporting Countries (OPEC), 151
Orthodox church, 46
Ottoman empire, 140, 160;
   collapse of, 160

Pacific rim, 116;
   solidarity, 68
Pacific union, 14–17
pacification, 186, 187, 191, 195, 207, 209
pacifism, 13
Pakistan, 154, 161
Palestine, 169
Pan-Africanism, 150

INDEX

Paris Exhibition (1900), 202
partition of states, 154
Pater, Walter, 201
Peace Keeping Operations Bill (Japan), 66
peace, zones of, 14
Peace Studies, 91
Pearl Harbour, attack on, 61, 62
Peking Legations, siege of, 58, 59
Pissaro, Camille, 201
planning, 14, 44, 50, 51, 118;
  and democracy, 51–4;
  central, 5, 6, 47, 50, 146
  (collapse of, 45, 115);
  five-year, 47, 48;
  in USSR, 46–51
  (masquerade of, 51);
  incompatible with democracy, 45;
  international, 182;
  retreat of, 54–6;
  sabotage of, 48;
  Soviet, 9, 10
Plekhanov, Georgii, 110
Poland, 77, 80, 141
politics, relation to economics, 110, 181
Portugal, 84, 143, 151
power-based theory, 22–5, 35–7
primary commodity markets, 173
protectionism, 182, 185
purges, in USSR, 48

racism, 213
Rafah party (Turkey), 168, 173
Rathenau, Walther, 119
rationalism, 144
rationality, 15, 94, 95, 96
Ravachol, 210
Rayyan finance companies, 167
Reagan, Ronald, 85, 101
realism, 21, 23, 37, 184, 185
Redon, Odile, 201
Renan, J.-E., 138
Renner, Karl, 189
Rhodesia, 143, 144
Ricoeur, Paul, 16
Roman empire, 22
Romania, 77
Rome, Treaty of, 81
Roosevelt, Franklin D., 31, 32, 112, 113
Roosevelt, Theodore, 36
Rousseau, J.-J., 15
Royal Air Force, 79
Royal Navy, 79

rubber: Japan's supplies of, 62;
  synthetic, Japanese production of, 63
Russia, 24, 43–57, 72, 86
Russian Revolution, 145, 146

Schacht, Hjalmar, 121
Schmidt, Helmut, 114
Schorske, Carl, 200
Schuman, Robert, 81
Schuman Plan, 81
secession, 145, 181
secularization, 158, 168;
  Islamic opposition to, 165
security, national, 32
self-determination, 77, 141, 146, 152, 153, 154
self-interest, rational, 13
Serbia, 76
Shakhty trial, 48
Shari'a, 165
Slovenia, recognition of, 155
Smith, Adam, 44
Snyder, Jack, 105
Social Democratic Party (Japan), 67
socialism, 43, 45, 53, 102, 116, 140, 143, 145, 152, 167, 168, 173, 179;
  African, 150;
  Arab, 165;
  demise of, 3–7, 10
South Africa, 14, 143, 144, 154
sovereignty, 140, 173, 177, 179, 185, 187, 189, 190, 192, 195, 204, 213;
  in Islam, 164;
  popular, 153, 210;
  shift away from, 191
Spain, 84
Spengler, Oswald, 211
Spinelli, Altiero, 79
Spykman, N.J., 32
stagflation, 113
Stakhanovite movement, 48
Stalin, Joseph, 37, 44, 47, 48, 49, 51, 52, 146
state, 114;
  and democracy, 55;
  and economic growth, 112;
  building of, 185;
  constitutional, 9;
  intervention, 112, 119;
  liberal, 11;
  misuse of monopoly powers, 195;
  mobilizing power of, 193;
  monopoly (of control of instruments of

violence, 183, 184, 186;
of right to taxation, 183, 184, 187);
nationalist, 184;
provision for the poor, 179;
relation to citizen, 193;
sovereign, inadequacy of, 213;
territorial, 177;
totalitarian, 47;
transformation of structures, 192;
weakened ability to control human identity, 188;
weakened bond with citizens, 188;
withering away of, 7
Strategic Studies, 93
steam, transition to, 28
steel-making, 24, 58
sterling, 124, 127, 128, 131;
floating of, 130;
overvaluation of, 122, 129;
restabilization of, 123;
valuation of, 125
Stimson, Henry, 30
Stirling, J.H., 177
strategic culture, 105
Strategic Studies, 91
Strong, Benjamin, 123
structural adjustment policies, 152
sub-national groups, 194, 195
submarines, 204
substantive theory, 97, 98
Sudan, 163, 171, 172, 174
Sun Yat Sen, 147
Sutherland, Alexander, 207, 210

Taiwan, 146
tariffs, 117
taxation, 115, 187
technological determinism, 98, 100
technology, 22, 99;
ambivalence of, 99;
as vehicle of liberation, 97;
as vehicle of reification, 97;
communications-, 93;
critical approach to, 105;
development of, 93–7;
nuclear, as autonomous force, 103;
viewed as neutral, 97, 100
terrorism, 209
Thatcher, Margaret, 115, 127, 128, 129
third world, 10, 26;
solidarity, 151
Thomas, Evan, 31
Thompson, Dorothy, 33

Thompson, E.P., 102, 103, 104
Thucydides, 23
time, meaning of, 8, 9
Tojo, Prime Minister, 62
trade, growth of, 120
transnationals, 121, 173
tribalism, 15
Truman Doctrine, 37
Tucker, Robert W., 28
Tunisia, 164, 166
Turkey, 15, 73, 75, 161, 168, 173

U Thant, 154
Umma, 162, 170
Uncertainty Principle, 94
unemployment, 116, 117, 122, 128, 130, 147;
benefit, 147
Union of Soviet Socialist Republics (USSR), 2, 4, 6, 13, 15, 20, 21, 22, 26, 32, 33, 35, 61, 66, 78, 79, 80, 86, 101, 102, 114, 143, 145, 150, 152, 167;
demise of, 3, 44, 55, 139, 155, 167;
German attack on, 61;
legitimacy of, 44
United Kingdom (UK), 22, 23, 24, 27, 33, 37, 58, 59, 61, 62, 74, 76, 78, 79, 80, 82, 84, 113, 114, 116, 139, 141, 142, 143, 147, 211;
and ERM, 126–30;
and gold standard, 111, 117, 121–6 (abandonment of, 125);
control of Atlantic, 27;
entry into Europe, 83;
hegemonic internationalism of, 181;
intervention in Latin America, 27;
rearmament, 126;
role in World War II, 32
United Nations (UN), 21, 29, 66, 144, 154, 155, 156, 162, 170;
as tool for US interests, 170;
Charter, 153;
increased active role of, 171;
Security Council, 146, 147, 155;
Universal Declaration of Human Rights, 153
United States of America (USA), 13, 20–42, 61, 64, 65, 66, 76, 77, 79, 82, 104, 105, 112, 122, 125, 126, 145, 147, 148, 150, 155, 161, 165, 168;
as model for Europe, 80;

contribution in world wars, 20;
decision to use nuclear bomb, 90;
Department of Energy, 92;
devaluation, 126;
discrimination against exports, 26;
entry into World War II, 32, 33, 34;
expropriation of assets of, 26;
foreign policy of, 22, 29, 35, 38;
Germany declares war on, 62;
investment abroad, 31;
Japanese treaty with, 66;
national security of, 27;
nationalism of, 38;
peace treaty with Japan, 65;
rivalry with Europe, 85;
standard of living of, 35

vaccination, 202, 211
Vagts, Alfred, 208
Verne, Jules, 203
Versailles, Treaty of, 77, 78
Vietnam War, 148
Voltaire, 15

wages, reduction in, 124
Wall Street Crash, 125
Wallace, Alfred, 45, 55, 202, 208, 209, 211
Wallerstein, Immanuel, 1
Walpole, Horace, 204
Waltz, Kenneth, 12, 23, 102, 103, 104
war: avoidance of, 14;
  major (fewer in number, 185;
  obsolescence of, 180, 185, 186, 192);
  total, forecast, 204
warfare, decline of, 207
Washington Conference, 60
Webb, Beatrice, 46, 210

Webb, Sidney, 46
Weber, Eugen, 200
Weimar Republic, 115
welfare, 148, 173, 179, 181, 182, 184, 185, 190, 195
Wells, H.G., 46, 203, 204, 205, 211, 213, 214
Western European Union (WEU), 86
Westernization, 158, 173, 191, 193;
  and Europeanism, 73;
  and Islam, 168–72
Wight, Martin, 23
Wilde, Oscar, 201
Williams, Raymond, 100
Williams, William Appleman, 25, 27
Wilson, Woodrow, 27, 30, 78, 141
women: seer role of, 205;
  treatment of, 208
working class, incorporation of, 117, 118
World Bank, 21, 29, 152
World War I, 20, 59, 76, 77, 140, 141, 142
World War II, 35, 43, 51, 53, 79, 95, 112, 140, 146

The Yellow Book, 201, 206
Yeltsin, Boris, 6
Young Egypt movement, 167
Yugoslavia, 77, 155

Zaire, 154
Zambia, 14
Zeitgeist, 200
Zimbabwe African National Union (ZANU), 144
Zimbabwe African People's Union (ZAPU), 144
Zola, Emile, 199, 204

www.ingramcontent.com/pod-product-compliance
Lightning Source LLC
Chambersburg PA
CBHW052036300426
44117CB00012B/1844